THE JUNIOR ASSEMBLY BOOK

Ther

more happiness

in giving

than in receiving

SIMON & SCHUSTER

LONDON • SYDNEY • NEW YORK • TOKYO • SINGAPORE • TORONTO

Consultants
Patricia Harrison, *Senior Lecturer in Primary Education,*
Liverpool Institute of Higher Education
Steve Harrison, *Advisor in Primary Education,*
Lancashire Education Authority
Dr Owen Cole, *Senior Lecturer in Religious Education,*
Bishop Otter College, Chichester

Artists
Studio Two
Lucy Su

Design
Michelle Cox

First published in Great Britain in 1989
by Simon & Schuster Young Books

Simon & Schuster Young Books
Simon & Schuster Ltd
Wolsey House, Wolsey Road
Hemel Hempstead, Herts HP2 4SS

Text © 1989 Doreen Vause and Liz Beaumont
Illustrations © 1989 Simon & Schuster Ltd

Reprinted 1990

Printed and bound in Great Britain by
BPCC Paulton Books Limited

British Library Cataloguing in Publication Data

Vause, Doreen
Junior assembly book.
1. Juniors schools. Morning assembly.
Themes
I. Title   II. Beaumont, Liz
377′.1

ISBN 0-7501-0086-9

INTRODUCTION

The Junior Assembly Book is a sequel to The Infant Assembly Book, but was written with the needs of slightly older children in mind. Some of the material contained in this book is also suitable for children in the top infant classes and some of the ideas could be developed further for even older children.

The book is written not only for those who have the responsibility for conducting school assemblies but will also prove useful for class teachers and students during initial teacher training. The book is envisaged as a collection of ideas which will give *starting points* which teachers can then develop according to their needs and interests.

The book is divided into four parts. The first three parts can be grouped and are intended to promote self-awareness, awareness of others in our communities, and awareness of wider world issues.

To promote self-awareness we consider feelings and values such as truth and love, to increase understanding and consideration of better relationships through stories which promote the virtues of honesty, courage, friendship and forgiveness. We try to promote spiritual growth from discussion of the wonder which we see around us in our world. We aim to encourage the children to contemplate on the responsibilities of leaving the world a better place by observing the damage which pollution causes and promoting the value of conservation.

The fourth part aims to *highlight* the beliefs and values of a cross-section of people living in a multi-cultural society. We look at the positive benefits to be gained from exchange of ideas in the belief that we are all able to learn from others.

In the first three sections there are natural connections between one topic and the next, although each topic could be considered to be a complete teaching unit. The topic 'Our World' brings together the issues raised in the previous topics and would prove useful as a topic to be used at the end of the school year.

With each topic suggestions are made for discussion, which is considered to be of importance to the development of the theme. Through the use of discussion we aim to increase knowledge, to encourage children to question and to promote thoughtful attitudes regarding their relationships with each other, with others in their families and communities and with the world community.

The stories are taken from a wide variety of cultural backgrounds and from resources which include folk tales, stories of contemporary life, fiction and non-fiction. Some of these are traditional whilst others are new and specially written for this book. A selection of poems, both old and new, is also included.

Suggestions are made for music but teachers will no doubt find that many of their own favourites will be suitable for use with the themes.

Activities are suggested with each theme. Whilst some of these activities are concerned with art and craft others link the teaching of religious education to other areas of the curriculum, such as mathematics, science, history, geography. Many of these activities involve the children in the development of language and problem solving skills.

For their friendly advice and criticism we wish to thank Patricia and Steve Harrison, and also Daphne Butler of Macdonald Children's Books. We also owe our thanks to the children and teachers at The Cedars Infant School, Blackburn who have inspired many parts of our work. We would like to say a special thank you to three families whose experiences provide the basis for three of the stories: The Casey family of Great Harwood, the Gonsai family of Blackburn, the Singer family of Bury.

Doreen Vause
Liz Beaumont
February 1989

Contents

OURSELVES AND OUR FEELINGS

Hope and Optimism

The aim of this topic is to encourage the children to think in a positive way. In our lives we meet people who look at life differently, some are very optimistic about what the future holds. They usually look on the brighter side, picking out all the good things they see. There are also the pessimists who pick out the small things which are wrong, this makes them anxious and fearful of what the future holds, and often their anxiety is passed on to others. The optimist thinks positively and greets each new day with hope, even when dark days come along.

Talking points

▶ Discuss with the children the hopes they have for their own future, and their hopes for the world.

▶ The snowdrop and the star are often regarded as signs of hope. Discuss why this should be so.

▶ Talk about special times of hope. For example: the New Year, (New Year resolutions – hoping to do better); a new term in school and other "new beginnings".

▶ Discuss the saying, "It is better to travel hopefully than to arrive".

▶ Optimists say that every cloud has a silver lining. Is this true? Discuss false hopes. Who would you prefer as a friend an optimist or a pessimist?

Hoping for a better life

Under a huge shady tree he sat
His empty hands stretched out
Begging for money he rarely gets
To give his bony body some food.

People went past him without a glance
His eyes filled up with sadness and hunger
But once in a while his face lit up
As generous hands and hearts went by.

Every bone in his body was visible
He didn't have the strength to stand
All the time his stomach made a sound
A sound which wealthy people never heard.

The days went by he did not care
As every day was filled with hunger
Hoping for a better life next birth
A life with happiness not with sorrow.

Samantha Paranahews, The Island Newspaper, Sri Lanka

The snowdrop

This is an outline story which children can use as a plot for drama. It includes dialogue between an optimist and a pessimist.

An old couple lived in a small isolated cottage. It had been a severe winter with much snow and the cottage was marooned by drifts. They had stored logs, fuel and food. They were too frail to try to reach help through the deep snow. The old man was pessimistic and thought that the food would run out before help could reach them. The old woman, an optimist, tried to calm his fears and anxiety. She opened the door and saw a tiny snowdrop peeping through the snow. She regarded this as a messenger of hope. She called the old man and said, "As sure as Autumn is followed by Winter, Winter is always followed by Spring, and the Creator sends the snowdrop as his messenger of hope."

Pandora's box

About 2,500 years ago a great civilization flourished in the land we now call Greece. The Ancient Greeks were very good at art, science and managing their affairs and people still use some of their ideas today. Many things that they couldn't understand they explained by inventing a whole family of Gods. These Gods quarrelled and squabbled and were responsible for all the ills of the people.

The Greeks thought that people had been created by a sort of junior God called Prometheus and that Prometheus had made them to look like the Gods and to live on Earth. Prometheus shut up all the nasty things of the World in a box and gave the box to his brother Epimetheus for safe keeping. So human beings did not suffer from things like old age, sickness, greed, envy and so on. In fact they were really doing rather well on Earth, especially after Prometheus stole fire for them from Heaven.

The king of the Gods was furious about all this. He thought that people were far too like the Gods and he plotted revenge. He made a clay statue of a woman and brought her to life calling her Pandora.

Make your own Pandora's Box

1. Paint the inside of a **shoe box** and its lid black. Sprinkle **glitter** inside while the **paint** is still wet.

2. Cut out different shapes from **card**. (Your own ideas of what you think would come out of Pandora's Box.)

3. Decorate them and thread a length of **cotton** through each one.

4. Attach the other end of the cotton to the lid of the box.

Don't forget to put a sprite of hope inside the box.

Pandora was very beautiful but she was also very foolish, mischievous and idle. The king of the Gods sent Pandora to Epimetheus as a gift. Epimetheus didn't really trust a gift from the Gods and wanted to send her back, but the Gods started to torture his brother Prometheus and Epimetheus thought he had better marry Pandora after all.

Epimetheus made Pandora promise never to open the box, but of course she was very foolish and, just as the Gods had planned, her curiosity got the better of her. One day she opened the box; all the evil things poured out to infect all people for evermore. Pandora quickly tried to shut the box but only succeeded in trapping one small bright shining sprite inside. This was Hope – all that was left to comfort people in an evil world.

Snowdrops

I like to think
That long ago,
There fell to earth
Some flakes of snow
Which loved this cold,
Grey world of ours
So much, they stayed
As Snowdrop flowers.

Mary Vivian

Things to do

▶ Write sentences beginning with "I hope", hopes for yourself and hopes for the world.

▶ Illustrate the story of Pandora.

▶ Make a small statue of Pandora out of clay or Plasticine.

▶ Compare the Greek idea of the creation with the story of Genesis in the Old Testament and the scientific explanation that people and animals evolved over millions of years.

▶ Make a frieze of the creation as told in Genesis. Different groups can take different parts of the story, for example, sun, moon and stars, animals, fish and birds.

▶ If the teacher draws a small dark circle on a large sheet of white paper and asks the children what they see, they often reply 'a small circle'. Point out that we often see the dark spots but so often neglect the brightness all around.

Joy and Sorrow

The aim of this topic is to encourage in children an awareness of their own feelings and empathy for the feelings of others. The stories show how simple things, co-operation and friendship bring joy, and sorrow is caused by denying them.

Talking points

▶ Are you feeling happy or sad today? Discuss happy and sad faces and the kind of things that might make you happy or sad.

▶ Discuss happy times like holidays, the birth of a baby, and an outing with friends, and contrast them with sad times like loneliness, separation and disappointment.

▶ Discuss special festivals like Christmas, Easter, Eid, Holi, Diwali, Passover, Hanukah. Ask children to think about what it is that makes them happy at such times.

▶ Discuss the sorrow caused by disasters such as earthquakes or famine, and the work of the voluntary agencies who try to bring relief.

The village cobbler

Have you ever seen a proper cobbler's shop – I mean one of those old-fashioned ones that smell of leather? In the past nearly every village had its own cobbler – someone who made the shoes for the entire village – and this story is about just such a cobbler.

His shop was tiny, and he was a happy jolly fellow always singing as he worked. Each day the children would come to visit him; staring with big round eyes as he worked with his hammer; chattering and laughing telling him stories about the village. The cobbler welcomed the children and looked forward to their visits.

One morning the cobbler found a note pushed under his door. It came from the man who lived up above the shop. "Come tonight" it read. "I have something important to discuss."

That night the cobbler mounted the stairs wondering what on earth the man had to talk about. He had never really met the man – hardly ever saw him in fact. Inside the upstairs room the cobbler was astonished to see several large boxes full of gold coins. He was even more astonished when the man said, "I can't stand the noise that comes from your shop – all that chattering and banging, take these boxes of money and you will never need to work again!" The cobbler couldn't really believe his luck. "No more work!" he thought. He quickly agreed to the bargain and hurried downstairs with the boxes before the man changed his mind.

In the morning the cobbler went straight into the workshop and tidied away his tools. When the children came they found a new sign on the door which read "Closed until further notice." That night the cobbler did not sleep too well. He kept thinking that someone might try to steal his treasure.

As time went by the cobbler became very tired, very sad and very lonely. During the day he missed the children and at night he could hardly sleep for fear of burglars. He became ill and miserable and daydreamed fondly about the past. Then, one night he came to his senses. He collected up all the boxes of coins and stamped upstairs with them. "These are no good to me," he told the man. "They just make me unhappy, you keep them."

The next morning the cobbler was back working at his bench. The sign on the door read, "Open – business as usual!". Soon the children came again, and the happy sound of singing and laughter was heard once more in the cobbler's shop.

The two-metre chopsticks

For thousands and thousands of years people have been living in the land that today we call China. Some Chinese stories are very very old and have been passed down from generation to generation. In fact, the Chinese probably have a tale to tell about most things, but this particular tale is about chopsticks. For those of you who don't know, chopsticks are utensils with which the Chinese eat their food, and they are usually about 30 centimetres long. Now let's get on with the story.

Long ago, when the world was still quite young, a very brave Warrior was killed in battle. The Gods sent a Messenger down to Earth to guide the Warrior to the gates of Heaven. Inside all the people looked happy, content and well fed, but the Warrior could not see any of his friends. So, he asked the Messenger where they

Make a happy face/sad face frieze

Make a list of happy words and sad words. Write some of these on strips of **card**. Decorate with dots, stripes, **sequins** or **glitter**. Make happy and

sad faces from **paper plates** to match the words on the cards. Mount it all on a large sheet of **paper** to make a frieze.

might be. The Messenger said that there was another place called the Underworld and if the Warrior wanted he could show him the way. The Warrior thought this was a good idea so they set off together.

When they arrived in the Underworld, the Warrior saw all his friends, but they looked very thin and very sad. They were squabbling and quarrelling, and even hitting out at each other. There were pieces of food all over the floor. It really was a dreadful scene.

The Warrior looked more closely to see what was causing all this rumpus and realized that all the people were trying to

eat with chopsticks that were two metres long. The chopsticks needed to be this long because the table was very long and very wide, but once they had picked up the food they could not get it into their mouths.

The Warrior asked the Messenger to take him back to Heaven because he wanted to see why there was such a difference. Once through the gates of Heaven the difference was very plain to see. The people were still using two-metre chopsticks, but they were feeding each other and not themselves. There was not a sad face to be seen amongst them.

A prayer from Chester Cathedral

Give me a sense of humour Lord
Give me the grace to see a joke
To get some happiness from life
And pass it on to other folk.

Anonymous

A smile

A smile is such a lovely thing
It brightens up your face
And when it's gone it's hard to find
Its secret hiding place.

Yet still more wonderful it is
To know what smiles can do
You smile at me. I smile at you
And then one smile makes two.

Anonymous

Things to do

► Make a frieze of happy and sad faces. Surround the frieze with children's writing about things that make them happy and things that make them sad.

► Organize a 'smile day'. Everyone makes and wears a smile badge, misery is banned, a magazine of jokes is published.

► Collect sayings which associate colours with happiness or sadness. For example: in the pink; feeling blue; green with envy.

► Dramatize the story *The village cobbler*.

11

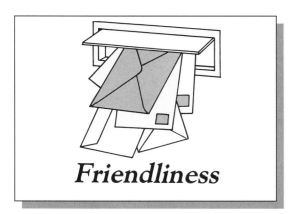

Friendliness

Friendliness towards people and animals is a very basic human feeling. One of the first ways we show this friendliness is with a smiling face and a warm word. At any particular moment, someone, somewhere is surely extending a greeting to someone else. The feeling of friendliness provides a way for children to explore how different cultures make this most fundamental of human gestures.

Talking points

▶ Discuss the various ways of making a greeting: verbal (face to face/telephone); written (letters and cards); physical (hugs, kisses, sending presents). Talk about the way customs vary with different cultures.

▶ Discuss how to say "good morning" in different languages:

Gaelic	French
Bengali	German
Gujarati	Spanish
Punjabi	Italian
Urdu	Russian
Greek	Chinese
Vietnamese	Japanese

▶ Discuss special greetings for festivals and anniversaries.

▶ Discuss different written greetings: letters, postcards, greetings cards for special occasions: birthdays, Christmas, Eid, Diwali, Lucia, Valentine, get well, congratulations, sorry ...

▶ Discuss different physical greetings: hugs, kisses and handshakes are fairly universal though customs differ in different countries as to exactly what is the polite way of doing it. There are special greetings in some cultures:

Inuit	rub noses
Sri Lankans	put their hands together and say "Ayoubown"
Maoris	put their foreheads together and shake hands

▶ Discuss the way customs change depending on how well you know the people, and whether or not they are your 'elders'. Discuss the need to do it the right way or risk giving offence.

Assalam-o-Alaikum

About 1,200 years ago Mohammed was living in Mecca where many of the people worshipped idols. Mohammed tried very hard to tell people that he believed that there is only one true God. Some of the people thought that Mohammed was a troublemaker, and they hated him. One such person was a little old woman who saw Mohammed every morning when she was sweeping her doorstep.

Each day Mohammed greeted the old lady with the friendly words "Assalam-o-Alaikum" which mean "Peace be with you". Each day the old lady sneered and swept her dust towards Mohammed. This went on week in and week out, and then one day the old lady was nowhere to be seen. She was not there the next day either. Suspecting that something must be wrong, Mohammed knocked on her door, and getting no reply, curiously opened the door and peeped inside. There was the old lady feeling very ill and miserable. She had been very nasty to Mohammed, but this did not stop him from wanting to help her. He called in the neighbours and between them they nursed her back to health. The old lady was very grateful and ashamed of her behaviour. Ever after when they met each morning, the old lady returned Mohammed's friendly greeting with her own friendly reply.

Today, people think about Mohammed as a great prophet and many of them follow his example. These people are called Muslims and their religion is called Islam. Each day Muslims greet each other with those same friendly words "Assalam-o-Alaikum" meaning "Peace be with you".

Valentine

Nearly 2,000 years ago Rome was a very powerful city. It ruled all the lands around the Mediterranean Sea and most of Britain which was very wild and uncivilized at that time. The Roman armies were strong and well-trained but they had great difficulty in defeating a fierce tribe called the Goths. The Goths lived on the northern and eastern borders of the Roman Empire. They attacked Roman towns and set fire to them, killing the people and stealing anything of value.

Make a Valentine card

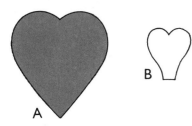

1. Cut a heart shape from a piece of **red card** (A). Cut five petal shapes from **white paper** (B).

2. Take each petal in turn and curl it by wrapping it round a pencil.

3. Put a spot of **glue** on the card and press the narrow parts of each petal on to this to make a rosette. Use tiny **beads** or grains of **rice** for the stamens. Make the frill by sticking small pieces of **doyley** around the edge of the card. Paint in tiny leaves, and write a message to your Valentine.

In 268, Claudius II became emperor of Rome. He was determined to stop the Goths once and for all. He decided that the Roman soldiers were spending too much time with their wives and families and not enough time fighting, so he made a rule that no soldier was to marry. He told the bishops and other churchmen to refuse requests to marry soldiers.

One of the bishops was called Valentine and he liked to see families living happily together. He believed that soldiers should marry and have children like anyone else. So, he defied Claudius and continued with marriage services for soldiers in secret. When Claudius found out about this,

Valentine was arrested and put into prison. His cell was cold, damp, and dark, and he had very little food. The jailor's daughter felt very sorry for him. At night, she used to creep down to his cell taking food, drink, and clean straw for him to sleep on. After a while Claudius decided to execute Valentine. The poor man was taken from his cell, beaten and then beheaded. That night, when the jailor's daughter crept down to the cell all she found was a message. It read "Thank you for making me happy – Valentine".

Today, we remember St Valentine on 14 February each year when people send messages to their sweethearts.

Hello

*Hello's a handy word to say
At least a hundred times a day
Without 'hello' – what would I do
Whenever I bumped into you?*

*Without 'hello' where would you be
Whenever you bumped into me?
Hello's a handy word to know
Hello! hello! hello! hello!*

Mary Ann Hoberman

Things to do

▶ Draw or paint pictures showing how people of different cultures greet each other.

▶ Work out the tune of *Happy Birthday to you* using chime bars, a xylophone, a recorder, piano or any other instrument.

▶ Search for ways of saying "hello" in different languages. Use these words to make a welcome poster for the entrance to your school.

▶ Make a long banner bearing the words "Assalam-o-Alaikum". Decorate the edges with patterned border.

▶ Find out more about the prophet Mohammed. Can you discover any more stories about his kindnesses.

▶ Make a collection of different kinds of greetings cards. Then design your own card, for example, a congratulations card for a new birth, or perhaps a Mother's day or Valentine card.

Tolerance

Everyone has their own way of looking at things. Children need to learn to seek out and to understand other people's points of view and to tolerate them even if they decide not to agree with them. People of different genders, cultures, and religions may see life differently. By sharing our ideas, our hopes and fears we can work together for a better world.

Talking points

▶ Talk about equality and the right we all have to be taken seriously. Likewise the responsibility we have to take others seriously.

▶ Discuss discrimination towards other people for whatever reason: their gender, their culture, their religion, the colour of their skin, the way they dress, the way they talk, and so on.

▶ Discuss how easy it is for us to discriminate without realizing we are doing it.

▶ Consider how difference is often equated with strangeness or oddity by some people.

▶ Discuss different types of homes around the world and how people have used the materials which were available to them. The type of material varies from place to place.

▶ Discuss different modes of dress and how the climate affects this. For example: no person at the equator ever wears a fur coat; and no person in the far north of Canada ever wears a thin sari.

▶ Discuss the different kinds of clothes we wear in Britain at different times of the year.

Abu Wahid

About 1,200 years ago Spain was invaded by people from north Africa. These people were called Moors. They were followers of Islam and they built many beautiful buildings and mosques. But the Spanish hated their conquerors and did their best to get rid of them.

In 1085 the people of the city of Toledo managed to overthrow the Moors and a Spanish king ruled the city once more. This king was a Christian, Alfonso VI, and he promised the leader of the Moors, Abu Wahid, that Muslims would be allowed to go to the mosque and worship as usual. Whilst Alfonso was away from Toledo on a visit, one of the Christian bishops persuaded the queen to break Alfonso's promise to Abu Wahid. When Alfonso returned to Toledo he found soldiers guarding the mosque day and night and the Muslims prevented from worshipping. Alfonso was so angry that he sentenced the bishop to death. On hearing about the death sentence Abu Wahid begged the king to

withdraw the death sentence and to pardon the scheming bishop. Alfonso was full of admiration for the tolerance Abu Wahid had shown in forgiving the bishop who had broken the promise.

Many years later a cathedral was built in Toledo. Statues of many Christian saints were placed on the reredos behind the altar, and along with them was a statue of Abu Wahid. This was to remind the people of the tolerant, forgiving and kind-hearted leader of the Moors.

No difference

Small as a peanut,
Big as a giant,
We're all the same size
When we turn off the light.

Rich as a sultan,
Poor as a mite
We're all worth the same
When we turn off the light.

Red, black or orange,
Yellow or white,
We all look the same
When we turn off the light.

So may be the way
To make everything right
Is for God to just reach out
And turn off the light!

Shel Silverstein

Ramakrishna

Ramakrishna was born in India in 1836. His family was a very poor Hindu family and so Ramakrishna never went to school. But Ramakrishna was very bright and was for ever asking questions. He wondered

Different outside
Same inside

▶ The aim is to demonstrate that even within a small group we find that people have different perceptions and preferences. We use the five senses here to illustrate this point.

Sight Provide a graph sheet showing four or five colours. Ask the children to mark their favourite colour.

Smell Provide five different perfumes, for example: soap, toilet water, perfume, talcum powder, air freshener. Mark them *A B C D E*. Ask the children to record their preferred smell.

Taste Provide four different fruits, for example: apple, orange, pear, banana. Ask the children to record on a graph their preference.

Touch Provide four or five materials, for example: wool, silk, Hessian, plastic, towelling. The children must touch each one and state which they prefer to touch.

Hearing Play four or five different types of music, for example: country and western, reggae, pop, ballet, brass band. The children need to listen to each kind of music and state their own preference.

In reading the graphs point out that although some children held similar views about colour they may hold different views about music, but there is no right or wrong, everyone's view is equally valid.

what God was like, and was always looking for an answer. All through his childhood he heard many Hindu stories and his family worshipped each day.

When he grew up, Ramakrishna decided to become a Muslim. He went to the mosque and studied the teaching of the prophet Mohammed. Later on, he moved to Calcutta and studied the teachings of Christ. Ramakrishna felt that each of these religions had something to offer to the others. He began to preach to the people and many came to Calcutta to hear him. He told his listeners that all people are God's children whatever their religion and encouraged them to tolerate each other.

Ramakrishna used to tell a story to explain what he meant. In this story three men went to the well and each began to draw some of the liquid from the well. The Muslim called this liquid *pani*, the Hindu called it *jal*, and the Christian called it *water*. The water was the same but each man had a different name for it. In the same way different religions have different words and different customs, but Ramakrishna believed they worship exactly the same God.

Greed

We all experience feelings of wanting things, but some people are always wanting and are never ever satisfied. As soon as they have obtained one thing they want another. We have probably all been greedy at times because we have wanted more than we needed. Sometimes greed has caused nations to go to war to conquer lands and territory which has then been used to amass wealth. The Buddhist religion teaches that it is only when we free ourselves from wanting things that we can reach the peace of Nirvana. This is why the Buddhist monk owns only his begging bowl, he has no worldly possessions to worry him.

Talking points

▶ Have we ever been greedy? (At festival times – do we eat more than we should? More than is good for us?).

▶ What is a miser? Do you think that misers are generally happy people?

▶ What are the basic needs of all people? Are they shelter, food, love, warmth, friendship etc? Do all people in our world today have their basic needs

met? Do some people have more than they need? Where do they live?

▶ Discuss how some people live below the level of basic need. Often these people live in nations that are still developing economically, but also a few people in the rich industrialized nations live below the level of basic need.

▶ Discuss the old Chinese proverb "Every key is a worry".

The little green bottle

Today, in Italy, in the city of Genoa there is a beautiful cathedral. Inside the cathedral, where everyone can see it, there is a little green bottle. This little green bottle is very old and once belonged to a King who lived in Italy many years ago.

The little green bottle contained a special medicine. It was supposed to cure all illnesses and anyone who drank it would live for ever. One day the King received a message from a man who was dying. The man had not seen his wife and children for several years and he begged for one drop of the medicine so that he could live long enough to see his children once again. The King thought about this request long and hard but decided he could not possibly open the bottle.

Then an old woman came to the palace. She could not walk and was carried by her friends. She told the King that her only son was dying; there would be no one to look after her. She begged for one drop of medicine from the green bottle, but to no avail. The King said he was keeping the medicine for somebody who really needed it. And so the old woman's son died.

Several more sick people begged for a drop of medicine, but each time the answer was the same. "The King is saving the medicine for someone who really needs it." People soon guessed that the King was being very selfish and keeping the medicine in the bottle for himself.

Years went by and the King himself became very ill. The doctors could not help him, and so, he asked for the little green bottle. Very carefully he removed the cork and put the bottle to his lips. Imagine his horror – the little green bottle was quite empty. The King had kept the bottle for so long that all the medicine had evaporated.

The King realized, at last, how greedy and selfish he had been. If he had shared the medicine he could have helped so many people. The King died, but the little green bottle was preserved. It was kept in a safe place and eventually put in the cathedral at Genoa to remind people that it is better to share than be greedy and selfish.

The man who wanted more

Nathalan was a farmer who lived by the sea. Every year he sowed wheat and in the late summer he collected in the harvest. One year the weather had been very good and Nathalan had a wonderful crop. The wheat had grown very tall and the sun had turned it to a wonderful golden colour. Somehow Nathalan couldn't quite bring himself to start cutting the wheat. He felt that if he left it one more day it would grow even taller and turn even more golden.

Then, quite suddenly, the weather changed, black clouds appeared in the sky and large drops of rain began to pelt down.

Make a Rich World/Poor World collage

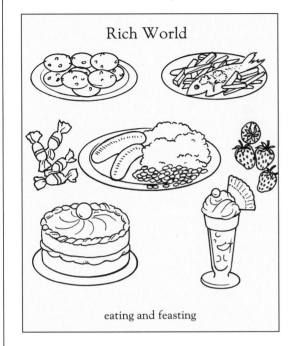

Rich World

eating and feasting

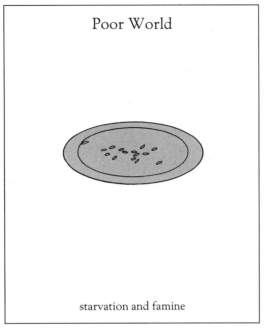

Poor World

starvation and famine

Nathalan's wonderful crop was ruined! Nathalan was furious with himself. "I have been a very stupid man" he raved. "God blessed me with a wonderful crop, but it wasn't enough I still wanted more. What a greedy fellow I am."

In his rage Nathalan decided to punish himself. He went down to the seashore and put a heavy chain around one ankle, fastening it with a lock. The key to this lock he threw out into the sea. He then set off on a pilgrimage to Rome. The journey was hard, the chain was heavy, and many times Nathalan regretted having thrown away the key. When he reached Rome he was tired and hungry and his clothes were worn and torn. He found his way to the market place and sat down. People thought

Nathalan was a beggar and a rich man tossed him a coin.

Nathalan was quite grateful for this and immediately went to buy food. He bought a fish from a fisherman who was selling his catch in the market square, and because he was so hungry he slit the fish open to eat it on the spot. As he pushed the knife into the fish it touched something hard – inside the fish he found a key. A key? No, *the* key. The one he had thrown into the sea!

Joyfully Nathalan undid the lock and freed his ankle from the chain. This time he threw away the chain and kept the key. He put the key on a cord around his neck to remind him of the time he had been so greedy and foolish, and he returned to his farm a wiser man.

Greed

There was once a young man called "Preedy"
And he was incredibly greedy
He ate lots of rump steak
Five buns and a cake
Then said, "Oh! my tum feels quite seedy."

There was a young lady, Miss Reedy
Her friends told me she was quite greedy
She hid all her sweets,
And never gave treats,
That selfish young lady – Miss Reedy.

There once was an old Mr Beady
He shared all his things with the needy
He gave things away,
And others would say
Mr Beady, will never be greedy.

Doreen Vause

Things to do

▶ Write and illustrate a limerick (a five line nonsense verse) about a greedy person.

▶ In connection with the story of Nathalan, make a frieze of the world under the sea. What sort of fish do you think could have eaten Nathalan's key?

▶ Ask the children to name all their favourite foods. For example: bangers and beans, fruit jelly and ice cream, jammy doughnuts, chocolate biscuits, fish and chips. Ask the children to illustrate these on paper plates. Use the plates to make a Rich World/Poor World frieze. Make the lettering round and fat for the Rich World and thin and straight for the Poor World.

Discontentment

People who are discontented never seem to be happy and what is worse, make other people feel unhappy too. The aim of this topic is to help children recognize discontentment when they meet it and to find ways of coping with it. Also, to help children differentiate a genuine grievance from discontentment with life in general.

Talking points

► Discuss the difference between a person with ambition and a person who is always dissatisfied with things.

► Talk about the effect that unjustified grumbling has on other people.

► Consider people who might have legitimate grumbles about their situation.

► Think about a situation where people are grumbling. What are they grumbling about? Are they right to do so?

► People in this country are often discontented with the climate, they grumble about the weather. Discuss the benefits of a climate such as ours.

► Would people be content if our country suffered from drought and famine like some countries.

Pete the lonely mongrel dog

Pete was a lonely mongrel dog
Who lived in Central Wigan.
He had a great thought one winter's day
While out for bones a-digging:
He'd change his life and he'd change his ways
And a sailor-man he'd be,
So he packed his tail and buried his bones
And off to sea went he.

He joined an English man-'o-war
As first mate to the captain,
They travelled far to many lands
Where the trees were tall and champion.
He roamed the seas until he found
It wasn't what he'd dreamed:
There was no place to bury his bones
And his tail was a permanent green.
He'd change his life and he'd change his ways
And a soldier he would be.
So he buried his bones in the ocean deep
And off to war went he.
He joined the Royal Artillery
As mascot to the battery.
Well he combed his hair and polished his tail
And did things very exactly.
Well they marched him up and down the
*   square*
And stood him to attention,
But when he chased the cook-house cat
They put him in detention.
He'd change his life and he'd change his ways
And an airman he would be,
So he swapped his guns for a set of wings
And off to fly went he.

He joined the Royal flying lads as assistant
*   navigator*
At finding his way from here to there
There never was anyone greater.
He flew through the air at incredible speeds
And sometimes upside down,
And after a while he thought it was
Much safer on the ground.

He'd change his life and he'd change his ways
And go back to his digging,
So he packed his tail and he left his bones
And sniffed his way back to Wigan.

He'd change his life and he'd change his ways
And he'd go back to his digging,
And spend his days in simple ways:
With his tail 'neath the trees of Wigan.

John Meeks and Colin Radcliffe

The clever Rabbi

This tale is about a Jewish man called Jethro who lived many years ago with his family in a comfortable house on the edge of a large city. His wife was a jolly woman and they had six healthy children, but Jethro for some reason always had a long miserable face and something new to moan about. His reputation as a grumbler spread far and wide, and people tended to avoid him.

One day Jethro was sitting in the park gazing miserably at the spring flowers when the local Rabbi joined him for a chat. The local Rabbi had heard a great deal about Jethro and his moaning and felt that he would like to help him. Jethro started complaining to the Rabbi about how his house was too small for his big family. The Rabbi was very sympathetic and suggested that perhaps the house would *seem* bigger if Jethro got the cockerel from the coope at the bottom of his garden and kept it inside the house.

Jethro hurried home to try this out, but he was soon back moaning to the Rabbi that his house was still too small. This time the Rabbi told him to take his donkey inside the house as this may be the answer to his problem. Jethro did as he was advised but once again returned to the Rabbi. This time the Rabbi told him to take the cow inside his house. Can you imagine the commotion? Jethro hurried back to the Rabbi to complain about the noise. "It's quite easy," said the Rabbi, "If you take out the cockerel, the donkey and the cow, then you will certainly have more room, there will be less noise, and you will have no need to grumble any more."

Jethro did as the Rabbi said and was most surprised to discover that there was quite enough room for his family to live comfortably. He was very grateful to the Rabbi and everyone was very pleased to see Jethro smiling.

A display of masks made by junior children

Sun and shadow

Who cares if April brings a shower
The birds sing in the sky
And keep on singing, knowing well
The clouds will soon pass by.
When clouds blow up, and thick and fast
Misfortunes fall like rain
We cheerfully will carry on till
The sun shines out again.

Doreen Vause

Things to do

► Make a list of all the things that make you feel contented.

► Jumbled Grumbles: make a list of grumbling words (for example, pessimist, grousing, discontentment, grumbling, moaning, complaining, dissatisfaction, faultfinding). When you have made your list jumble up the letters in each word (for example, nanigom for moaning) and let your friends sort them out.

► Write a story which ends with "in future, don't grumble, count your blessings instead".

► Find out what sort of work a Rabbi does. There are many amusing stories about a Rabbi being ingenious. Perhaps you could make a collection.

► Make a play out of the story of *The clever Rabbi*.

► Make animal masks to use in the play. You will need a cockerel, a donkey and a cow.

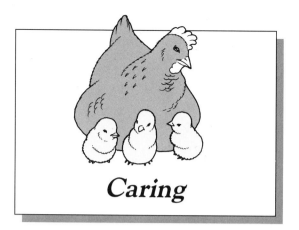

Caring

Caring is the cornerstone of all relationships; without caring there is nothing. All religions encourage their followers to care about the needs of others. The aim of this topic is to make children aware of what it means to care. Caring about the quality of our work, how we spend our time, caring for those we love, for those in need, the less fortunate, the weak.

Talking points

▶ Everyone of us needs someone to care for us. Who cares for you? Talk about how babies, elderly people, and the handicapped may need special care.

▶ Discuss the voluntary agencies who 'care'. For example: the Samaritans, Save the Children Fund, Oxfam, UNESCO, the Red Cross.

▶ Talk about emergency relief: caring for people after natural disasters like earthquakes, famine and flood.

▶ Talk about the special initiatives of Bob Geldof in raising both money and public awareness of famine in Africa.

Days

I wasted it
It's gone
And I repent
The precious day
You gave me
Came and went!
It wasn't really mine
To throw away
I'm sorry that I
Used it up that way,
Remind me that my days
Are just on loan
Forgive me
When I treat them
As my own.
But here's another,
Fresh and clean
And new.
Help me to use it
Wisely Lord, For You.

John Gowans

The street children of Bogotá

Luis is now 16 years old and goes to a secondary school, he hopes eventually to get a good factory job and marry. Luis has been very lucky but he remembers a very unhappy childhood spent wandering the streets of Bogotá in Latin America. Listen to his story.

I cannot remember having a father or a mother. I grew up like many other children in Latin America. I had only a city pavement to call home. We spent our time in little gangs swarming across the rubbish covered streets, picking pockets, stealing purses and watches or food in order to survive. Sometimes we managed to earn honest money by shining shoes.

At night we slept in doorways or beneath park benches. I remember the cold wind which whips down from the Andes mountains at night and how we often found a piece of cardboard to curl around our bodies to keep off the chill. Some of my friends would be wakened by armed police and 'taken in'; their crime was having no home, no parents, no place to sleep. They were children of the streets.

I once asked about my parents and I was told that many families from rural backgrounds left the country plots they worked and were lured to the cities by the promise of factory jobs, but most of them were disappointed because they lacked the industrial skills which were necessary. They found themselves in a trap of poverty and parents full of despair neglected and even abandoned their children. I was told that there are about three million homeless street children in Latin America, children just like me.

One night in 1986 I was walking the street in one of Bogotá's worst slums when I met a young friendly guy, the first person in my whole life who seemed to want to know me. After that I met him several times and we became friends. One night I was suffering from a terrible earache and along came my new friend. He took me along to a large courtyard where he obtained medical attention for me and I was given a meal, after which, I returned to the familiar streets.

That was the beginning of my journey away from the street community. I was soon to realize that my new friend was working as a 'street teacher' for the United Nations project. This project has organized groups of 'street teachers' who bring

Kum ba yah

1 Kum ba yah, my Lord, Kum ba yah. Kum ba yah, my Lord, kum ba yah, Kum ba yah, my Lord, kum ba yah, O Lord, — kum ba yah.

traditional

Things to do

▶ Make up your own words to fit the song *Kum ba yah*. For example:

Someone's hungry Lord
Kum ba yah
Someone's lonely Lord
Kum ba yah
Someone's caring Lord
Kum ba yah

▶ Find out if any of the class have family links with other countries. Make a display of drawings of the flags of these countries.

▶ Find out about the work of the Red Cross and about its flag. Why is a different flag used in some countries?

▶ Find out about the work of the voluntary agencies. Choose one and make a special study of its work.

▶ Arrange for a social worker, district nurse or similar person to talk about their caring role with the children.

▶ Establish a link with a local special school. Bring children together in joint activities, each to learn from the other. This will help children see that others have contributions as well as needs.

▶ Organize a drama activity based either on a story, or based on the children's imagination, or based on real life description from social workers.

▶ Talk about pride in oneself: caring about the quality of our work and how we spend our time.

abandoned children into a care scheme. Many residencies have been set up and at first boys and girls can come and go as they wish. The routine and discipline were too strict for me at first, because I had always been used to doing things just as I liked and when I liked. I enjoyed playing team games, I enjoyed the hot meals and hot showers. On the first night when I stayed I was given a clean pair of pyjamas and I did not know what I was supposed to do with them.

Eventually I lived at the residence all the time and helped in the grounds by cutting the lawns, tending the plants and sweeping the paths. I also carried out certain chores within the house itself. Some of the boys wanted the benefits but were not prepared to play their part in doing the chores and they returned to the streets. I have never regretted the night I met my friend 'the street teacher', the one who showed he cared. Now I am a 'street teacher' helping the United Nations to care for some of the homeless children who wander the streets of Bogotá in Latin America.

Generosity

Everyone likes receiving presents – particularly children – but it is important that children come to realize that it is the act of giving and the attitude of mind that is of value. All religions encourage their followers to give to the less fortunate. There are different ways of giving: money, goods, time and effort. It is not necessary for the gift to be expensive, what is important is that the gift is offered for the right reasons.

Talking points

▶ Talk about the times that people give presents: birthdays, festivals, special occasions.

▶ Talk about why people give presents: to show their love and affection, to say thank you for an act of kindness. Discuss the sending of 'Thank you letters'.

▶ Flowers and garlands are traditional gifts in many cultures, both between individuals and as offerings in temples, shrines and churches. Talk about the different occasions on which flowers are given.

▶ Discuss 'Thanksgiving' festivals. What are people giving thanks for?

▶ Talk about the simple gifts which cost nothing and can mean so much: a friendly smile, a helping hand, ten minutes to stop and listen to someone's problems.

Super-walk '88

On my way to the Super-walk I felt very excited. I went with the Cedars Crawlers a group from my Mum's school. While I was walking I felt very happy and proud. I wished I had worn another pair of shoes because I got a blister on my little toe. I kept on asking my Mum "How far is there to go?", my Mum kept saying, "Not far."

I didn't make it to the finish because I felt sick, but my Mum did. We raised a lot of money for the Scanner Appeal, which will help to buy a scanner for people suffering from cancer.

David Grimshaw aged 9 years

The Gift of love

About 2,500 years ago a great teacher lived in India. He was the son of a nobleman but he rejected his comfortable life and wandered from place to place instead. He persuaded people to show love and respect for all living things. He became known as the Lord Buddha, and Buddhism, the religion he founded, spread throughout India to Sri Lanka, Thailand and China. There are many statues of the Buddha, but the statue in this story stands in a temple in China.

Long ago, the people living near the temple decided that they wanted a new statue of Buddha. The monks went out and about, far and wide, collecting gifts from the people so that they could make the statue. The youngest of the monks was very keen. One day he visited the house of a rich merchant. The whole household was assembled to hear the monk talk about the wisdom and gentleness of the Lord Buddha. This included the smallest servant girl who helped with the household chores. She worked hard all day long in return for her food and her clothes. The only thing that she owned was a worthless copper coin.

They all listened carefully to what the young monk had to tell them: the stories of the Lord Buddha, and the request for contributions to his statue. The rich merchant gave gold and silver coins and huge ornate vases; the ladies offered their gold jewellery, silver bracelets and brooches; friends gave silver ornaments and gold rings. The young monk was very pleased with all these things and wrapped them up carefully. As he was leaving, the tiny servant girl stopped him and offered her only treasure – the worthless copper coin.

"Take this," she said, "It is all I have, but I want to give this for the wise, gentle Buddha." The monk was very young and he didn't really stop to think. He was in a hurry to get back and show the other monks what he had collected. He waved the servant girl aside.

When the monks had collected many precious gifts they melted them all down to make the statue. They poured the liquid metal into a mould and waited anxiously for it to set. When all was ready, they broke open the mould. Imagine their disappointment, for the statue was very very ugly. They decided to start again, but exactly the same thing happened.

"The metal was very badly mixed," one wise old monk said, "I fear this is a sign that one of us has not shown sufficient love and kindness." The young monk courageously stepped forward and confessed that he had refused the small gift from the servant girl at the house of the rich merchant. "Go back and accept the gift," advised the old monk, "Although the gift was small it was given with a kind and loving heart." The young monk hurried back to the merchant's house and asked the servant girl if she would still give her small coin for the statue of the Buddha. The girl was thrilled to think that her small coin was needed after all and she willingly handed it to the monk.

For a third time the metal was melted down and poured into the mould, and for a third time the monks waited anxiously to see the result. But they need not have worried so. This time the statue was perfectly beautiful – and on the chest of the Buddha there was a small copper coin – the gift of the servant girl – the gift offered with a loving heart!

Temple flowers for a Buddhist festival

 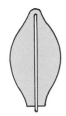   

1. Cut 10 petal shapes out of **coloured paper**. Make a petal by taking two shapes and gluing them together with **fuse wire** in between. Make 5 petals altogether.

2. Make a stamen out of a strip of **yellow crepe paper**. Roll the strip between the fingers to twist and splay it out at the top. Make 5 stamens.

3. Gather the petals around the stamens and bind them tightly together with **cotton**. Open the flower out and bend the petals back. Make a shrine like the one in the photograph and decorate it with your flowers.

A prayer for giving

Help us, dear God:
To be more ready to give than to receive;
To be more willing to help other people;
To be more thoughtful for the needs of others;
To be more ready to share those things we have;
And, in doing so, to find for ourselves
The true happiness that money can never buy

From *Dear God* by Rowland Purton

Things to do

▶ Make gift-wrap paper and matching gift tags suitable for gifts for different occasions.

▶ Make gift tags from old birthday cards and Christmas cards.

▶ Write a story entitled 'A most wonderful gift'.

▶ Learn the poem *A smile* which is on page 11.

▶ Make paper flowers and use them to decorate a shrine for a Buddhist festival.

▶ Encourage chidren to adopt a charity. Ask them first of all to select the charity through discussion, and then decide on ways to raise money to donate to the charity. This should be a classroom activity with benefits both as a learning activity and for the chosen charity.

Anger

Anger is a very natural human feeling but all too often people try to suppress their anger and sometimes it can erupt totally out of control. This topic aims to make children aware of their own feelings and to realize the consequences of uncontrolled anger. If we recognize feelings of anger we are more able to control them and avert disastrous consequences. We may even be able to do good.

Talking points

▶ Discuss times when you have been angry. Analyse when and why with the children. Encourage children to do the same.

▶ Discuss the kind of things that make us angry.

▶ Discuss what it feels like when someone is angry with you.

▶ Talk about the colours associated with being angry. For example, 'seeing red' or "showing a red rag to a bull".

▶ Discuss times when you think that anger is justified.

Coloured feathers

Old Thaddeus lived in a small house which was one of several surrounding a courtyard, one of many such courtyards to be found in Kwara State in Nigeria.

Thaddeus sat outside his little home. It was evening and as the sun sank down he was reminiscing over the day's events. He spoke in the language known as Yoruba and said, "I'm so glad that I was able to help that young lad, I remember when I was his age." Thaddeus thought he was alone and talking to himself but he was startled when a voice said, "What do you remember grandfather?" There behind him stood Abiodun his grandson.

"Alright! Come here my boy and I will tell you." Thaddeus began his story, "It seems a long time ago now, but when I was young I had my troubles. You see, Abiodun, I had a very bad temper and I soon became agitated when things went the slightest bit wrong for me. What is more, when my temper got the better of me, I would rashly say angry words to anyone who happened to be around me. The result of this was that I was losing many friends and becoming more lonely everyday. One day my father said that my bad temper and anger were defeating me and that he felt we should go to discuss the matter with the wisest old person in the village. He was a sort of farmer chief whose name was Sepho. We went along and Sepho asked me one or two questions about how I felt when I went into a silly rage, then old Sepho said that he knew the answer."

"To my surprise the old farmer handed me a bag of coloured feathers. 'What shall I do with these?' I said. Sepho replied, 'Listen carefully Thaddeus. Later tonight when all is dark and still, you must go and place one feather at the entrance to every dwelling in the village. Tomorrow before the crack of dawn you must return here, and I will give you further instructions.'"

"Did you do that grandfather?" asked Abiodun. "Yes, I went round to each house and placed a coloured feather outside each door. Then very early next morning Sepho sent me to pick up and collect the feathers but this was impossible for there had been a strong breeze all night long. I went and stood before Sepho and told him that the task he had set was impossible."

"'Yes, Yes,' Sepho said, 'Remember this, Thaddeus. The angry words you speak in rage are like those feathers. Once said they cannot be retrieved, they hurt someone and the damage is done – it is impossible to cancel words once they are uttered, but it is possible to be aware of our feelings and control our anger.'"

Thaddeus then smiled at his grandson and said very slowly, "I learnt my lesson Abiodun, and I'm glad I did, or today I would be a friendless and lonely old man."

Gelert the wolfhound

There was a time when Britain was not a united kingdom and England, Scotland and Wales each had their own kings and princes. Life was much harder and wilder than it is today. Wolves roamed in the forests and people hunted animals for food. In Wales at this time, Prince Llewelyn and his followers went out hunting with huge dogs called wolfhounds. These dogs helped them catch animals for food but they also protected them from the wolves.

Llewelyn had one favourite hound called Gelert. He also had a baby son. Llewelyn

Make a shadow puppet show

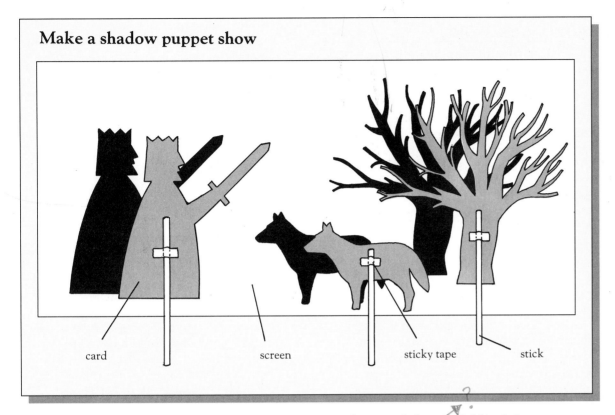

card screen sticky tape stick

handwritten marginal notes:

always to find his son
safe on the lambskin
one guarded her
by faithful
not found Gelert.

became very afraid that whilst he was out hunting, a wolf might wander into his home from the forest and harm his child. So Llewelyn started to leave his favourite hound behind to guard his son. The child lay on lambskin on top of a small wooden platform and faithful Gelert lay in front.

Each time the prince returned in the evening he went straight to see his baby son. One day to his horror he returned to find neither Gelert nor his baby son, just a trail of blood on the floor. Llewelyn was a quick tempered man and immediately thought that Gelert had attacked the baby and then run off. The prince in a great rage drew his sword and set off in pursuit. He followed the trail of blood, and before long he came across Gelert trotting down the path towards him with blood dripping from his mouth. Without a second thought Llewelyn ran forward and killed the faithful hound.

Then, Llewelyn looked around wildly for the body of his son. He followed the trail of blood. And, just round the corner he found a mangled body, not of his son, but of a wolf. At that moment messengers arrived to say that his son had been found alive and well. Llewelyn was devastated. He had killed his friend because of a mistake.

Llewelyn buried Gelert at a place he named 'Beddgelert'. If you ever go to north Wales you can still see this place where almost 700 years ago a prince buried his most faithful friend having acted too quickly in anger.

A grudge

There isn't much point in nursing a grudge,
For the one who will suffer is you;
It clouds all the sunbeams that make life
  worthwhile,
And blights every happiness too.

So bury it deep as you possibly can,
Dig with a smile on your face,
And you'll find where that grudge used to
  wrankle and burn,
A flower will grow in its place.

Doreen Vause

Things to do

▶ Write sentences beginning:

I become angry when I see   _ _ _ _ _ _

I become angry when I hear   _ _ _ _ _

I become angry when I feel   _ _ _ _

I become angry when I know   _ _ _ _

▶ Make simple cut-outs for the characters in the story *Gelert the wolfhound*. Use these to put on a shadow puppet show for your friends to enjoy.

Write the story of a play for your shadow puppets.

▶ Put yourself in the place of Llewelyn. How would you feel if the same things happened to you?

▶ Read the poem *If* by Rudyard Kipling.

25

Kindness

A little kindness can go a long way towards making life easier for everyone. We all need kindness; even those who seem strong, like Mum, Dad or teachers get tired, ill or down-hearted and will be grateful for a kind word or deed. We can show kindness in many ways sometimes this means giving our time, or money or giving just a smile or friendly word.

Talking points

▶ Ask the children about times when people have been kind to them.

▶ Discuss cruelty as the opposite of kindness. How would the children feel if they knew they had been cruel or missed an opportunity to be kind.

▶ Discuss kindness to animals and the work of the RSPCA.

▶ Talk about different ways of showing kindness, some involve giving time, money, a friendly smile or word.

▶ Who needs our kindness most? The young and the old, people with special needs, the sick, the lonely.

The Pingalwara

Puran Singh was the son of a Sikh banker, but when he was a young man his father fell on hard times and the family business collapsed. Puran Singh was then left without a job to earn him a living. He moved to Lahore thinking that he may find employment there. He found free food and lodging in the Gurdwara of Guru Arjan Dev. He helped each day to serve food from the Gurdwara's kitchen to the many poor and sick people who came there to be fed. He noticed how many of these people were in need of medical treatment and would accompany them to a nearby hospital.

One day, as he went about his work, he noticed a small child at the entrance to the Gurdwara. As he came closer to the child he noticed that the little boy was crippled and later realized that the child had been left there all alone with no one to care for him. Puran Singh was a kind person, and took care of this little crippled boy and decided that from that day onwards he would not look for a job, he knew how he would spend his life. He would work to help the poor, the crippled, the sick and lonely. These people needed someone to show them kindness.

In India, in 1947, hospital treatment was not free. Puran Singh went to Amritsar, which is well-known for its Golden Temple, and there he encouraged other people to show kindness by giving money so that his work with the sick and poor could continue. Puran Singh bought several tents and pitched these a small distance from the hospital. Soon the tents were full of people, for the poor and sick came in large numbers and Puran Singh cared for them, taking them to the hospital when they needed treatment.

When people heard of the good work in this small settlement they sent along gifts of money, food and clothing. Eventually doctors and nurses went to the settlement to work with the poor and as the news spread further, more money began to pour in. In 1950 Puran Singh was able to build a large home which he called a Pingalwara. It became known as Bhagat Puran Singh's Pingalwara. Bhagat means Saint and Pingalwara means a home for the crippled.

The kind gorilla

We often hear stories of people who have done kind deeds, but this is a story about an animal who showed kindness to a human being.

On 2 September 1986, the newspapers and television news told a story about a family who went to spend a day at a zoo in Jersey. It should have been a very happy time but a terrible accident happened which could have had very serious consequences. Listen to the story.

Mr and Mrs Merritt and their son, Levan, arrived at the zoo. Levan, was just 5 years old and wanted to see all the animals but especially the monkeys, baboons, apes and gorillas which we all find quite amusing.

The family walked over towards a large enclosure in which there were gorillas. Father lifted Levan so that he could have a good view of the animals, which were safely enclosed in a huge deep pit, surrounded by a small wall.

The little boy had seen the animals but wanted to have another look and decided to climb up on the wall once more. Father turned away for just one second and Levan toppled from the wall and fell down forty

Make big and little animals

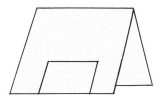

1. Cut out the shaded area through both bits of **card**.

3. Draw a head for the body. Cut out and push the neck edge into the slit. Make a tail from **paper** or **wool** and place it between the fold.

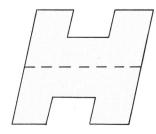

2. Open out. Paint or print the animal's coat.

4. The shape of the animal can be adjusted by cutting off the shaded areas.

Different textures such as **gummed spots**, pieces of **material** and strands of **wool** can be added.

---

feet, into the pit amongst the animals.

Everyone around was horrified. The incident happened so quickly, but now poor Levan was lying motionless and injured. There he was, down at the bottom of the deep pit and surrounded by wild and unpredictable animals.

Then the animals gathered around Levan. The largest animal which was seven feet tall walked slowly over to the little boy, it towered over him, the spectators were filled with fear. What was going to happen now?

The seven foot gorilla sniffed around and then stroked Levan gently. The other animals were inquisitive and came closer but the large gorilla could be seen to warn them to keep away. The huge gorilla stood guard over the injured boy whilst the other gorillas looked up at the watching crowds. They appeared to be appealing to the crowd for help.

As little Levan came conscious he screamed, and the animals backed away. Zoo workers then carried Levan to safety.

Levan was extremely lucky. The large powerful gorilla had shown such kindness and gentleness. Mr and Mrs Merritt and Levan will never forget their day out at Jersey zoo.

Things to do

▶ Find pictures of apes, gorillas, baboons and monkeys. Where do they live and what do they eat?

▶ Scan newspaper reports of people who help others.

▶ Find out more about the Sikh community in Britain.

▶ Find out about the work of organizations like the RSPCA, the PDSA and the NSPCC.

Truth and Honesty

Truthfulness and fair play are important aspects of all cultures. Children must develop a regard for the rights of others and set standards for their own behaviour.

Talking points

▶ Discuss the idea of 'pretence'. Pretending to be better than we are, pretending in order to avoid work, fakes, forgeries, cheating. Discuss the telling of lies and how it is always better to be truthful even when the consequences are not very nice. How when we lie we only cheat ourselves.

▶ Discuss the saying "Honesty is the best policy".

▶ Discuss how we feel when we find out someone has lied to us.

▶ Discuss how communities can help combat crime in the neighbourhoods. Talk about 'Crime Watch Posters'.

▶ Discuss the saying "crying wolf" and the telling of lies in order to play a joke on someone. Is this kind of lying justified?

The reward

Long ago in the larger towns and cities, town criers went up and down the streets reporting the latest news to the townspeople. One night a particular town crier told the listeners that a bag containing a large number of gold coins had been lost and the finder would be given a reward of half their value.

When the townspeople knew the value of the reward they became diligently watchful, and eventually a poor man found the bag of coins. Although he was in need of the money himself, he was a very honest man, so immediately he hurried along to find the town crier. He asked to whom the bag of coins should be returned and how he should claim his reward.

The town crier sent the poor man to the home of a rich merchant. When the merchant saw the man he was delighted to know that his gold coins were safe. He invited the finder into his house and when the bag of coins was handed over the merchant emptied the contents on to a huge table.

The merchant then decided that the reward which he had offered was too high and wanted to keep all the coins for himself, so he quickly thought of a plan to avoid having to pay the reward he had promised.

"What has happened to the precious stone?", the merchant asked.

"I have seen no precious stone. I am returning to you the bag of coins which I found", said the poor man.

"You rascal", said the merchant, "You are not an honest fellow, you are a thief, go away quickly or I will have you imprisoned."

The poor man knew that he had been

entirely honest and therefore did not fear the merchant's threat. "Come then", he said, "We will go to the court together so that the matter can be settled".

Inside the courtroom each man was given the opportunity to tell his own story. The merchant insisted that the bag of coins which he had lost had also contained a diamond, whilst the finder of the purse said that the purse contained only coins.

The judge looked carefully at each man and thought deeply then he said, "I have solved the problem. This bag of coins which this man has found cannot possibly belong to the merchant. The merchant's bag contained a diamond and this bag did not." The judge then turned to the merchant and said, "I hope that you will find your purse before very long."

To the poor man the judge said, "You are a honest and trustworthy man, if this purse is not claimed within the next four weeks, you shall become its new owner, the purse and the money will be yours."

The dishonest merchant left the courtroom with nothing.

The enchanted bell

It's a horrible feeling when someone breaks into your home and steals your things. It's even worse if you know that the thief must be one of your neighbours. Once, long ago, in China in a village on the banks of the Huang He River the people had a problem. Someone in the village was a thief; the villagers could no longer trust each other; and, although, there were several suspects locked up in the village jail, they all claimed to be innocent.

The head of the village sent for the village elders and they discussed the problem for some time but could find no

Lino-cut printing for Neighbourhood Watch stickers

1. Work out your own design for a Neighbourhood Watch sticker.

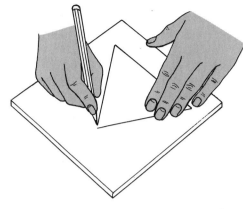

2. Draw out the design on a piece of linoleum.

3. Cut carefully along the lines to make a groove.

4. Spread printing ink on to the linoleum using a roller.

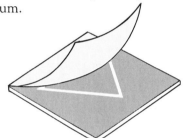

5. Press paper carefully on to the linoleum. Peel off the paper and let it dry before you cut it out.

6. Try a repeat pattern on a large sheet of paper to make a poster.

---

solution. Eventually, however, the headman had an idea. He ordered that a huge tent should be erected, and inside the tent on a platform an enormous bell was placed. All the villagers turned out to watch. The headman told the crowd that the bell was enchanted and would ring out loudly if a thief was to touch it.

When all was ready the suspects were brought from the village jail. The headman told them that they were to enter the tent one at a time, touch the bell, and then come out again and wait. One by one the men entered the tent to touch the bell. One

by one they came out again, but the bell did not ring. People were beginning to think that the bell had no magical powers.

Then the headman asked the suspects to show their hands. All of them had dirty black marks on them, except for one. "You," shouted the headman, "You are the thief. You didn't dare to touch the bell because you knew you were guilty. I know because I put black soot all over the bell and your hands are still clean!"

And so, the dishonest thief was caught and punished and the villagers could trust each other once again.

Things to do

▶ Make lists of 'good' words and 'bad' words.

▶ Design and build a burglar alarm. The alarm could ring when the door was opened, a mat trodden on, or a cup lifted.

▶ Make Neighbourhood Watch stickers and posters.

▶ Dramatize the story *The reward*.

Loyalty and Friendship

Relationships with other people demand truthfulness, honesty and loyalty. Friendships involve certain responsibilities; loyalty requires a duty to others. If we belong to a club we get benefits from our membership, but at the same time it demands our time and places certain expectations on us. Sometimes we may not want to fulfil our obligations, but we must give as well as take.

Talking points

▶ Discuss what it means to have a friend. What are your duties towards your friend?

▶ Talk about two sayings "The strength of a chain is its weakest link" and "A friend in need is a friend indeed".

A friend remembered

The days were drawing shorter and winter was coming fast. Soon the snow would start to fall. This year yet again the harvest had been poor; there would not be enough to eat right through the winter. Farmer Roth said a fond goodbye to his two eldest sons. "You will be better in the city," he said sounding more cheerful than he felt. "You will both find good jobs, and if we are careful here, we will have enough to eat until the spring."

The two boys set out westwards on foot. It was a hard journey and took several weeks. Their clothes were ragged and they had hardly any money. One night they knocked on the door of a large house. They were cold and tired and all they wanted was to sleep in the stable with the horses; but they were turned out into the rain with the dogs growling menacingly from the warm lighted doorway. Further down the road they had more luck. The blacksmith was just shutting his forge for the night. He called the boys over and invited them in, offering food and a bed for the night.

In the morning the young men thanked the blacksmith and tried to give him what little money they had. But the blacksmith would take nothing. Instead, he simply wished them well and sent them on their way. "If you ever come this way again, don't forget to call in," he said pumping the air into the fire in his forge.

At last the boys reached the city, they settled down and worked hard. Several years passed and they had become rich and very famous. One day, whilst travelling between cities they neared the village where the hospitable blacksmith still tended his forge. As the brothers approached, a servant appeared in great haste. He brought an invitation from the rich man with the big house. "This is a fine invitation," said one of the brothers, "It seems we are offered a banquet, a bed, and a stable for the horses." "Return to your master," said the other brother, "Tell him, last time we came here we were very poor. He had no time for us then, and we have no time for him now. We are going to stay with our friend the blacksmith."

The old brown horse

The old brown horse looks over the fence
In a weary sort of way;
He seems to be saying to all who pass:
"Well, folks, I've had my day –
I'm simply watching the world go by,
And nobody seems to mind,
As they're dashing past in their motorcars,
A horse who is lame and half-blind."

The old brown horse has a shaggy coat,
But once he was young and trim,
And he used to trot throught the woods and
  lanes
With the man who was fond of him.
But his master rides in a motorcar,
And it makes him feel quite sad
When he thinks of the days that used to be,
And of all the times they had.

Sometimes a friendly soul will stop
Near the fence, where the tired old head
Rests wearily on the topmost bar,
And a friendly word is said.
Then the old brown horse gives a little sigh
As he feels the kindly touch
Of a hand on his mane or his shaggy coat,
And he doesn't mind so much.

So if you pass by the field one day,
Just stop for a word or two
With the old brown horse who was once as /young
And as full of life as you.
He'll love the touch of your soft young hand,
And I know he'll seem to say –
"Oh, thank you, friend, for the kindly thought
For a horse who has had his day."

W K Holmes

How to draw a horse

1.

2.

3.

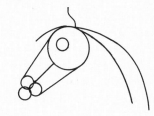

4.

5.

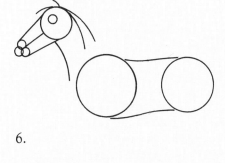

6.

7.

8.

Almost a Friend

I almost phoned,
I almost spoke,
I almost invited
the next-door folk.
Oh! What a pity
No-one knew
All the good
I meant to do.

Doreen Vause

Things to do

▶ Illustrate the poem *The old brown horse*. Horses are not that easy to draw so there are some tips to help.

▶ Imagine you are the horse and write about the way you feel.

▶ Draw a portrait of your best friend and underneath describe why you chose this person for a friend.

▶ Write a letter to a friend whom you have not seen for some time but whom you are soon going to visit. Try to recall a time when you enjoyed yourself in the past and let them know how much you are looking forward to seeing them again.

▶ Try to make contact with another school where the children are of a different cultural background or environment to your own. You could try to enlist the help of your advisory service. They may know of a school which would be a good match.

Justice and Injustice

Charles Dickens wrote "In this world in which little children exist there is nothing so finely perceived or so finely felt as injustice." Children in the junior age range are keenly aware of rules when playing games. The aim here is to help the children to the realization that fair-play is for the benefit of all.

Talking points

▶ What are rules? School rules, why we need rules, unfair play, gaining at the expense of others.

▶ Talk about the laws of our land. Why must we drive on the left? Who makes our laws? Who enforces the law? What happens if you break the law?

▶ Talk about "The scales of justice" the symbol of justice on the Old Bailey, Why blindfolded?

▶ Talk about Libra a sign of the Zodiac. Discuss with the children the difference between astronomy and astrology. Point out that some people deplore beliefs in astrology whilst others see it as fun.

Solomon and the baby

King Solomon was the son of David and Bathsheba, he reigned over the land of Israel in the 10th century BC. He was noted for his wisdom and during his reign the people knew peace. Through his wisdom King Solomon was able to make alliances with Phoenicia and Egypt and trade and commerce expanded. During his reign many palaces and temples were built, the most famous building which was erected was the Temple at Jerusalem.

In those days if people could not find a solution to their problems, they brought them to the attention of the King who would act as adviser or judge. Thieves were often brought before the King and his judgement was final.

One day two women were brought before Solomon and a tiny child was carried into the royal throne room. One of the King's ministers told the King that the women were both claiming the child as their own. Solomon was asked to decide which woman was the rightful mother.

The King spoke to both women in turn and found that each woman appeared to be equally fond of the baby. Solomon thought for a long time then he turned to the women and said, "One of you only can be the child's mother, which one of you does not tell the truth?" Neither woman would say that the other woman was the true mother so Solomon called one of his soldiers to him. "Take out your sword", he said. "The only fair thing that I can possibly suggest, is that the child should be cut into two, then each woman may have a half."

At that moment one woman screamed out, "No, no, do not hurt the child, let her take it", and the woman fell down sobbing at the feet of the king. "I love the child dearly but I do not wish to see any harm come to it, give it to the other woman."

Solomon smiled and told the woman to stand up and dry her eyes. He then said, "It is very obvious that the child is yours, rather than see the baby harmed you were prepared to give it to the other woman. You are the real mother, take the child."

The child was placed in its mother's arms and the real mother left King Solomon's palace a happy woman. The King and his courtiers were also happy because they knew that justice had been done.

Saki Macozama

Saki Macozama is a quiet friendly young man. His home is in South Africa but he has recently visited England. When Saki is at home he works to care for the families of people who are detained in prison.

If people are arrested in our country they must be given a fair trial before they can be committed to a long sentence in prison. In some other countries people can be imprisoned for long spells without having had a trial. Some people in South Africa today feel the laws are harsh and repressive and unfair to the black population. Reports tell us that people have disappeared; young people have been arrested on their way to school or to the shops, for no other reason than they were at the right place at the wrong time and just happened to be black. Some of these young people have been detained without a trial, or sentenced to long terms of imprisonment. In some cases probably wicked acts have been committed and in these cases imprisonment is fair and just, but many suffer from injustice.

Whole families are affected because in may cases their 'breadwinner' has been taken from them and this brings about a situation of poverty. Families become desperate in their efforts to survive. The prisoners are very lonely because their families often cannot afford to visit relatives in prison because they cannot raise the cost of travel from the villages to the larger towns and cities.

Saki and others in his team care for these families, but they themselves, live and work under unimagineable pressures as they carry out their pastoral duties but as Christians they keep in mind the words of the Bible, "Keep in mind those who are in prison as though you were in prison with them. Remember those who are suffering as though you were suffering with them" (Hebrews 13:3). The purpose of Saki's visit to England was to ask for the prayers of people here for himself and his fellow workers, for the families who live in poverty, and for the young people who have suffered from injustice and those who are imprisoned without trial.

Things to do

▶ The ancient Egyptians believed that after death each person was given a book to help them to make the journey into the afterlife. This book recorded the person's deeds during their life time. The Egyptian god Osiris used this book to judge whether a person was worthy to enter paradise.

Draw or paint a picture of yourself. Use collage materials or paints. From the hands hang the pans of scales. On strips of paper write down deeds you have done. Use one colour for good deeds and one colour for wrong ones. Glue the good strips into one pan, and the wrong strips into the other.

▶ Write a short play entitled 'The day of judgement'.

▶ Make a visit to the local courts. You may be allowed to enter the courtroom when the court is not sitting.

▶ Make a class scrap book using cuttings from newspapers about events which happen in South Africa.

▶ Find out all that you can about Archbishop Desmond Tutu.

▶ Find out which laws have been passed to stop discrimination against certain groups of people.

▶ List the kinds of actions which would break these laws.

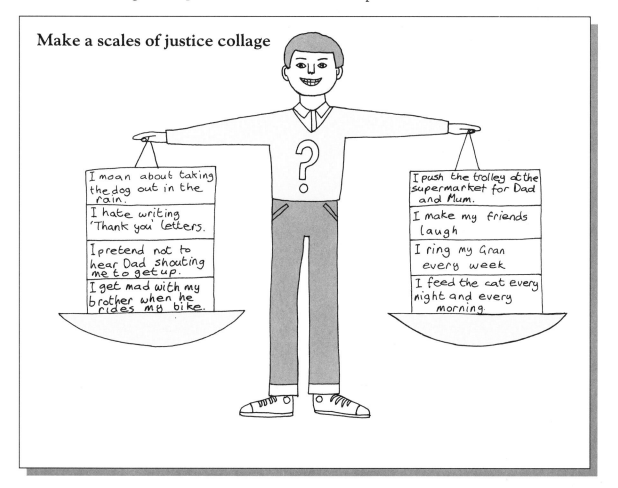

Make a scales of justice collage

I moan about taking the dog out in the rain.

I hate writing 'Thank you' letters.

I pretend not to hear Dad shouting me to get up.

I get mad with my brother when he rides my bike.

I push the trolley at the supermarket for Dad and Mum.

I make my friends laugh

I ring my Gran every week

I feed the cat every night and every morning.

Perseverance

The aim is to help the children to face difficulties they meet and try to overcome them.

Each one of us, at some time in our lives, meets a difficult task. People through the ages have conquered difficult tasks. Pioneers, inventors, musicians and scientists have persevered in the face of difficulties and as a result have been able to leave the world a better place for us today. Some very ordinary people have shown perseverance and determination when faced with difficulties. Today many people suffer the effects of unemployment and have to show great perseverance when seeking jobs. There is an old saying which says "If at first you don't succeed, try, try, and try again." There is a great deal of satisfaction gained when we feel that we have tried our best.

Talking points

▶ Ask the children to tell of times when they have found things very difficult.

▶ Ask the children how they felt when they were first learning to swim or ride a bicycle. Was it easy? Did they have to persevere?

▶ Discuss with the children how their younger brothers and sisters can be seen to persevere when learning to walk or tie shoes.

▶ Talk about how one must persevere and practice when learning to play a musical instrument.

▶ Discuss the saying "Where there's a will there's a way".

▶ Discuss the sense of fulfilment when we complete a task and feel that we have achieved, for example, the last piece of a difficult jigsaw puzzle.

Mary McLeod Bethune

Mary McLeod Bethune was born in the southern part of the United States in 1875. This was just at the time of the end of slavery and her mother was overjoyed that her seventeenth child was born free.

Because there were no schools for children in black villages, Mary went picking cotton from a very early age. One day a visitor suggested that she should go to the nearest school which was five miles away. Mary wanted so much to learn that she was willing to walk the ten miles a day, and she still found the energy in the evenings to teach her brothers and sisters all that she had learned that day.

She continued to love learning and finished her schooling when she was fifteen. It then looked as if she would spend the rest of her life back in the cotton fields, there seemed no other chances for her. During her time at school, though, she had formed her own ideas about equality and education, and she believed that everyone whether black, white, rich or poor should have a chance in life.

Mary was lucky, a dressmaker heard about her determination and paid for her to continue her education and she went on to college. She earned some money by making speeches and talking to meetings. Mary was a good orator. She eventually became a teacher.

For many years Mary wanted to have her own school, but all her money had gone back to her family who were still very poor. She found an old house in Florida which needed a great deal of repair, but she needed money to turn this into her school. She enlisted the support of local churches and with their help she collected enough money to make a start, but the struggle continued for some time. When the children came they used elderberry juice for ink and sticks for pens, Mary begged for lamps and books, her furniture for the building came from the town's rubbish dumps.

After a while the school became overcrowded and she started fund-raising again. She bought a plot of land where she built a college, and later went on to build a hospital for black people too. The Bethune Cookman College is still there today because of Mary McLeod's determination and perseverence. In 1934 Mary was put in charge of a government education programme for black youth, so she could make it possible for even more black children to be given a chance.

Robert Bruce

In the past the people of England and Scotland often fought each other. At the beginning of the 14th century, King Robert, who was known as Robert the Bruce, led his armies into battle against the

Try again

Have you seen the little spider in the corner?
She will spin and she will weave and she will fall;
The thread is thin and breaks, but however long it takes,
She will hang her shiny web upon the wall.
So I'll imitate the spider in the corner,
If at first I don't succeed I'll try again.
Though the way is very long, I will say, when things go wrong,
If I try, I'm bound to get there in the end.

Think about the salmon from the ocean;
They must swim against the tide and stand the test:
Leaping rocks and waterfalls, through streams and icy pools
Till, in gentle rivers they can take their rest.
So I'll imitate the salmon from the ocean . . .

Remember, too, the swallows in the sunshine:
Halfway round the world they have to fly;
Blown by stormy winds and rain. But they'll do it all again
To soar and swoop into a blue and summer sky.
So I'll imitate the swallow in the sunshine . . .

words and music by Sandra Kerr

English. The Scottish armies were defeated and as the King was returning home he sheltered inside a small cottage. He was tired and very depressed.

Many battles had been fought against the English but the result was always the same. King Robert wondered what he must do in order to win. He looked up and saw a spider above him. The spider was weaving a web and swinging itself between two adjacent beams. King Robert watched intently. The spider failed many times, but the little creature did not give up. So persistent was the spider that eventually the web was constructed. King Robert then knew what to do, he had learnt a lesson from a tiny creature. "If at first you don't succeed, try, try, try again."

Things to do

▶ Find out about the life history of the salmon. Why are they well known for their perseverence?

▶ How did Robert Bruce's fortunes change after his experience with the spider?

Bravery and Courage

All children will experience opposition to their views at some time or another. They often need courage to speak out when they know themselves to be in the right, or to speak out in defence of a friend. They need to appreciate the different kinds of courage: courage to overcome handicaps, physical bravery on behalf of others and the courage of their own convictions in the face of considerable opposition. They need to understand how changes in society can be accomplished by discussion.

Talking points

▶ Have you ever felt afraid? What makes you feel frightened? Are you afraid of the dark?

▶ Talk about awards for bravery and rescue work.

▶ Talk about heroes and heroines, martyrs and people who have died for a cause.

▶ Talk about pioneers in exploration who have shown bravery and courage, for example, the first astronauts – their feelings as they left Earth.

▶ Talk about people who have courage to defend the rights of others even if it means unpopularity.

▶ Talk about the courage which people need to overcome obstacles which they meet in their everyday lives, for example, blindness, deafness, immobility, poverty, separation.

Helen Keller

Helen Adams Keller, was born in 1880. She was a fine active baby, but at the age of nineteen months she caught a terrible fever. When she eventually recovered her mother discovered that she was both blind and deaf.

Little Helen was therefore living in a dark and lonely world, she could neither hear nor see. The little child became very frustrated and showed the frustration she was feeling by terrible tantrums in which she tore her clothes, destroyed anything in her environment or attacked anyone who went near her. Helen's parents sought help from many doctors but were told that Helen was a hopeless case.

When Helen was about seven years old her parents enlisted the help of a teacher named Anne Sullivan. When Anne first met Helen, the little child appeared to be rather wild, but Anne Sullivan did not despair. Helen was given different articles to hold in one hand whilst Anne traced out the name of the article on to the palm of her other hand. One day Anne splashed water on to Helen and traced out the letters of the word 'water'. At this point Helen realized what was required of her. She learnt the names of many things and from then on Helen and Anne could communicate with each other. Later Helen learnt Braille.

By the time Helen was eleven years old she had also learnt to speak by touching the throat of her teacher as she made sounds. This learning had taken perseverence on the part of both Anne and Helen, but it was a great achievement. Helen began to write stories at the age of twelve and later attended College. Whilst she was in College, in the year 1902, she wrote a book entitled *The Story of My Life*, which was translated into many different languages.

Helen Keller graduated from Radcliffe College, Cambridge, Massachusetts, in 1904, and went on to lecture in many countries and raise money for the education of people with special needs. This demanded great courage for someone who was both blind and deaf.

Helen Adams Keller died in 1968, she is remembered today as a writer, lecturer and social worker, but above all, as a person of courage and determination.

Votes for women

From time to time elections are held in Britain in order to select our local Councils and also for the selection of Members of Parliament. Men and women over the age of eighteen years have the right to cast a vote. This has not always been the case in Britain, at one time only *some* men were allowed to vote.

Some women felt that it was an injustice for men to be treated differently to women. In the 1860s a number of women organized committees and pointed out this injustice but they were ignored. No changes took place. So in 1903 Emmeline Pankhurst gathered together a group of women who decided that they must take

Make peg doll suffragettes

1. Wrap the end of a **clothes peg** in **cotton wool**. Cover with a piece of **flesh coloured material**. Tie tightly to make a head and neck.

  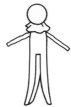

2. Wrap a **pipe cleaner** or a piece of covered wire around the neck to make arms. Paint a face and add hair. Gather a piece of **coloured material** around the neck and tie to make a waist and a long skirt. You can make more clothes from **bits of material, ribbon** or **paper**. Make lots of dolls.

3. Paint a street scene and arrange your dolls to hold a protest meeting.

A prayer for courage

Dear God, give us courage:
  Courage to go on when in difficulty,
  Courage to face all our problems with
    cheerfulness,
  Courage to stand up for what is right,
  Courage to be true to our beliefs.

At all times when we need that extra courage,
  dear God grant us your help.

From *Dear God* by Rowland Purton

Things to do

▶ Use your reference library and find out all you can about Anne Frank and her famous diary. Was she a person of courage?

▶ Helen Keller wrote a book entitled *The Story of My Life*. Write your own life story and illustrate it with photographs.

▶ Blindfold a friend. Try to communicate by writing words with your fingers on the palm of your friend's hand.

▶ Imagine a law was passed which ruled that only people with red hair could vote. Write about how you would feel. What would you do about it?

▶ Try to discover which countries in the world still discriminate by only allowing certain adults to vote.

▶ Use newspapers to find stories about people who have acted with great bravery and courage. Use your collection to make a book about brave people.

stronger action. These women went to political meetings and heckled the speakers. Some of them chained themselves to railings at Buckingham Palace and Downing Street, others were very violent and organized a window smashing demonstration in Oxford Street, London. One woman, named Emily Davison, even gave her life for the cause when she threw herself under the hooves of King Edward VII's horse during the running of the Derby Race in 1910.

The hecklers were treated badly by men, some were whipped, and others roughly handled and thrown out of meetings. The window smashers were arrested and sent to prison. Once in prison these women did not give up, as a protest against their sentences they went on hunger strike. At first the authorities forcibly fed these prisoners but there was a public outcry against this barbarity. Parliament then passed an Act in 1913 which was known as 'The Cat and Mouse Act', it allowed the release of a hunger striker, only for her to be re-arrested when she had recovered her health.

In 1918 a new law was passed through Parliament which allowed all men over twenty-one to vote and all women who were over thirty. It was not until 1928 that women in England were allowed to vote on the same terms as men.

The women who worked to gain votes for women, and remedy this injustice, became known as the Suffragettes.

Further Resources

This page contains a list, by topic, of additional ideas to follow up. These include songs, poems, hymns, stories and useful addresses.

page 8
The Pessimist, *Oxford Book of Poetry for Children*, OUP.
One more step along the world I go, *Someone's Singing Lord*, A & C Black, 1973.
Lord of all hopefulness, *Come and Praise*, BBC Publications, 1978.

page 10
When you're smiling, *Ta-ra-ra Boom-de-ay*, A & C Black, 1977.
If you're happy and you know it, *Apusskidu*, A & C Black, 1975.
Spread a little happiness, *Boomps-a-Daisy*, A & C Black, 1986.
Grandad, Kitt Wright, *Rabbitting On*, Puffin.

Page 12
St Valentine's Day, *A Musical Calendar of Festivals*, Ward Lock, 1983.
David and Jonathan (1 Samuel 20).
The Good Samaritan (Luke 10).

page 14
The prayer of St Francis of Assisi.

page 16
King Midas and the touch of gold, Aesop's fable.
The goose that laid the golden egg, Aesop's fable.

page 18
Grumblers, L. Clark, *The First Poetry Book*, OUP.
The shirt of happiness, *Together with Infants*, Robert Fisher, Evans, 1982. (Suitable for dramatization.)

page 20
When I needed a neighbour, *Come and Praise*, BBC Publications, 1978.
Look out for loneliness, *Someone's Singing Lord*, A & C Black, 1973.
Kind deeds, *Book of a Thousand Poems*, Evans, 1959.

page 24
Maggon the bad tempered dragon, *Apusskidu*, A & C Black, 1975.
Hindu prayer, *Assembly Stories from Around the World*, William Dargue, OUP, 1983.

page 28
The Indian boy and the robbers, *The Infant Assembly Book*, Doreen Vause, Macdonald, 1985.
The bag of gold, *The Assembly Year*, Robert Fisher, Collins, 1985.
The boy who cried wolf, Aesop's fable.

page 34
Give me oil in my lamp, *Come and Praise*, BBC Publications, 1978.

The prayer of Sir Francis Drake.
The story of Sir Edmund Hilary and Sherpa Tensing's ascent and conquering of Mount Everest.
Try again, E Cook, *Book of a Thousand Poems*, Evans, 1959.

page 36
Whenever I feel afraid, *Apusskidu*, A & C Black, 1975.
When a knight won his spurs, *Someone's Singing Lord*, A & C Black, 1973.
The story of Captain Oates on Scott's expedition to the Antarctic.
Stories of saints and martyrs on appropriate days throughout the year.
Stories of brave deeds which appear in the Press.

THE
COMMUNITY

Families and Homes

The aim of this topic is to help children appreciate family relationships and the part which members of a family play in providing a secure environment. Furthermore, to help children view the family as the basic social unit and to extend this idea so that they perceive themselves as member of a world family.

Talking points

▶ Discuss the variety of patterns of family life, the varied sizes of families, one parent families, family life in other countries, and extended families, as in some Italian families for example.

▶ Discuss the various roles played by members of the family, the roles of wage earning, providing food and shelter and domestic duties. The importance of sharing, caring and contributing Relations and the extended family.

▶ Talk about special family customs and traditions.

▶ Discuss forenames and their meanings family names, and ancestors.

The old woman

There was an old woman
Who lived in a shoe,
And all her grandchildren
Played there too.
She laughed at their jokes
(When they were funny)
And kept a green jar
Of bubble gum money.
She rode with them
On the Carousel
And played Monopoly very well.
She taught them to paint
And how to bake bread.
She read them riddles
And tucked them in bed.
She taught them to sing
And how to climb trees.
She patched their jeans
And bandaged their knees.
She remembered the way
She'd felt as a child,
The dreams she'd had
Of lands that were wild,
Of mountains to climb
Of villains to fight,
Of plays and poems
She'd wanted to write.
She remembered all
She'd wanted to do
Before she grew up
And lived in a shoe.
There was an old woman
Who lived in a Shoe
And lived in the dreams
She'd had once too.
She told those she loved,
"Children be bold.
Then you'll grow up
But never grow old".

Joyce Johnson

Soraya's blanket

Soraya lived in a village called Darwaza in India. Most of the time it was hot and sunny, and she was happy to run around the village streets and alleyways barefoot, saving her sandals for her trips into town when she wanted to look especially good. The hot weather also meant that Soraya could sleep up on the roof of their flat-topped house. She loved the cool air and the bright stars of those nights. Grandmother's charpoy was next to Soraya's, and she would sing Soraya to sleep or tell her the stories that she had heard as a child. Soraya loved her Grandmother and spent all her time with her apart from when she was at school.

One day, Soraya realized that things were about to change. Her Dad explained that he had heard from Uncle Ashraf and Auntie Shaheen in Britain. Their business was doing well and they needed help to run it. It was an exciting idea and Soraya's Mum and Dad were looking forward to joining the family business.

Soraya felt mixed up. She was excited to think of a new country and glad to see that she would be with her cousins again, she hadn't seen them since their visit to Darwaza over a year ago. She was sad, too, because she knew that she would be leaving her family and friends behind in the village. Tears filled her eyes as she hugged and kissed Grandmother "Good-bye".

As Soraya's plane flew half-way round the world, she thought about her Grandmother and wished that she could have come with them. Then, as the plane landed, Soraya's head filled with the new sights and sounds, and there were her cousins waiting to show her round her new town. The sadness left her.

Can you find sixteen ancestors?

	parents	grandparents	great grandparents	great-great grandparents
HRH Charles Prince of Wales	HRH Prince Philip Duke of Edinburgh	Prince Andrew of Greece	George I King of the Hellenes	King Christian IX of Denmark
				Princess Louisa of Hesse-Cassel
			Grand Duchess Olga of Russia	Grand Duke Constantine of Russia
				Princess Elizabeth of Saxe-Altenburg
		Lady Alice Mountbatten	Louis Mountbatten First Marquess of Milford Haven	Prince Alexander of Hesse-Darmstaat
				Julie de Haucke, Princess of Battenburg
			Princess Victoria of Hesse	Louis IV, Grand Duke of Hesse
				Princess Alice of Great Britain
	HM The Queen	HM King George VI	HM King George V	HM King Edward VII
				Princess Alexandra of Denmark
			Princess Mary of Teck	Francis, Duke of Teck
				Princess Mary of Cambridge
		Lady Elizabeth Bowes-Lyon	Claude, Fourteenth Earl of Strathmore and Kingborne	Claude Thirteenth Earl of Strathmore
				Frances Dora Smith
			Nina Cecilia Cavendish Bentinck	Reverend Charles Cavendish Bentinck
				Caroline Louisa Burnaby

1. Rule out a chart like the one above and insert your own name on the left.

2. Ask your parents and grandparents to help you fill in the chart.

She began to go to school with her cousins and though it was hard at first to make sense of it all, Soraya knew that she would like it here. Oh, but it was so cold. As she shivered she thought she would never get used to the cold British weather. It was only at night time that Soraya felt lonely, when she looked at the sparkling frost patterns on the window pane in her bedroom. She dreamt about the warm nights sitting close to Grandmother under the stars. Every night Soraya missed Grandmother and wished she were next to her, then she wouldn't be cold.

A few weeks after they arrived, Mum and Dad wrote to Grandmother to tell her about their new home. Soraya asked if she could write a sentence too. She wrote: "I love you and miss you. Naanee, especially at bedtime".

Weeks passed then one day the postman handed Soraya a parcel with her name on it. The postmark and stamps told her it was from India. She opened it as fast as she could. Inside she found a beautiful woollen blanket knitted so finely in the brightest colours. As she wrapped it around herself she found a note pinned to it that said, "My Soraya, I have made this for you. Put it on your bed and think of me every night. In the blanket is my love for you, it will always keep you warm. Naanee."

Night times seemed to get warmer for Soraya from that day.

Things to do

▶ Collect photographs of grandparents and other relations.

▶ Visit a Reference Library. View the microfilm of 1841–1871 Census. Examine old Rate Books and Polling Lists. Find people with similar surnames to your own.

▶ Design a Coat of Arms for your own family.

▶ Make a genealogical table.

▶ Make a list of surnames of members of your class and try to ascertain how they came into being. For example:
Johnson = son of John,
Lancaster = place names,
Slater = occupations,
Patel = farmer,
Choudray = leader,
Singh = lion,
Kaur = princess.

▶ Use the database and make a file showing the names and addresses of the children in your class and the names of their parents. Make graphs to show the number of people with similar forenames, the number of people living on any one street.

▶ Discuss the different homes of animals and how the parents make a home and prepare for the young. Make a list of these. For example:
squirrel – drey;
fox – lair;
beaver – lodge;
bird – nest.

Friends and Neighbours

We all need friends but friendship places certain demands on us. Friendships demand learning to share, to tolerate and make allowances, to give as well as to receive. The idea of friendship can be extended to neighbourliness in the immediate, and then the wider, community.

Talking points

▶ What is a friend? How do we make and keep our friends? By caring, sharing not only possessions but our thoughts and ideas, and by being a good friend.

▶ Who has a pen-friend, or friends in other countries?

▶ Neighbours. "Who are our neighbours?" Discuss the Story of the Good Samaritan.

▶ Discuss the feelings of people who have recently moved into a neighbourhood, the old and the lonely.

▶ Discuss how your neighbourhood has changed in the last 100 years. Are these changes for the better?

▶ Talk about people who have been friends of children, for example: Benjamin Waugh founder of the London Society for the Prevention of Cruelty to Children (NSPCC today); Lord Shaftesbury; Dr Barnardo; The Princess Royal (Save the Children Fund); Mother Theresa of Calcutta.

▶ Discuss the saying: "A friend in need is a friend indeed".

The two friends

In Canada during the winter the ground is often covered with thick snow and the tracks of animals can be seen quite easily.

One day two friends, Pierre and Mike, were out hunting in the forest. They were searching the snow for tracks. When they looked up they saw a great bear moving slowly towards them. Both the men were afraid and began to run hoping to find somewhere to hide. Pierre slipped on the icy ground but his friend climbed up the nearest tree. The bear was still some distance away and Pierre lying on the ground pleaded with his friend to help him. However, Mike was so afraid he stayed just where he was, safe up the tree.

Soon the bear approached Pierre who was still lying on the ground. He lay still, and although the bear sniffed around him and licked his ear, it did not attack him and eventually lumbered away in the same direction from which it had come.

When Mike saw that the bear was out of sight, he got down from the tree and went to his friend. Jokingly he said, "I thought the bear was whispering something in your ear." "Yes," said Pierre, "The bear said that she wouldn't like to have a friend who deserted her in *her* time of need."

Billy Dreamer's fantastic friends

The Incredible Hulk came to tea,
Robin was with him too,
Batman stayed at home last night
because his bat had flu.
Superman called to say hello
and Spiderman spun us a joke,
Dynamite Sue was supposed to
come but she went up in smoke.
The invisible man might have called,
But as I wasn't sure,
I left an empty chair and bun
Beside the kitchen door.
They signed my autograph book,
But I dropped it in the fire.
Now whenever I tell my friends
They say I'm a terrible liar.
But incredible people do call round
('Specially when I'm alone),
And if they don't and I get bored,
I call them on the phone.

Brian Patten

The Samaritans

If we are ill we can go to a doctor who will try to make us better but the unhappiness which some people experience cannot be treated so easily. There are people who feel that they have no one to care about them and that no one would worry if they died, and this makes them very depressed. Some of these people have probably moved away from their families and been attracted to the larger towns by offers of better jobs, but soon they find that they are without friends and very lonely.

A man called Chad Varah, realized that very often people who are lonely and sad,

Friends and neighbours collage

OUR WORLD
FRIENDS
AND NEIGHBOURS

Prepare three backing sheets:
1. Our friends and neighbours
2. Our world friends and neighbours
3. Our neighbours in space

Use **photographs** or drawings of friends or neighbours. For the space version use imaginative drawings of space creatures.

Don't complain

You can't do mathematics?
You're poor at sport?
An artist you're simply not?
If these things you cannot do
Then don't complain a lot.
Maybe you're born to ease the load
Of some old neighbour down the road.

Doreen Vause

Things to do

▶ Make a plan of your own neighbourhood. Number the houses in the streets. Mark on it the homes of people you know.

▶ Find out about the Home Help service and Meals on Wheels.

▶ Is there a Community Centre in your neighbourhood? Find out what activities take place there. Do they cater for the needs of both young and old?

▶ Write down your ideas about how your neighbourhood could be improved.

▶ Find out what your neighbourhood was like one hundred years ago. What changes have taken place in that time? Use old maps, school log book, photographs and newspapers to help you.

▶ Interview old people and ask which changes they think have been for the better and which changes they think have not.

just need someone to talk to about their worries and fears.

Chad Varah had the idea of setting up a telephone service with a special number which people could call if they were in distress or worried. He received so many telephone calls that he needed helpers to assist him in his work. This service was called "The Samaritans" because Chad Varah and his helpers were like the Good Samaritan in the Bible story. They were ready to help anyone whenever they were required. The Samaritan service proved worthwhile and has spread not only to other towns and cities in Britain but to other countries in the world.

43

Towns and Cities

Towns and cities are busy, throbbing centres of trade and commerce where many people work and earn their living each day, but also where there are problems of the jobless, homeless, poor and lonely.

The aim of this topic is to help the children to focus on the problems of the inner cities and also to help children realize that we are all responsible for our immediate environment.

Talking points

▶ Start the discussion with a 'brain-storming' session about all the things the children would see in the centre of their own town, public buildings, traffic, people, places of worship, schools, offices, shops, a market, hospitals, green areas, roads, rivers, bridges, toll-gates etc.

▶ Discuss why and when some of these buildings were erected and by whom? Compare styles of architecture.

▶ Discuss change: how small shops have become supermarkets; service in a small shop and in a supermarket;

commodities in the shops, how they arrive there, and the places from where they come; commodities available in the past. How were they packaged and sold?

▶ Is your home town as you would wish it to be? Are the buildings spoiled by graffitti? Is there evidence of vandalism or is there litter in the streets?

I live in the city

I live in the city, yes I do,
I live in the city, yes I do,
I live in the city, yes I do,
Made by human hands.

Black hands, white hands, yellow and brown,
all together built this town,
Black hands, white hands, yellow and brown,
all together make the wheels go round.

Repeat putting in the name of your own town.

Ralph Mactell

Father Borelli and the orphans

Father Borelli was a young priest living in Naples in Italy. After his ordination he took up a teaching appointment and during the day went about looking very respectable and wearing his priest's collar. The priest led a double life for as soon as night fell, off came his respectable clothes and the young priest put on tatty old trousers and a flat cap. The disguise was necessary for each night Father Borelli went down into the city of Naples. In the city all kinds of crime flourished, and gangs

of homeless boys wandered the streets. The boys begged and thieved to keep themselves alive.

The young priest knew that the boys would take no notice of anyone whom they considered represented "Authority" and he decided that if he wanted to help them he would have to become one of them.

The first night that Father Borelli went into the city he noticed that some of the boys were sitting on and around a pipe which brought warm air from a baker's shop. The young priest went and sat amongst them. The gang leader demanded to know his name, but Father Borelli did not answer. In a rough voice he replied, "Got a right to a bit of warmth, like you, haven't I?", then pretending to be tough, he spat in the gang leader's face.

Night after night the priest became a tramp drifting around the alleys and streets of Naples, talking to the members of the street gangs, and sleeping on the pavements. Sometimes he became involved in fights between the boys and hardships that they faced.

Father Borelli realized that something must be done to help the street boys. Whilst he went on seeing them each night, he was secretly making arrangements with other to provide a shelter for them. The priest acquired an old church and his friends whitewashed it and installed electric light. They provided straw mattresses, blankets and oddments of furniture and boxes for seats. When all was ready the friends of Father Borelli told the street boys that the place was ready for them to use a shelter.

At first the boys went along in ones or twos, they could not understand why these people should want to give them a little food and a mattress for the night. They did not trust them, for no-one had ever shown an interest in them before. Soon the number of boys using the hostel increased. They were encouraged to help to run the hostel themselves by collecting scrap-iron which could be sold to provide food and furniture.

Still Father Borelli wore his disguise each night. One night a boy looked very closely at the priest and then said, "I have seen your picture in a newspaper. You are not really a street boy. You have been disguising yourself all the time. You are Father Borelli." The priest was astonished and did not know what the gang members would do. He was very pleased when they all crowded around him and showed appreciation for all the things he had done for them. Although the boys were not his own children he was like a father to them.

Workers in towns and cities

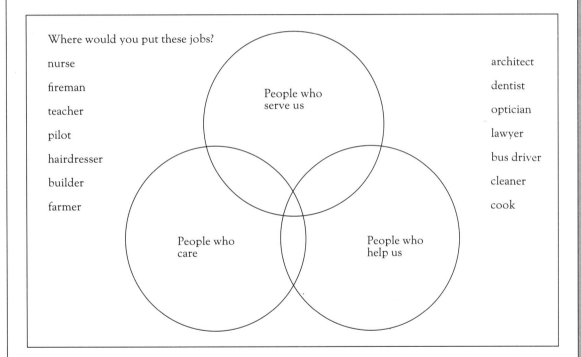

Where would you put these jobs?

nurse

fireman

teacher

pilot

hairdresser

builder

farmer

architect

dentist

optician

lawyer

bus driver

cleaner

cook

People who serve us

People who care

People who help us

1. Prepare a chart like the one above with three overlapping circles.

2. Make a list of different jobs people do and write them on **cards**.

3. Discuss the roles represented by these jobs.

4. Put the cards in the appropriate place on the diagram.

Rainy nights

I like the town on rainy nights
when everything is wet
When all the town has magic lights
and streets of shining jet!

When all the rain about the town
is like a looking-glass,
and all the lights are upside down
below me as I pass.

In all the pools are velvet skies,
and down the dazzling streets
a fairy city gleams and lies
In beauty at my feet.

Irene Thompson

Things to do

▶ Find a street map of your town. Find out where you live. Trace the route you take on your journey to school.

▶ What was it like in your town a hundred years ago? Find old photographs and drawings.

▶ Take a traffic census on a particular road in your town at two different times. Would you expect the traffic to be heavier at one time rather than the other?

▶ Visit your local town hall or council chamber. Find information about your town's coat of arms.

▶ Look around the immediate vicinity of the school for litter. Examine the litter and try to detect where it may have come from.

45

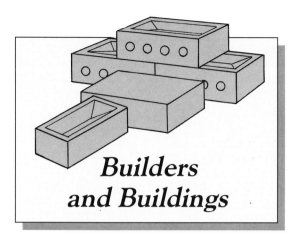

Builders and Buildings

The aim is to encourage children to observe different types of buildings in their environment and to recognize their purposes, and then to form a link between the laying of sound foundations for a building and laying foundations for later life.

The story of St David the Builder is useful for an assembly on St David's Day which is 1 March.

Talking points

▶ List the different sorts of buildings which the children pass on their way to school.

▶ Name the different shapes which we see when observing buildings.

▶ Discuss the purposes for which different buildings are used. Have any of the buildings in your town changed purposes over the years?

▶ Discuss different types of buildings used for worship by different religions and communities.

▶ List different building materials used in this country and other parts of the world.

▶ Discuss the importance of sound foundations and the consequences of inadequate foundations.

The Golden Temple

Every religion has special places for worship. Places of worship are often beautiful buildings where people can feel close to God. At Amritsar in India is a Golden Temple, which was built by a leader of the Sikhs named Guru Arjan. Many thousands of pilgrims visit this wonderful temple every year. The Golden Temple stands in the middle of a great artificial lake.

When some of the Guru Arjan's followers saw the plan for the temple they were very disappointed. They felt that the temple should have been a tall building reaching up towards the sky and towering over everything in the surrounding area. Guru Arjan disagreed with this, and commanded that the Temple should be a low building and built in such a way that anyone entering it would have to descend several steps. Guru Arjan explained to the Sikhs that this would remind all those entering the temple for worship that they must humble themselves in the service of God.

The plan of the temple also showed four doors and the Sikhs wondered why this should be so. Guru Arjan explained that the four doors were incorporated into the plan to remind all worshippers that God is everywhere and also that the temple was open to people of different castes, which meant that God's temple was there for everyone.

In the centre of the Temple at Amritsar a space is specially reserved for the Guru Granth Sahib, (the sacred book of the Sikhs). The centre of the temple is the most important place and the book was placed there to prevent anyone else from claiming this spot as his own.

When choosing a person to lay the foundation stone for the beautiful temple Guru Arjan chose not a Sikh, but a friend who held the Muslim faith.

When the building of the temple was complete a great Emperor named Akbar came to view this place of worship and wished to make contribution towards its up-keep and maintenance. At that time many of the Emperor's tenants were very poor and suffering from the effects of a severe famine.

Guru Arjan did not accept the offer from the Emperor but pointed out to him the plight of some of his people and suggested that instead of giving money for the temple he could return one year's rent to the tenant farmers.

St David

On the first day of March you may see people wearing a daffodil. Do you know why?

It is because 1 March is a special day for the people of Wales, when they think about their history and ancestors. The daffodil is a special emblem for the people of Wales which reminds them of their country. Strictly speaking the emblem is a leek, but on the 1 March the wild daffodil is usually in flower. Another symbol of the Welsh people is the big red dragon which appears on the Welsh flag.

St David is the special saint, or patron saint, of Wales. "Who was St David?" you

Daffodils for March

1. Draw a small pentagon and put a dot in the centre.

2. Draw a circle around the pentagon. From the centre dot draw guidelines to the edge of the circle.

3. Draw in petal outlines using the guidelines as the centre of the petal.

4. Take a strip of **yellow crêpe paper** and roll it round your finger. Cut slits in the base.

Fold out tabs and crimp the top edge with your fingers.

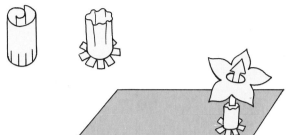

5. Stick the tabs down on to a sheet. Cut out the centre of the flower and place it over the trumpet.

6. Paint on stems and leaves.

may ask. "Was it David who was the shepherd boy?" The answer is "No, the David whom the Welsh people remember was born in Wales 1,200 years ago. Yes! he was a Welshman."

When David was young he went to the monastery school. There he learnt that whatever work people do they must have patience and take great care to see that it is always the best they can offer.

When David grew into a man he worked as a Christian missionary and went throughout the land of Wales encouraging the village folk to help to clear the ground and build monasteries. If the villagers wanted to rush their work David would always remind them that they should take great care to lay sound foundations. Do you think that he might have told them the bible story about the wise man who built his house upon the rock?

David often told the people stories. At times the crowds who came could not see David because he was a very little man, but they could always hear him because he had a very strong clear voice. Many Welsh people have very tuneful singing voices and music is always part of their special festival of St David's Day, which is held each year on 1 March.

Things to do

▶ Make a plan of the classroom or school buildings, show entrances, windows etc. Use a simple scale.

▶ Visit a building site; look at the materials being used, and at the way these are being put together. How are they brought to the site? What sort of dangers are present on a building site? What skills do the builders need? What sort of tools and machines are used by the builders?

▶ Make a display of building materials:

▶ Using a building brick, take its measurements, measure the amount of water it displaces.

▶ Make constructions of different shapes with Meccano, for example, square, rectangle, triangle, hexagon. Test which is the strongest shape.

▶ Make a scrapbook of different types of buildings.

▶ Make a graph to show the different types of homes of the pupils in the class. Show the number of semi-detached, detached, bungalows, flats, terraced homes. Make another graph to show the same information for their grandparents when they were young. Compare the two.

▶ Set the children the task of designing a machine which could be used by builders to lift building materials to a second floor. Use Baufix, Meccano or something similar.

Government and Leadership

Leadership, and the election of leaders involves responsible thought and action. Children need help to sort out their ideas and form their own sensible judgments. This is not always easy.

Talking points

▶ Discuss the role of group leaders, team leaders, house captains, class teachers, headteachers. What sort of things should a good leader do? Should we always follow our leaders unquestioningly?

▶ Discuss how Moses acted as a leader when he led the children of Israel from captivity in Egypt, and how Muhammed acted as a leader when he led the first Muslims from Mecca to Medina.

▶ Do we have people to lead our country, and our towns? Who are they and what sort of things do they do? Discuss the work of elected members and paid officials.

▶ Discuss the difference between a leader and a representative.

▶ Discuss the role of women during the Long March in 1934 when 100,000 Chinese communist soldiers covered 8,000 kilometres on their retreat from Chiang's troops.

▶ Discuss how the British parliament has two houses: the House of Lords, and the House of Commons. Talk about how laws are made and how laws are changed? What do we do about things we disagree with?

Confucius the leader

About 500 kilometres south of Peking in China was the province of Shantung. It was there in the small village of Tsou that Confucius was born over 2,000 years ago.

Although Confucius' family was very poor he taught himself to read and write, and later spent a great deal of his life studying all kinds of things. Confucius is thought by some people to be the wisest man who ever lived and many of his sayings and writings have been handed down to the present day. One of these sayings is: "Without learning the wise become foolish; by learning the foolish become wise."

Confucius was interested in the way people were governed and had many ideas about what makes a good ruler or leader. He was never able to persuade anyone to try out his ideas on a large scale, but he was appointed as mayor of the city of Chang-tu. During the time that Confucius was the leader the people were happy because he used his wisdom, abilities and skills to manage the affairs of the city in a responsible way.

Confucius said that all people should be careful of many things:

"Their eyes, so that they may observe;
Their ears, so that they may learn;
Their face, so that it may always reflect kindness;
Their manners, so that they might show respect for other people;
Their words so that they may be true;
Their dealings with other people, so that they may be fair."

About leadership Confucius said that leaders must possess many virtues and wisdom to use these at the appropriate times. Good leaders always remember that, kindness is a great virtue but that it is not always the answer to a problem. That bravery is a virtue but can sometimes spur us to rash action when caution is needed. That it is important to know when to act swiftly and when to move slowly and when it is best to do nothing at all. That it is important to know when to be dignified but it is also important to know when to relax and be friendly.

Confucius was once asked how people could live together successfully and to this he replied, "Do not do to other people what you would not want them to do to you."

Harriet Tubman

Harriet Tubman was born on one of the cotton plantations in the Southern State of Maryland in North America. From the moment of her birth she was a slave. Harriet would never go to school, for there were no schools for slave children. As soon as she was old enough she would be made to work.

Life was harsh on the plantations and slaves were whipped or beaten for the smallest thing. A slave family was often split up because the masters bought and

Make rosettes

1. Cut out a circle of **card**.

2. Cut out a circle of **crêpe paper**, diameter 6 cm. Fold the paper over to cover the small circle and stick down.

3. Cut out a piece of **crêpe paper** 12 cm × 50 cm and stitch along the top.

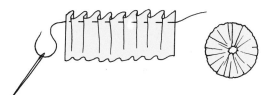

4. Draw up into pleats. Form a circle and tie the ends firmly.

5. Glue a coloured circle in the centre of the rosette. Cut out two **ribbon** tails and glue them into place.

---

sold their slaves, as and when they pleased. Harriet had no security of any kind for she knew that on any day she could be sold to another master who may be even more cruel than the one she had at present.

Although Harriet could not read or write she knew that she lived in a very unjust world, and decided to run away and go to one of the Northern States where slavery was illegal. She made her way to Pennsylvania and looked for a job as a housemaid or in the kitchens of one of the larger hotels. For the first time she was in control of her own life.

As time passed she desperately wanted to see her friends again and some of her family whom she had left behind. She knew it would be dangerous to go back to Maryland and arranged her journey so that she would arrive there after dark. Her family and friends were overjoyed to see

her and begged her to take them with her to freedom. They all knew they would be punished if they were caught but the little band set out and Harriet led the way. When the slave owners realized what had happened they were furious and they offered rewards for the capture of Harriet Tubman. Nevertheless Harriet repeated her journey many times, and if danger threatened she always knelt down and prayed.

When the Civil War broke out in 1861 Harriet joined the Northern army to nurse the wounded. She still made the dangerous journey to the Southern States as she had done so many times before. Eventually the Northern States won the war and all the slaves were freed. Much later Harriet's courage in helping the slaves to freedom became known and she was called "The Moses of her People."

Things to do

▶ Dramatize the story of Harriet Tubman. Let part of the drama show scenes on the cotton plantations and sing Negro Spirituals.

▶ Dramatize the story of Moses, with Moses asking the Pharoah for permission to leave Egypt. Tell the stories of the plague and the Israelites' escape after the baking of unleavened bread.

▶ Find out more about the food eaten by Jews today at the Passover meal. Find out more about the Torah and the Talmud.

▶ Draw up a 'Classroom Constitution'. Hold a brainstorming session where everyone identifies possible items. Each child then votes for six items to be included in the 'Classroom Constitution'.

Discuss what the class hope it will achieve; what sanctions should be used when the Constitution is not adhered to. (Stress *should* rather than *shall*.) Plan a time when the constitution will be discussed to see if it is working fairly. Have the children helped each other to stick to the rules?

Hold a 'Mock Election'. The children to devise their own campaign: choose candidates, write speeches, make posters, rosettes, badges etc, make ballot papers and boxes, have an 'Election Day', hold a declaration ceremony, discuss whether the Election was *fair*.

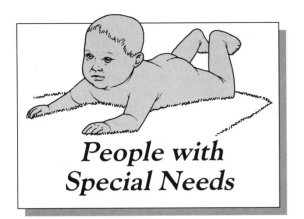

People with Special Needs

Not everyone is healthy or has the full use of their limbs or senses. Some people may need a wheelchair to get around or they may be partially or completely blind. These people have special needs: they can manage their lives very well and make a positive contribution to society provided certain practical things are arranged specially for them. For example wheelchairs can't climb steps, they need ramps. The aim of this topic is to help children to empathize and be aware of the needs of *all* other people, and also to show how some people have persevered in order to overcome disabilities.

Talking points

▶ Talk about the five senses.

▶ Discuss safety and road accidents.

▶ Talk about people with special needs: The very young and the very old; those who are blind, deaf, or with other physical disabilities.

▶ Discuss guide dogs for the blind and how these dogs are trained.

▶ Think about arrangements in the neighbourhood for people with special needs, for example slopes, ramps, lifts.

▶ Discuss with the children the adaptations that might need to be made to their own classroom in order to meet the needs of a blind or partially-sighted pupil, or a child in a wheelchair.

Two busy people

Kathy was born a fine healthy baby. When she was old enough she went to nursery school and joined in all the activities and fun. Just before her sixth birthday her parents moved house to a new home on a busy road. On the day of the removal her parents were busy arranging things in the new house and Kathy went out to play with her ball on the driveway. Suddenly the ball bounced out of her hands and rolled out on to the road. Without a thought Kathy ran after it into the path of an on-coming car. Kathy was badly injured and spent many months in hospital. The surgeons carried out several operations but eventually Kathy's parents realized that Kathy would never be able to walk un-aided again.

During the time that Kathy spent in hospital she was visited by a girl named Mary. Mary needed a wheelchair to help her get around, but she cheered Kathy up every time she visited her.

Eventually Kathy returned home and a wheelchair was provided for her. The day came when she was to return to school and she wondered what the reaction of the other children might be to one of their classmates in a wheelchair. As Kathy and her mother entered the classroom the children turned and looked at her. Kathy stared at them too, then suddenly everyone seemed to smile, and from that moment Kathy was "another girl in the class".

Kathy is now grown-up. She drives a special car. She goes to work each morning with her wheelchair in her car. She works in the Accounts Department of a very busy office and has a very responsible position in the firm.

Alongside Kathy there is another young lady who also has special needs. When Margaret was born she was found to be blind. Wherever she goes she is always accompanied by her guide-dog, Bruce. Margaret attended a school for children with special needs. She worked very hard to acquire the skills of reading Braille and typing. Margaret is now an excellent typist, and deals with a great deal of correspondence each day. Both Kathy and Margaret take part in all kinds of events to help other people.

Jimmy Savile

Jimmy Savile is a well-known disc jockey and television entertainer. He is the star of the television series *Jim'll Fix It*. On this programme he asks people to write to him of something they have always wished to do, and if it is at all possible he will make arrangements for them to have their wish.

Jimmy Savile is a person who obviously likes to spend his time in bringing happiness to others. Apart from his work on television, he spends some of his spare time helping at the Stoke Mandeville Spinal Unit, which cares for people who have to spend time in wheelchairs. He also takes part in many charity events, such as sponsored walks and cycle rides to raise money for people with special needs.

Christy Nolan

In January 1988 Christy Nolan won a valuable literary prize. He was 21 years old and his book called *Under the Eye of the Clock* – a book about his life – won him the famous Whitbread Prize.

Christy's first book, *Dam-burst of Dreams*, was published when he was only 15. What is even more remarkable is that Christy has produced these marvellous books in spite of very severe disabilities. When he was born he suffered brain damage which left him paralysed and unable to talk.

In order to write his books Christy needs the constant help of his mother. While Christy taps out the words of his stories on to a typewriter using a stick strapped to his chin, his mother is there supporting his head all the time.

In spite of being unable to speak, Christy has developed a very effective way of communicating with his mother. By using sounds, facial expressions and gestures Christy can express, through his mother, his thoughts and feelings to those around him, including the television and newspaper reporters who paid him a great deal of attention at the time of his award.

The Whitbread Book of the Year 1987

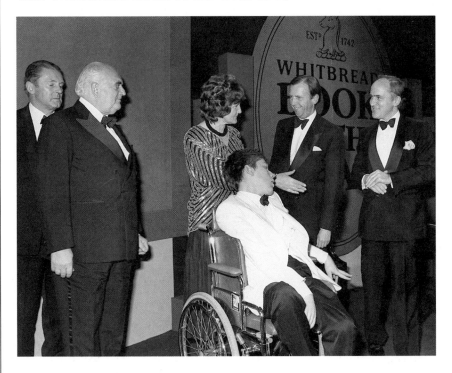

Things to do

▶ Find pictures of toys for young children. Sort out the ones that would prove difficult for children with special needs – share ideas about how these could be adapted to make them better for these children. Consider physical disabilities, problems of hearing, sight, movement etc.

▶ Design a toy or a game that would be especially good for a partially-sighted or blind child (toddler). Think about helping the toddler explore its other senses, for example, touch, hearing, smell, taste.

▶ Find out more about the Stoke Mandeville Hospital.

▶ Find out how a guide dog is trained and how much it costs to provide a dog.

▶ Find out what you can about Louis Braille. Can you find an example of Braille? Can you compose an alphabet which is based on a raised pattern of dots? Use your alphabet with a friend to send messages to each other.

▶ How do people who cannot hear or speak communicate with each other? Could you invite someone to come to school to show you how this is done?

▶ Try to make a painting without using your hands. Some people can paint beautifully using their feet or mouths to hold the brush.

▶ Consider using television schools broadcasts on this particular topic.

People on the Move

Many families have friends or relatives who have gone to live in another country. A number of British workers are to be found amongst the work-forces in Middle Eastern countries. Some children will have family living in such countries as Australia, Canada, the United States, Pakistan, Hong Kong, and Jamaica. These links may be the best starting point for dealing with this topic.

Talking points

▶ Discuss what we mean by emigration. How might people who emigrate from this country feel when they arrive in a new country?

▶ Discuss the 'two-way traffic' of immigration and emigration.

▶ Discuss the reasons for such moves, for example, better opportunities.

▶ Discuss the strange surroundings, possibly a different language, different money, few friends, possibly traffic moving in a different direction, a new home, a new job and a new school for children.

▶ Ask the children to think of any occasion when they have felt strange, lonely, isolated or very confused by new or strange surroundings. For example, have they ever been lost?

▶ Ask the children whether any of them speak a language other than English at home. Encourage them to talk about their language and their lives outside of school, their festivals, and whether they have visited their relatives in other countries.

Dr James Kodwo Aggrey

Just over a hundred years ago Kodwo Aggrey was born in Ghana. He went to a small Methodist school and was baptised and given the name James.

James Kodwo was clever and studied hard. When he was about fifteen he taught the children in the village school. After school, he spent the evenings studying science, Greek, Latin and Religion.

James left Africa and went to the United States where he studied at a college in North Carolina and eventually became a Methodist minister. His congregation was comprised of poor black people who were treated as inferiors by the whites. James Aggrey believed that God had created all people equal, and he felt that he must use his talents, as a speaker, to help people of different cultures to understand each other.

He travelled around the United States and his fame as a speaker spread. People came and packed the halls to listen to him. Dr Aggrey was very clever and often tried to persuade people by using parables and amusing sayings. He once said, "God knew what he was doing when he made me

black. He did not want me to be grey or white. He wanted me to be black. On a piano you cannot make a good tune using only the white notes, and you cannot make a good tune using only the black notes. For real music you must use both the white and the black notes".

In 1920 Dr Aggrey returned to Africa. By this time he was renowned as a great thinker and speaker. He was welcomed by black people wherever he went. He tried to persuade white people to share responsibility with black people but he was not successful in changing the attitudes of the majority of white people. He made some friends and many enemies because of his belief in equality. He died in 1927 in the United States.

The visitor

It was Friday afternoon, Mr Hussain knocked on the Headteacher's office door. "I know it's not usual but I wonder if Shahid could be allowed to leave school a few minutes early today?" "Well, really we don't like our children to miss any school," said Mrs Kahn, "is there a special reason?" "Yes," said Mr Hussain, "a very special reason. You see, I've just had a phone call to say that my mother's plane from Pakistan has landed early at Manchester airport. She's waiting there for us to collect her in our car. I'd really like Shahid to come with me and my wife. Shahid has never met Grandmother and he's really excited. I hope you'll let him out early just this once."

Mrs Kahn agreed, so Mr Hussain and Shahid hurried out of school to where Mum was waiting. It took about an hour to drive to the airport, the family hardly spoke to each other. They were so busy

People on the move

Bedouin near Beersheba, Israel.

thinking about Grandmother.

The airport looked huge as they drove on to its multi-storey car park, and Shahid thought suddenly, "What if we can't find Grandmother?" Soon they were through the doors and into the airport building. Shahid was surprised as Dad set off running across the large hall waving both arms. Then he spotted an elderly lady wearing a shalwar and kameeze waving back at Dad. By the time Shahid and Mum caught up, Dad and Grandmother were hugging each other. Shahid was introduced to his Granny and soon they were hugging each other too.

Driving home to Blackburn the family weren't at all quiet, they all had so much to talk about.

Back at school on Monday morning Shahid's teacher asked him to tell them all about meeting Grandmother. Shahid told the class about the airport and what had happened. He told Miss Marsh that his Grandmother had been the village school teacher when she was younger and that she would love to see Shahid's school. Miss Marsh thought this would be a good idea and said that Grandmother could visit the school the next day.

Tuesday was a great day. Grandmother stayed all morning, she looked around the school and talked to everyone. She asked lots of questions and told them about her schools in Pakistan. She had a turn on the computer and thought it was fun. At the end of the morning Grandmother said goodbye. She had enjoyed her visit. It had been very interesting, and a lot of fun.

Things to do

▶ Make a display of artefacts which people have brought from other countries. Display books and newspapers in a variety of languages.

▶ On a large map of the world find the countries from which other people have come to Britain and also countries to which people from this country have emigrated. Make a table for the classroom wall showing the names of these countries, their currencies, their festivals, the size of their population and the type of climate which they have and the language or languages spoken by the people.

▶ Explore the High Street of your town. This could be a 'Town Trail' approach. Look for the following:

Food: A variety of foods from other countries. Speciality shops: for example, Polish delicatessen, Indian 'sweet centre'; interview the shopkeepers if they are not too busy to talk.

Restaurants: Look at the variety of restaurants around the town, for example Italian, Indian, Chinese. Try to get copies of the menu.

Clothes: Notice different types and styles, look for shops which sell sari lengths.

Places of Worship: Look for temples, mosques, synagogues, gudwaras and different churches serving diferent faiths.

53

Changing Things

Most societies in the world today are constantly changing and developing. In all societies there are injustices: some people are privileged and others exploited. Some people are trying to control change in society to make things better, others have self-interest at heart.

Injustice is overcome through the dedicated efforts of extraordinary men and women with insight and commitment, but we can all lend a hand and support their work. Children need to appreciate the ways in which change can be brought about in society, and how many small voices saying the same thing can bring about change. (Human rights are separate topics on pages 78 to 81.)

Talking points

▶ Discuss the ways in which we can make changes in society, for example, by voting at elections, by writing letters to our representatives such as Members of Parliament or Local Councillors.

▶ Discuss how people can protest in a democratic society: peaceful demonstrations, sit-ins, marches, enlisting co-operation of others in a

good cause, persuading people to a particular point of view, not agreeing with a point of view if we consider that any injustice has been done.

▶ Discuss strikes in industry. Encourage the children to see that there are two sides to any dispute. Encourage the children to think about what we mean by 'rational judgement' and making our own decisions.

Women in India

Sometimes, if the father of a family dies, the mother is left with several children and may not have the skills with which to get a job. Consequently, some women may become destitute if their relatives cannot support them. In Madras, India, a Hindu lady, Mrs Krishna Rao, felt that she would like to help women earn a living.

Mrs Rao had very little money but she was respected in the community and she had many friends whom she asked to help her in order to achieve her aim.

Mrs Rao rented a room for homeless mothers and children and set about training the women. They were given food and a mat to sleep on at night. During the daytime while the mothers worked, the children played in the nursery. Soon the one room was not big enough for everyone so they moved to a larger building, but this in its turn became too small as more mothers and children joined. A schoolroom, a nursery and a place to eat and sleep were built and Oxfam gave money for more building.

The women start with easy work and are then trained to carry out more difficult tasks. They learn tailoring, puppet making, batik, printing, typing, traditional Indian

crafts and electronics. To help pay the expenses the women make dolls and educational toys which are sold. Oxfam buy some of these and sell them in their shops.

Mrs Rao's work means that women who might have become beggars can earn a living and their children are cared for and go to school.

Martin Luther King

Martin Luther King was born in 1929 in the southern part of the United States of America. His father was a minister, and although at one time Martin wanted to become a doctor, he decided to become a minister like his father. He grew up in Georgia where signs reading, "Whites Only" or "No coloured" were commonplace. This troubled him because he felt that all people should have equal rights as citizens.

Martin Luther King began his work as a minister in the city of Montgomery. The local bus company did not allow black people to sit in the same seats as white people. There were special seats for white people only, and black people had to sit at the back.

In 1955 a lady called Rosa Parks had finished her day's work and was travelling home by bus. The bus driver told Mrs Parks to give up her seat to a white passenger. She refused. For this she was arrested and put into prison.

The black people were very angry and a meeting was called which was attended by their minister, Dr Martin Luther King. Dr King believed black and white people should have equal rights but he encouraged the people to use peaceful means to fight for their cause. The meeting decided to persuade black people to stop using the buses. For over a year the black people of Montgomery refused to use the buses and walked until they were allowed to sit where they wished when travelling by bus.

This was just the beginning, the fight went on for votes and jobs and the right to mix with white people in all public places such as cinemas, libraries, shops and cafes. Dr King was a talented speaker and spoke out on many occasions against this injustice of inequality. He was often attacked and was thrown in jail many times but still be carried on, gaining more and more followers.

Dr King once said, "I have a dream, that one day this nation will rise up and live out its belief that all men are created equal. I have a dream that my four little children will one day live in a nation where they will not be judged by the colour of their skin but by their character."

Dr King was awarded the Nobel Peace prize in 1964. His campaign contributed to the passing of the Civil Rights Act 1964 and the Voting Rights Act in 1965.

The fame of Dr King spread but as he made many friends he also made enemies. In 1968 he was shot by James Earl Ray, as he stood on his hotel balcony in Memphis, Tennessee. All through his life he had taught the way of peace and love, and had given himself in the service of others.

Wax resist techniques

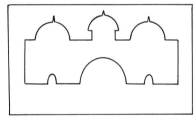

1. Draw an outline on to paper.

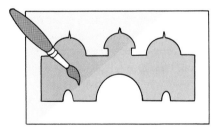

2. Using an ordinary **wax candle**, fill in the image. Then wash over the paper with different colours of **paint**.

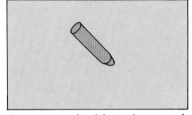

1. Apply **crayon** thickly in layers of different colours.

2. Using the end of a sharp instrument such as a **screwdriver**, make your own picture.

Things to do

▶ Find out all you can about the traditional crafts of southern India. How are batiks made? Try out the two methods of wax resist techniques explained in this page.

Find out the cost of goods made in India when sold in Britain. How much money does the person in India receive?

▶ Find out more about what life was like in the city of London in the early 19th century.

▶ Interview a grandparent or elderly friend/neighbour about life for them when they were your age – ask about:

health – vaccinations, hospitals, medicines;

school – leaving age, buildings, the school day;

leisure – clubs, sport, music;

family life – roles, extended family, routine;

Ask about the changes they have noticed in this country and which are for the better and which for the worse.

Write a story about the person you have interviewed and include a photograph.

▶ South Africa still has many of the injustices that Dr King fought against in the United States. Discuss how you might feel is you were a black person in South Africa.

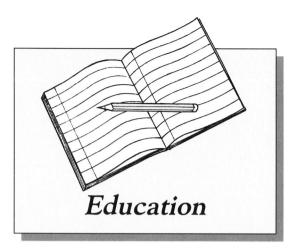

Education

Education is more than the learning of subjects and facts, it also involves learning how to live successfully and responsibly with others. Children do not always realize that once, education was available to only a few children in Britain and that even today it is not available to all children in all parts of the world.

Talking points

► What would your school have been like 100 years ago? What sort of work would you have done in school?

► What did the children do if they did not attend school? Discuss the children who worked in factories and mines, the long working day and poor conditions.

► Why do we come to school? Do we learn in other places than school? For example at home, Cubs and Brownies, Sunday school, mosque schools, Polish School, watching television, reading books and newspapers.

► Who are the people who visit our school regularly? What sort of work do they do? How do they help us?

► Discuss special days in the life of the school for example Open Days, The School's Birthday.

► Talk about the role of supplementary schools for example Chinese Saturday school.

Education Sunday

In some Christian Churches one Sunday is often marked as Education Sunday. Education Sunday usually falls at Septuagesima that is in January approximately 70 days before Easter. Special services are held and are attended by people interested in education. On this day prayers are said for pupils, their parents and teachers.

Sarasvati

Sarasvati is the Hindu Goddess of learning, wisdom and knowledge. The Goddess is usually shown holding a book and a musical instrument. Some children in India carry a picture of Sarasvati in their school bags. In some parts of India a special festival is held in honour of Sarasvati. This usually takes place on the day of Basant Panchami – the Spring Festival. Hindus visit the temples and place pens and books before the statues of Sarasvati, incense is burnt in order to offer praise to the Goddess.

Sarasvati was the wife of Brahma who created all things, the father of all gods. When Brahma created the world he wanted someone to share it with him and created Sarasvati, who was young, graceful and beautiful. Manu (the first man in the world), was the offspring of Brahma and Sarasvati. Sarasvati is therefore regarded as the mother of all people, and this is the reason why her festival is still held in some parts of India in the Springtime.

Tuskgee Institute of Education

Booker T. Washington was born on a plantation in Virginia, in 1856. He was born into slavery because his mother was a slave and, as soon as he was old enough, he was set to work. There was no time for play and no time for schooling. One day an important looking person arrived on the plantation and read a proclamation from the President of the United States saying that all slaves were now free.

Booker and his family moved away from the plantation. He was about ten years old and was sent to work in a mine. The hours were long but the wages, though pitifully small, were helping to feed the family.

There was great excitement in the village one day. The people heard the news that a school was to be opened. Booker was very keen to attend but his stepfather would not allow him to study during the day, as this would mean a loss of wages.

Some months later, night school classes began and Booker was able to attend. He was a keen pupil and very soon learnt to read and write. When he was older he heard of a high school many miles from his home. By agreeing to work as a caretaker he was allowed to become a student.

Booker worked extremely hard, eventually passing his examinations and becoming a teacher. Although penniless, Booker started a school of his own in a rickety old building. The people who had worked on the plantations and had never had a chance of education before, poured into Booker's school. Word spread across

Make a school poster

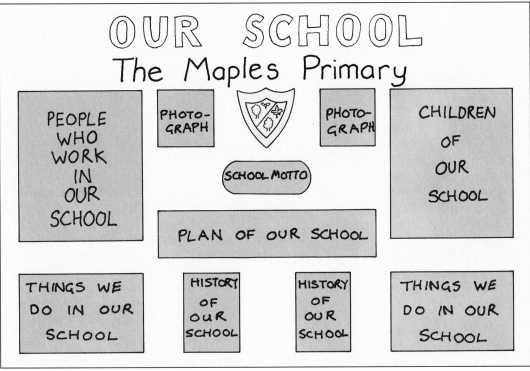

Create a wall display like the one above for your school entrance hall. Add your school Crest and Motto to the display. If you do not have one, design your own.

Research the history of the school and find out about the people who work there. Include photographs and drawings. Write about the children and what they do in school.

the States and his school became oversubscribed. A former plantation owner helped Booker to raise money and together they travelled to New York and Boston to collect money for a new school. Several years later the little rickety building had been replaced by forty buildings which formed the campus of the Tuskegee Institute of Education.

Booker T. Washington spent his life in working to make the Tuskegee Institute a school where poorer children would receive a first-class education. When he died in 1915 there were more than a hundred buildings and 1,500 students. Many people had been able to gain knowledge and live happier and more interesting lives.

Things to do

▶ Find out when your school was built and how many pupils were there on the first day your school opened. What were the names of the teachers? Has your school a foundation stone? What kinds of building materials were used?

▶ Make a graph to show how many children there are in each class.

▶ How many adults work in your school? Write about the jobs they do.

▶ Ask a school governor to come and speak to the children about the role he or she plays in the life of the school.

▶ Find out about schools in other countries and schools of long ago.

▶ Ask a grandparent to come to school and tell the children about his or her experiences in school.

▶ Write a prayer for your school which you could read in assembly.

▶ Take photographs of the different things you do in school and mount these for a display in the school entrance.

▶ What have you learned to do that you are most proud of? For example, to swim, to knit, to ride a bicycle.

Draw a strip cartoon to show how you managed to do it in the end. You could make a "Look what I've done" classbook, or a similar book of what you are trying to learn now.

The News

News plays an important part in the life of a community. Each day our newspapers are delivered and we receive news by radio, television or letter. We receive good news and bad news about accidents and catastrophes. Technological innovation means that news is now passed swiftly around the world and people are far more aware of what is taking place in other parts of the world than they were several years ago. There is a responsibility when passing on news to report truthfully and accurately and avoid distortion. This applies to radio, television, newspapers and individuals. Gossip itself leads to distortion and can be very dangerous in communities, causing trouble and sadness.

Talking points

▶ Discuss the many different ways of passing on news, for example, letters, telephone, handbills, posters, newspapers, television.

▶ Talk about the Royal Mail Trains, the first stamps, the Mail Coaches of long ago and the post boys on horseback. Point out to the children how pigeons have been used to carry important news.

▶ Discuss different kinds of news, for example, world events, local events, sports news, gossip columns.

▶ Discuss magazine and newspaper advertising and television advertising. Is it possible to set up fair tests to check the truthfulness of all advertisements?

▶ Discuss the sort of things we could consider to be good news and what constitutes bad news. Also the effect which good news or bad news had on a community.

▶ Discuss the news that the angels brought to the shepherds at the first Christmas time and the effect that it must have had on the little community at Bethlehem. How would people react?

The story of the cock

The usually proud and strutting cock sat sulking in a corner of the farmyard. He was wondering what he could do next to impress the hen he loved. She had ignored him for weeks no matter how hard he had tried to make her notice him.

Then he had an idea. "Keep calm and play it cool," he told himself as he strolled across the yard to where the hen was scratching in the soil. She looked up curiously. With a flourish he pulled out a feather from his breast and bowed gracefully as he handed it to her.

The goat looking over the fence was amazed to see the proud cock trying so hard to impress. She thought that she must let the other animals hear the news, they would be most interested.

"Guess what?", the goat whispered to the horse "the cock has just pulled out two of his feathers to give to the hen."

The horse, too, was eager for the others to hear the news, so he trotted over the cow. "Would you believe it?" he declared, "the cock is so madly in love with the hen that he has just pulled out six of his finest feathers to give her."

The cow was intrigued and thought deeply about the event. She ambled across the field to the pond to tell the duck of this incredible happening.

"You must hear this," she told him, "I have it on good authority that the cock has pulled out twenty feathers to give to the hen."

The duck hurriedly made his way to the farmyard, nearly bursting to tell the news. The first of his friends that he met was the cock. "What do you think of the latest news? The cock has pulled out all his feathers to give to the hen."

"Ha," the cock sneered, "the things some poor creatures will do for love."

Good news

"Yes, Reuben, I was only a young man, but I was there," said David. "We were round the fire, Joshua and I were keeping watch, although we were very drowsy. The flock had settled well that night. There was a chill in the air and I was pulling my cloak around me, when suddenly, I thought I saw a star moving across the sky. I glanced up and then said to Joshua, 'Look there!' As we watched the darkness seemed to part and brightness shone all about us. Abe, Isaac and Nathanial were wakened by the sudden brightness. Then we were all aware that something very strange was happening. The air seemed to move around us and we felt a strange presence. There was the

Messenger – the angel – standing before us. We were terrified, we clutched and clung to each other and then the angel spoke."

"Be not afraid – Good news I bring, For unto you is born this day in the City of David, A Saviour."

"Then we heard the music, beautiful sweet music, such as we had never heard before. The news that the Messiah had been born had been given to us poor shepherds. We hurried down the slopes to Bethlehem rejoicing."

Reuben then said, "I only wish that the King had accepted the news as you did. Look what terrible events followed the night when the travellers from the East visited the palace with the news that a new king had been born. Elisha was on guard duty that night. He told me how these travellers arrived at the palace gate on camels. They said that they were searching for a new king and had therefore come to the palace. Where else would they find a royal child?

King Herod had them brought to him and he questioned them. Elisha said that he pretended to be pleased about the news of the birth of a baby king. He asked the traveller to bring him news when they had found the child and said that he wanted to worship him also."

"Aye, Reuben, it was a nasty trick," said David, "And when they did not return to his palace, things became worse. Just imagine, sending out his men to slaughter innocent children in order to satisfy his own jealous desire. But I suppose more harm could have been done if the news of his plan had not travelled as fast a it did."

"When Jacob passed on the news, about the killing of all male children under two years of age, to Joseph the carpenter, he acted quickly. In no time at all he had all their belongings packed and that night, under the cover of darkness, he took Mary and the young child to safety in Egypt."

Make a news scrap-book

Make separate scrap-books for local news, news from overseas, school news and sports news.

Using cut-outs from **newspapers** and **magazines** make your own collage poster to advertise a school event or to provide issues for group discussion.

Things to do

▶ Make a class or school newspaper with news reports of school happenings. In schools where an intercom system exists appoint newsreaders to read the school news each week.

▶ Write a well known Bible story in the form of a news report, for example David and Goliath, Moses, Noah. Compare the different accounts of the same story.

▶ Make a School Bulletin Board. Collect news from all classes. Include photographs, drawings etc. Change the news regularly.

▶ Play the game of 'whispers'. One child whispers something to another, and this is passed on around a large circle. Compare what was said initially to what the last person hears.

▶ Arrange a visit to a local radio station or newspaper office to find out how news is collected and selected. The children could record their visit in the form of either a radio programme or the front page spread of a newspaper.

▶ Use cuttings from local newspapers concerning a particular local issue, for example, a cinema closing, a building being pulled down, road building. Look at different points of view represented. Discuss the way it has been reported, try to decide on the 'fairest' outcome.

Find an advertisement and examine it critically.

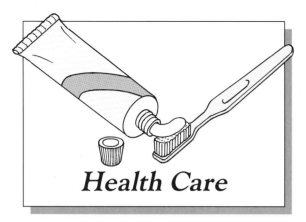

Health Care

The aim is to show the debt of gratitude we owe to people who have committed their time and energy to medical research, founding hospitals and often risking their own lives when dealing with infectious diseases. Because of medical research much suffering can be prevented by the use of antibiotics, anaesthetics and vaccination.

Talking points

▶ Talk about a visit to the hospital. Have the children ever spent time in hospital?

▶ Discuss the reasons for keeping all medicines out of the reach of young children.

▶ Discuss vaccination, anaesthetics, antiseptics. What must medical treatment have been like before these were developed?

▶ Discuss the work of doctors, nurses, radiographers, pharmacists, health visitors. Mention all the other people who work in hospitals and who are often forgotten, the cooks, the cleaners, the porters, the ambulance crews, clerical assistants and receptionists.

▶ Discuss the measures which we can take to avoid infection and keep our bodies healthy.

▶ Discuss the types of food that are good for us and the ones that are bad for us.

▶ Discuss the need for better medical services in some parts of the world today. Do we pay for the services of a doctor if we are ill? If not, who pays?

Mary Seacole

Mary Seacole was born in Jamaica in the first part of the 19th century. In 1850 there was a cholera epidemic and Mary nursed many of the sick with no thought for her own safety.

She developed a medicine during the epidemic which was successful in combatting this terrible disease. News of the new cholera medicine spread to many other countries.

In 1854 war broke out in the Crimea between Turkey and Russia and an English nurse called Florence Nightingale volunteered to lead a band of nurses to work in the military hospitals there. Mary Seacole heard about the poor conditions in which the men were being nursed and decided that she wanted to help. First she travelled to London, but was told that she could not go to the Crimea because she was "coloured".

This did not deter Mary. She travelled on to the Crimea. When she finally arrived the army authorities would not allow her to open a hospital because she had dark skin. Mary was disappointed but nothing could stop her in her determination to help the wounded.

Instead of a hospital she opened "The British Hotel". This looked like a café downstairs but upstairs it was a hospital. The wounded came, and soon she was nursing hundreds. The soldiers called her "Mother Seacole" because she cared for them like a mother. Mary was extremely brave and often went out to the trenches on the battle fields looking for the wounded, she was always ready to be of service to others.

Baba Amte

The poorer people of India find work by carrying out the dirty and unpleasant jobs, such as collecting rubbish and taking it to the rubbish tips at the end of the day.

Baba Amte was born a Brahmin which is the highest caste in India. He was studying at College, when he decided that he wanted to get to know the poorer people and if possible to help them. He left his books and his student days behind and went to work clearing rubbish.

One night as he had dumped his load in the tip he saw a human body. He looked a little closer and at first thought to his horror that it was a dead leper. At that moment, the man's eyes moved slightly and Baba Amte realized that the man was not dead. He ran away in fear, and felt that he could not possibly go on with the work. However, he couldn't think of anything else only the sight of the poor man who needed help.

Baba Amte gathered himself together and with new courage he returned to the refuse tip. He found the poor leper still alive. He comforted the sick man, cleaned him up and took him to a home for lepers.

Healthy eating

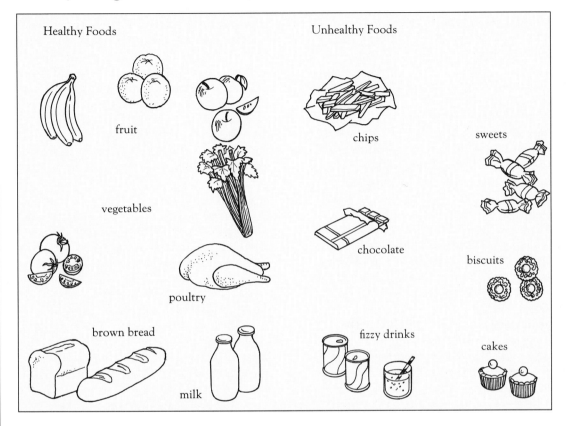

Healthy Foods

fruit

vegetables

poultry

brown bread

milk

Unhealthy Foods

chips

chocolate

sweets

biscuits

fizzy drinks

cakes

Make a classroom wallchart showing two lists of foods: one list of healthy foods and one list of unhealthy foods. Add illustrations of the foods.

After this experience Baba Amte went to medical school to learn more about leprosy. At the end of his training he started his first leprosy clinic at Warora, near Nagpur, and gradually a community grew up around the clinic. There was a farm, worked by the lepers and workshops where lepers could earn their living. Baba Amte married, and with his wife Sadhana, set up new settlements for lepers at Anandwan, Ashokwan, Somnath, and Hemalkasa.

Baba Amte once said of himself: "I want to be a man who goes round with a little oil-can and, when he sees a breakdown offers his help."

Eat good food

Eat good food, don't eat junk,
Eat good food, don't eat junk,
Crunchy granola, yogurt and cheese,
Cracked wheat cereal,
More milk please.

Eat good food, don't eat junk,
Eat good food, don't eat junk,
Lettuce is good, celery too,
Meat and potatoes
But don't eat Goo.

Eat good food, don't eat junk,
Eat good food, don't eat junk,
No more doughnuts, pies or cakes,
No more chocolate bars
For your health's sake
Eat good food, don't eat junk,
Eat good food, don't eat junk,
NO MORE JUNK!!

Lois Birkenshaw

Things to do

▶ Find out all you can about the World Health Organization. What sort of work is it involved in?

▶ From your reference library find out more about Anton van Leewenhoek, Edward Jenner, Louis Pasteur, Joseph Lister, Dr James Simpson, Florence Nightingale, and Marie Curie.

▶ Design a logo which could be used in your home to warn people against dangerous medicines.

▶ Make a chart of healthy foods and unhealthy foods.

Pets

Many children come from homes where there is a family pet. Children need to be aware that when we accept an animal as a pet we also take on the responsibility of caring for that animal throughout its life. We also have a duty to other members of the community, we must ensure that our pets are kept under control and do not cause a nuisance to others. For example: dogs on a leash on busy roads; or rabbits in a neighbour's garden.

Talking points

▶ Make a graph of the different kinds of animals that are kept as pets.

▶ Discuss the needs of pets: food, clean water, exercise, decent housing, regular brushing to keep them clean, love, care and sometimes the services of a veterinary surgeon.

▶ Discuss the costs involved in keeping a pet, and the inconvenience that pets can cause.

▶ Discuss the work of the RSPCA and the PDSA (People's Dispensary for Sick Animals).

▶ Do you know of anyone with an unusual pet? Find out about its country of origin. What kind of environment would it have there?

▶ Discuss the interdependence of people and their pets.

An unusual pet

The fawn lifted its face to his. It turned its head with a wide, wondering motion and shook him through with the stare of its liquid eyes. It was quivering. It made no effort to rise or run. Jody could not trust himself to move. He whispered, "It's me."

The fawn lifted its nose, scenting him. He reached out one hand and laid it on the soft neck. The touch made him delirious. He moved forward on all fours until he was close beside it. He put his arms around its body. A light convulsion passed over it but it did not stir. He stroked its sides as gently as though the fawn were a china deer and he might break it. Its skin was softer than the white coonskin knapsack. It was sleek and clean and had a sweet scent of grass. He rose slowly and lifted the fawn from the ground. It was no heavier than old Julia. Its legs hung limply. They were suprisingly long and he had to hoist the fawn as high as possible under his arm. (He put the fawn down.) .... He remembered his father's saying that a fawn would follow that had been first carried. He started away slowly. The fawn stared after him. He came back to it and stroked it and walked away again. It took a few wobbling steps toward him and cried piteously. It was willing to follow him. It belonged to him. It was his own. He was light-headed with his joy.

From The Yearling, *by* M. Kinnan Rawlings

In memory of Bobby

Rebecca took a short cut through Greyfriars Churchyard every morning and evening. It was the quickest way between home and the hat shop where she worked.

Even though she was late almost every day she just had to stop and give the crust she had saved from her breakfast bread to the dog. It was a tiny Skye terrier, a favourite breed in Rebecca's city, Edinburgh.

When she was very small Rebecca had often stood watching the old newspaper man on the corner outside the churchyard. He sometimes sang in a croaky old voice and Bobby sitting at his side would set off howling. It had made Rebecca chuckle. Bobby had stayed at the side of the old man right up until the day he had died.

She remembered the day of the old man's funeral, the shopkeepers and neighbours round about were watching as he was buried in a grave in the churchyard. It seemed right he should end up there, since he had spent most of his life just outside.

What Rebecca remembered most about that day was Bobby, how he kept close to the procession, was part of it, how he couldn't stand to be far away from his lifetime companion. No matter how hard she and her mother had tried to coax him away that night, he would not leave the graveside. Everyday for weeks they tried everything to tempt him from the cold graveyard to the warmth of their fireside. They weren't the only ones. Lots of the old man's friends were trying to adopt Bobby. He was loved by them all and each family would have been glad to have him. It was impossible, the terrier knew where he wanted to be.

Rebecca had an idea. Why not build a shelter there at the graveside for Bobby, it need not be too big, just enough to keep out the rain and the cold winds.

As Bobby grew older he was glad of the kennel and of the snippets of food that Rebecca and his other friends provided. As Rebecca grew up Bobby was as much part of her life as collecting up the pins in the hat shop. Stuffing bread, a chunk of cheese or a bit of left-over meat into her handkie for Bobby was a normal ending to her meals.

Leaving work on one dark winter evening she hurried home trying to dodge the rain. As she stooped to drop the scraps from dinner for Bobby her heart skipped a beat. He'd gone. "Bobby isn't there," she called as she opened her front door. Her mother was sitting in front of the fire mopping her red eyes with her apron. "I know love, he died today, Mr MacDonald found him and he's taken him away," her mother explained sadly. "Where's he taken him to? You know he couldn't bear to be away from that churchyard."

Rebecca burst into tears.

Her mother explained that everyone felt the same way about Bobby and the people round about had made plans to have something done in his memory.

Later, Rebecca often took her own children to the street corner in their city. Later still, she took her grandchildren too. They have all looked up at the top of the fountain to where a bronze figure of Greyfriar's Bobby sits proudly, and they listen spellbound over and over again to Rebecca's story.

Weird and wonderful pets

1. Work in groups of four. Each person takes a piece of **paper** and draws a different pet.

2. When the pictures are finished cut each animal into four pieces. Head, tail, legs and body. Then mix the pieces up.

3. Take four new parts and stick them on to background paper to make a new pet.

4. Invent a name for your creation, either a new name, or one made up by mixing the parts of the names of the four animals.

Things to do

▶ Organize a school pet show. Make posters advertising the event. Decide on the classes for entries, the cost of an entry. Buy some small prizes or make rosettes. Make suitable arrangements for receiving the animals in school. Organize judges etc. Invite parents and organize refreshments.

▶ Find as many poems as you can about animals and pets. Write your own poems and then mount them so that they can be stapled together to form an anthology.

▶ Carry out a survey and make graphs to show the different pets owned by children in school.

▶ Invite a member of the RSPCA to talk about the care of pets.

▶ Make a visit to a pet shop. Make a list of the variety of pet food and other articles on sale. Ask if it is possible to speak to the customers about their pets.

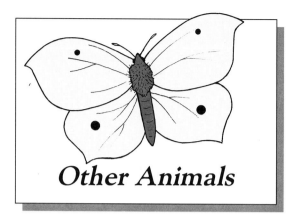

Other Animals

This topic introduces children to the concept of interdependence of people and animals. The poem, the Badger, raises issues about the behaviour of people towards animals, and could form a basis for discussion of fox hunting, bear baiting and cock fighting with older children. (Issues of conservation and protection of animal species are raised under the topics on pages 90–95.)

Talking points

▶ Discuss with the children how we obtain our food from animals, for example, milk, cheese, butter.

▶ Discuss the bad things about factory farming, and the reasons why nevertheless it is allowed to continue.

▶ Discuss how we obtain wool and leather from animals for our clothing.

▶ Discuss how animals have worked and helped people, for example horses, dogs. Make reference to animals around the world like camels, bullocks, elephants and the role they play in helping people.

▶ Talk about the changing attitudes in Britain towards working animals, for example, pit ponies. Are attitudes different in other countries?

▶ Discuss how worms help the gardener and farmer. Talk about making a wormery to discover how their contribution is made.

▶ Discuss the things which some animals can do better than people, for example, because of their keener sense of smell.

▶ Do we always care for the needs of animals?

▶ Do you think that fox-hunting should be illegal?

▶ Discuss the role of animals in different religions. For example: Ganesh the elephant, Hauman the monkey God, the sacred cow (Hindu); goat sacrifices (Eid – Muslim); the dove, the donkey (Christianity); elephants in a Buddhist perahera.

A festival day for pets and animals

The 17 of January is a day when people remember St Anthony of Egypt. St Anthony lived in Egypt between 251 and 356, and is regarded as a healer of men and animals.

In Mexico, people take their pets along to churches on this day to receive a special blessing. Prayers are also said for the protection of all animals.

In some very rural areas, the peasant farmers also take insects and worms to be blessed in the churches, because they are aware of the part which these small creatures play in the growing of crops.

The badger

When midnight comes a host of dogs and men
Go out and track the badger to his den,
And put a sack within the hole, and lie
Till the old grunting badger passes by.
He comes and hears – they let the strongest
   loose,
The old fox hears the noise and drops the
   goose,
The poacher shoots and hurries from the cry,
And the old hare half wounded buzzes by.
They get a forked stick to bear him down
And clap the dogs and take him to the town,
And bait him all day with many dogs,
And laugh and shout and fright the
   scampering hogs.
He runs along and bites at all he meets:
The shout and holler down the noisy streets.

He turns about to face the loud uproar
And drives the rebels to their very door,
The frequent stone is hurled where'er they go;
When badgers fight, then every one's a foe.
The dogs are clapt and urged to join the fray;
The badger turns and drives them away.
Though scarcely half as big, demure and small
He fights with dogs for hours and beats them
   all.

The heavy mastiff, savage in the fray,
Lies down and licks his feet and turns away,
The bulldog knows his match and waxes cold,
The badger grins and never leaves his hold.
He drives the crowd and follows at their heels
And bites them through – the drunkard swears
   and reels.

John Clare

Dolly and the donkeys

There was one old fellow I once knew, his name was Dick and he was a real animal lover, but he particularly loved horses. He was a character and all the folks for miles around knew him and said that he slept in the stable with his horses. He delivered coal around the village and he had a reputation for being able to manage any horse.

Old farmer Shutt had a good looking mare named Dolly. Dolly was a good worker but if the farmer left her in the field she always wandered off. Bolt the gate as they might Dolly would still get out.

Knowing Dick's reputation as he did, old farmer Shutt asked Dick if he would have a word with Dolly, so the next day Dick turned up at Shutt's farm. He had with him two rough looking donkeys. The poor creatures had been badly treated. One of them had a huge scar and sores and the other was very thin indeed. Dick had acquired them from an Animal Rescue Society.

"Shutt! Shutt!" shouted Dick, "I've fetched ye these two to put with your Dolly." farmer Shutt looked in amazement and said "What do I want with two scruffy donkeys?" "You might not want them, but your Dolly does," said Dick. "They'll only cost you their keep."

Farmer Shutt allowed Dick to put the two poor donkeys into his field, and immediately Dolly neighed and came over to greet her new friends. Dick then left calling out "She'll be alright now – you'll see. Be sure to look after them well and they will solve your problems."

True were his words, for after that day, Dolly never strayed again. She needed company, no longer was she lonely. The two donkeys soon began to look healthier because of good food and a little kindness.

A few months afterwards farmer Shutt was wakened very early one morning by Dolly neighing loudly. When Shutt looked from the window he saw her galloping and cantering around the field. "What's up with her now?" he thought, "I'd better go and see." Down he went and as he entered the field he saw the cause of Dolly's excitement, – no longer had she two friends but now there were three. The newly-born donkey was lying next to its mother.

Farmer Shutt met Dick down at the smithy and told him the news of the new arrival. "Well! you've solved your problem and made a profit in the bargain," said Dick. "It always pays to treat 'em well, they give as much back as we give them."

Horse power

At one time in Britain big strong horses were used for heavy work. Now lorries are used instead. A few horses remain as symbols of the past.

Things to do

► Find out all you can about badgers. Write their life story.

► Collect information about the ways in which animals help people in special ways. For example: sniffer dogs; guide dogs, bullocks; horses; sheep dogs.

► Why are elephant orphanages necessary today? Who are the people who work there? How are they funded?

► Write a prayer of thanksgiving for our animal friends.

► Find out about the Jains of India.

► Read the stories of Androcles and the Lion and the Bell of Atri.

Music

Music has been part of the lives and feelings of people from early times, it plays its part in may religious ceremonies. Examples are the Shofar horn, drums, bells and horns at Buddhist temple pujas, organs in churches and chapels and instruments from around the world.

Talking points

▶ Discuss how music is to be found in nature, in the song of the birds, the swish of the tides and the sound of the wind in the trees, the humming of bees.

▶ Compare musicians who play in orchestras and members of a team. What qualities are necessary? For example: perseverance; patience to practise until perfect; co-operation.

▶ Discuss the benefits of modern music equipment. Encourage children to realize that other people may not want to hear their music.

▶ Talk about the children's own preferences for different kinds of music for example, rock, reggae, orchestral, brass band, pop, jazz, heavy metal, country, steel band. Discuss how music is used in religious worship.

▶ Discuss the different types of songs for example, ballads, sea shanties, spirituals, psalms, bhajans. Talk about where these came from.

Music for the world

In December 1984 the Band Aid song *Do They Know It's Christmas?* topped the charts. The record raised about eight million pounds for famine victims in Africa.

Bob Geldof, who was singer with the Boomtown Rats saw the horrific news film of the effects of drought in parts of Africa and decided that he must do something to help. Millions of people were facing death.

Bob was impatient to get things going and thought that through rock music he could reach people and raise money. With fellow musician, Midge Ure, he composed the song *Do They Know It's Christmas?* Then he persuaded thirty six of the most famous rock stars in Britain at that time to become part of Band Aid and record the song. Sting, Wham and U2 were just some of the participants.

From the record Bob went on to help other groups organize similar records. Still not satisfied he had an even greater idea. On 13 July 1985 the *Live Aid* concert linked Britain and the USA in a day of rock music that was heard around the world. The event was so fantastic that by the end of 1985 it had raised over fifty million pounds for the famine victims in Africa. There were also many spin-offs, such as *Sport Aid* and *Comic Relief* in the years that followed.

When the concert was over Bob declared, "It was the world's day". So many musicians and technicians had come together to help the hungry victims of famine using the power of their music, and the response of modern technology.

Wolfgang Amadeus Mozart

Wolfgang Amadeus Mozart was born in Salzburg, in Austria, on 27 January 1756. When he was only three years old he started music lessons. At four years old, he was already a skilful pianist. By the time he was six years old, he could also play the harpsichord and violin, and by the time he was seven, he composed music and played a wide range of instruments. Mozart became famous as a child prodigy.

Mozart gave concerts in Austria and audiences were astounded at the skill of such a young musician. The Emperor of Austria invited Mozart to play at the palace in Vienna. Later Mozart's father took him to France where the King and Queen were part of the audience. They listened spellbound and at the end of the performance they pronounced that little Mozart was undoubtedly a genius.

From France, Mozart and his family moved to London, where a performance was given for King George III. The King was himself a lover of music and was delighted with Wolfgang's playing on the harpsichord and organ.

Mozart spent his whole life composing music. He was a genius but he never learnt to handle money wisely and was often too poor to buy food. He became ill and caught typhoid fever. He died when he was only thirty five years old and was buried in a pauper's grave in Vienna, but he left behind many musical treasures for the world to enjoy.

A string of sounds

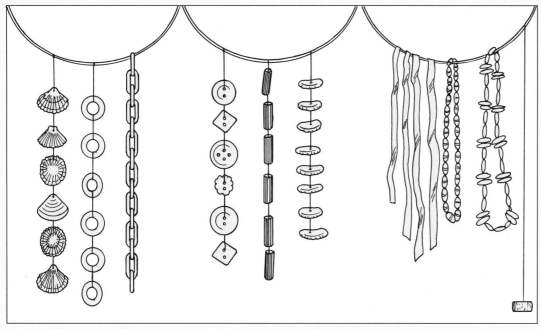

shells   chain   buttons   bottle tops   paper and foil   pull
washers   macaroni   necklaces

1. You need to secure a strong **string** to a low ceiling, or across a corner.

2. String together collections of interesting sounds. Attach to the main string.

3. At one end fasten a 'pull' string. This will produce a variety of sounds.

4. You can experiment with other objects. Change them around and make different combinations.

Things to do

► Listen to *The Young Person's Guide to the Orchestra* by Benjamin Britten. Examine pictures of each instrument, or if possible the instruments themselves.

► Discuss different ways of making music. For example: scraping, blowing, tapping, plucking, beating.

► Make musical instruments such as shakers, pluckers, strikers, blowers.

► Make music using a suitable computer. Use the computer handbook and from the instruction try to compose a short well-known tune. Play it to the rest of the class to see if they can recognize it.

► Divide the class into small groups. Give each group the name of a composer and ask them to research their life story and listen to some of their music. Each group can then give a talk to the rest of the class.

► Find out all you can about St Cecilia the patron saint of music.

► Play the music, *The Magic Flute* by Mozart or the *Sorcerer's Apprentice* by Dukas. Tell the story, ask the children to illustrate it.

► Read the poem *The Pied Piper of Hamelin* by Robert Browning.

► Involve the children in creating a musical programme to perform for the rest of the school.

Sport and Games

The aim of this topic is to show the value of sporting activities and also how the principles of being good at sport can be applied in our communities and in the world.

Talking points

▶ Discuss the different ways in which people participate either as competitors or spectators in many different kinds of sport and games.

▶ Towns and cities have football teams or rugby teams. Name some of the teams you know and your favourite players.

▶ Discuss how sport and games provide us with entertainment in our leisure time, both by participation as players and as spectators. Talk about the benefits of television to sport.

▶ Discuss the importance of giving of one's best, playing fairly, and learning to be a good loser. Is it more important to win or is it more important to take part?

▶ Discuss what it means to be a member of a team. Talk about the need to co-operate with others in working towards agreed ends.

▶ Discuss what we learn through taking part in sports and games, for example, to share, to think of others, to be patient and to persevere.

Portrait of a sportsman

Conrad Hunte was born on the island of Barbados in the Caribbean and like many other boys learnt to play cricket when he was very young.

Conrad's father wanted him to be clever and often nagged him for playing cricket instead of studying. It was clear that Conrad had all the skills needed to make a fine cricketer, and he was asked to play for his island team.

Conrad came to England hoping to further his career in cricket. Life was hard for him at first but after a time he was offered a job with Enfield Cricket Club. Later he was asked to join the West Indies Cricket Team to play against Pakistan, and even later was chosen for the West Indies Test Match Team. This meant that Conrad would now visit countries all over the world. On his travels he saw much poverty; he saw people who were being unfairly treated, he saw hate and violence, and this worried him a great deal.

In 1967, Conrad Hunte was back in England and very concerned. Black people in Britain felt that they were being unfairly treated and race riots seemed very likely. Conrad was black and he understood how black people feel. He knew that society needed to change but he did not agree with using violence.

Conrad explained that violence was futile, it would bring harm and death upon both black people and white people, and in the end the hatred would still be there. The only way forward was through forgiveness, understanding and tolerance.

Conrad wanted to do more to help black people and white people understand each other but his career in cricket took up most of his time. He started to think about giving up cricket but he didn't know how he would earn his living.

One day he was walking along a London street when suddenly a small voice seemed to say to him, "Look up Conrad." He looked up and saw a sign which said, "Take Courage". Had God spoken to him? Conrad went into a church and prayed. Afterwards he sent a letter of resignation to the West Indies Cricket Board.

He was now free to start his new work helping people to lose their hate and encouraging people from all races to live happily and peacefully together.

Adapted from Stories of Great Lives: Test Match *by John Pedley – itself based on* Playing to Win *by Conrad Hunte*

Boys only?

In 1988 a Manchester Primary School protested against the English Schools Football Association's ruling that they should drop their girl player from the school league football team.

The headteacher and the ten male players rebelled against the league's "boy's only" rule by refusing to participate in a Cup Match replay without her. They all agreed that she was one of the team's best players. The league, however, ruled that if the team kept her they would only be

Games of chance

Long ago in ancient Rome people were fascinated by dice. Dice were easily obtained because they were so easy to make. Many games were played with dice. When the Roman legions crossed the empire they took dice with them. The emperor Nero was thought to be addicted to the game.

Many of the games we play involve the use of dice. Each time we throw a die it gives a random number from one to six.

A French mathematician called Blaise Pascal who lived in the seventeenth century realized that the probability of any one number turning up could be predicted. Although we cannot say which number will turn up next time we throw the die, we can predict the pattern if the die is thrown many times. After many throws, each number will appear once in every six throws on average.

A game of heads and tails

1. Two people each have a coin.

2. They both toss the coin 20 times. For each pair of tosses the result could be:

3. Record the results.

Heads	Tails
卌 ‖	卌 ‖‖

allowed to play in friendly matches.
When a similar case was taken to court a few years ago, the judge ruled that Schools Football Associations are not covered by the Sex Discrimination Act.
Soccer is now beginning to be popular in the United States where it is common to see boys and girls playing together in mixed teams, but there are also girls' teams and leagues. In the United States it is illegal to run a team which bans girls and schools have to spend equal amounts of money on boys' and girls' sports. Local newspapers also give equal coverage to sports for boys and girls.
What do you think?

Things to do

▶ Find out all you can about the Olympic Games. How and where did they begin? What kind of sports were included? When and where will they be held next?

▶ Make graphs to show favourite sports and games.

▶ Find out what you can about the old ring games which children used to play, for example, *Ring O' Roses*, *In and out the windows*.

▶ Hold a games afternoon with dominoes, draughts, chess, ludo, snakes and ladders, monopoly, and other suitable games.

▶ Examine a map of your own town. Find out where there are facilities for sport or games. For example: swimming baths, tennis courts, football pitches, cricket grounds, ski-slopes, opportunities for water sports. Do you think these facilities are adequate?

▶ Divide into groups. Each group is a committee responsible for the organization of a Sports Day. Consider the preparation and the things you will need on the day.

▶ Make rosettes, posters and programmes for Sports Day.

▶ From the Radio Times work out the amount of time devoted to sport on television each week.

▶ Draw athletes in action.

Further Resources

This page contains a list, by topic, of additional ideas to follow up. These include songs, poems, hymns, stories and useful addresses.

page 40
Stories of family festivals, for example: Mothering Sunday, Raksha Bandhan, the Hindu festival that depicts 'ties of protection', the Japanese Boys' Festival, Girls' Festival and Children's Festival.
The building song, *Come and Praise*, BBC Publications, 1978.
The family man, *Come and Praise*, BBC Publications, 1978.
Come and Praise, on record REC317, on cassette ZCM317.

page 42
About Ben Adhem, James Leigh Hunt, *Emscote Book of Verse*, The Greville Press.
Au claire de la lune, traditional French folksong.
I'd like to teach the world to sing, *Apusskidu*, A & C Black, 1975.
When I need a neighbour, *Come and Praise*, BBC Publications, 1978.
Cross over the road, *Come and Praise*, BBC Publications, 1978.

page 44
Skyscraper Wean, *Tinder-box*, A & C Black, 1983.
Milk bottle tops and paper bags, *Someone's Singing Lord*, A & C Black, 1973.
City beasts, *Tinder-box*, A & C Black, 1983.
Penny Lane, Lennon & McCartney.

page 46
A hill is a house for an ant, *Tinder-box*, A & C Black, 1983.

page 48
The story of Dick Whittington.
Rules, Brian Patten, *Gargling with Jelly*, Puffin.

page 50
Prayer of St Teresa of Avila, see page 116.

page 52
You and I we're far apart, *Tinder-box*, A & C Black, 1983.
Jamaica Farewell, *Ta-ra-ra Boom-de-ay*, A & C Black, 1977.
One more stop along the world I go, *Come and Praise*, BBC Publications, 1978.
Liverpool Maritime Museum have material and project packs on the theme of emigration. Visits can be arranged for school parties.

page 54
Story of Elizabeth Fry.
The story of the Suffragettes and votes for women.

page 56
The ink is black, *Come and Praise*, BBC Publications, 1978.
The homework machine, Shel Silverstein, *A Light in the Attic*, Harper and Row.

page 60
The story of Florence Nightingale. Stories from the Gospels, for example: Jesus heals the leper, Blind Bartimaeus, Jesus and Jairus' daughter.
Stories from the Gospel according to St Luke (Patron Saint of doctors and nurses).

pages 62 and 63
I love God's tiny creatures, *Someone's Singing Lord*, A & C Black, 1973.
All things which live below the sky, *Someone's Singing Lord*, A & C Black, 1973.
Stand up clap hands, *Someone's Singing Lord*, A & C Black, 1973.
Who put the colours in the rainbow?, *Come and Praise*, BBC Publications, 1978.

page 66
Praise the Lord in the rhythm of your music, *Come and Praise*, BBC Publications, 1978.
The music man, *Okki-tokki-unga*, A & C Black.
You'll sing a song and I'll sing a song, *Tinder-box* A & C Black, 1983.
Whistle a happy tune, *Apusskidu*, A & C Black, 1975.
I'd like to teach the World to sing, *Apusskidu*, A & C Black, 1975.
Do they know it's Christmas?, Band Aid.
We are the World, USA for Africa.

page 68
The cricket match, *Ta-ra-ra Boom-de-ay*, A & C Black, 1977.
Football crazy, *The Jolly Herring*, A & C Black.
In our work and in our play, *Morning has Broken*, Schofield and Simms.
The story of the Olympic games.

THE WIDE WORLD

Myth and Legend

From the earliest times people have wondered where they came from and how the world began. They wondered about the sun, the moon and the stars and have asked questions about the rainbow, thunder, and lightning. To help themselves to understand all these things, they told stories about gods and spirits. These stories were passed down from one generation to the next. As time went by people gained new knowledge and they discarded some of these early beliefs but some of the old stories were written down and remain as myths and legends.

Talking points

▶ Discuss with the children how people worshipped the sun as a god and called him Sol. Talk about Stonehenge and sun worship and the Winter and Summer Solstices.

▶ Ask the children if they are afraid of thunder and lightning. Explain how the Norse people thought there was a god called Thor who caused the thunder when he was angry. Talk about what we know are the causes of thunder and lightning?

▶ Talk about the seasons and how the lives of people are affected by them, how did early people explain these changes? For example the ancient Greeks told the story of Persephone.

▶ Discuss the names of the days of the week and how early people wanted to please their gods and gave each day of the week a god's name. For example: Sun (Sunday), Moon (Monday), Tyr (Tuesday), Woden (Wednesday), Thor (Thursday), Freya (Friday), Saturn (Saturday).

The anger of Thor – a Norse legend

Long ago in the Northlands there lived a little boy whose name was Olaf. Olaf's people were known as the Norsemen. Many of them were fishermen and they often had to battle against wind, storm and rain but they were always strong and brave. At the end of each day Olaf and his family would sit around the fire and the elders would tell stories to pass away the long hours of darkness and to share their beliefs with their children.

Olaf's favourite story was about the great God Thor the Thunderer who was big, strong and powerful and protected the people of the Northlands from all dangers with his great hammer, the Thunderbolt.

One day Olaf was out fishing at sea with his father in their small boat when a terrible storm blew up. Olaf was afraid. The sky darkened and suddenly the thunder roared. "Do not be afraid," said Olaf's father, "Thor is angry but the God of Light will soothe him very soon."

Just then the dark sky brightened and a beautiful rainbow appeared. It stretched

across the sky between the earth and heaven. Olaf had never seen anything so beautiful before.

"What is that, Father?" Olaf asked. "It is a bridge that links the Heaven and the earth, and a sign to all people that Thor is no longer angry," said father.

The storm died away and Olaf and his father returned safely to the shore.

Ceyx and Halcyone – a Greek legend

The shortest day in our year is the 21 December. At this time the earth is tilted so that the northern hemisphere is further away from the sun. Also around this time the Mediterranean Sea is usually very calm and the Ancient Greeks had a story to explain this.

Halcyone, was the daughter of Aeolus, god of the winds. She was very beautiful and married King Ceyx of Thessaly. Halcyone and Ceyx loved each other very much and they lived happily together.

The time came when Ceyx needed to make a long journey across the sea to Delphi. Halcyone wanted to go with him but Ceyx knew that the journey would be dangerous and insisted that she stay behind.

Halcyone went to the temple of Juno each day and prayed that the goddess would take care of her husband. Whilst Ceyx was at sea there was a terrible storm and he was drowned. Halcyone dreamed of Ceyx' death. She dreamt that he was calling to her from the depths of the sea. The next morning she went to the seashore full of grief and threw herself into the waves. Juno took pity on them both and changed Ceyx and Halcyone into two beautiful kingfishers so that they were together once more. Zeus, the chief amongst the gods, decreed that the winds should not blow for a week on either side of midwinter's day. This is the time when the eggs of the kingfisher are hatching in their floating nest.

Another name for the kingfisher is the halcyon and today when people speak of 'halcyon days' they mean days of peace and tranquillity.

The little squirrel – an Indian legend

This story is about a little squirrel. Long ago Lord Rama lived in India with his beautiful wife Sita. Across a narrow stretch of water on the island of Sri Lanka lived Ravana, the wicked Demon King of Lanka.

Ravana kidnapped Sita and carried her off to his island. Lord Rama wanted to rescue her and asked the monkeys to help him build a bridge.

The monkeys worked very hard carrying large stones and rocks. Backwards and forwards they went with their loads. Suddenly they realized that a tiny squirrel was helping as well. One large monkey stopped the squirrel. "What on earth are you doing here?" he said. "I am helping Rama to build his bridge," the little squirrel replied. "You, you are too little to help anyone," said the monkey. "No, I can bring little pebbles and every little will help," replied the squirrel. All the monkeys began to laugh at the squirrel and told her to stop being so silly and to go back home.

The little squirrel wouldn't listen and she carried on as before. One large monkey became very angry, grabbed hold of her and flung her out of the way. She went soaring up into the air but when she came down again Rama was there to catch her. Rama had seen and heard all. He held the little squirrel close to him and called the monkeys to gather round. He told the monkeys that they were wrong to cast aside the weak for even tiny creatures can show their love, and all can serve in different ways.

Gently Rama put the squirrel on the ground and patted her on the back saying, "Little one, be blessed by me, you have loved and served me well." He stroked the squirrel on her back and left his finger marks there on her brown fur for all to see. To this day the Indian squirrel has three white stripes on its back.

The Indian squirrel

Three-striped palm squirrel eating coconut.

Things to do

▶ Search for books in your library containing myths and legends. Make a class book of myths and legends from around the world.

▶ Make drawings of the planets, name them and find out more about the Roman gods after whom they were named.

▶ Find out why our seasons are like they are. Find out how the seasons in Australia and South America are different to those in Britain.

▶ Choose one of the seasons and write a paragraph beginning "Winter is . . ." or "Autumn is . . ." Illustrate your work.

Religion

Many human societies have a belief in a divine purpose which is greater than themselves and provides a focus for their lives. The practices and customs of this belief are called a religion. There are many religions active in the world today. They have evolved in different parts of the world at different times responding to the needs of the cultures in which they flourish. Britain is basically a Christian country but people are free to follow whatever religion they choose. Nevertheless people do find it hard to understand an unfamiliar religion and children in particular need help and guidance to practise tolerance towards the beliefs of others. A summary of each of the major world religions is to be found in the section starting on page 103.

Talking points

▶ Discuss the variety of religions represented amongst the children present.

▶ Talk about the different places of worship in the immediate area of the school.

▶ Talk about times of worship, prayer, praise, thanksgiving. (Saying grace before meals.)

▶ Talk about festivals of different faiths. For example: Christmas, Easter, Eid, Holi, Wesak and the stories associated with these.

▶ Discuss the time when early people began to live together and the need for certain rules to help them to live together peacefully.

▶ Discuss how religions aim to help people to care for their fellow human beings.

▶ Discuss religious tolerance. Should people be able to worship as they wish? Talk about the times in Britain when this has not been possible. Discuss the places in the world where it is still not possible to worship as you choose. Consider why this is so?

The wonderful universe

Robert and Jane are twins and they always look forward to a visit from their Grandfather. Grandfather has retired now, but he used to be an engineer and spent all his life working on ships. He travelled all over the world and he always tells wonderful stories of the fascinating places he visited and the interesting people he met.

Grandfather had just arrived and it was 23 December – almost Christmas. At bedtime the twins begged Grandfather to take them up to bed hoping for one of his stories. Robert went over to the window and gazed out at the sky. "I like the stars," he said. "I wonder why we have so many stars?" Jane added quickly as she struggled with her dressing down. "They always seem to make the same patterns in the sky."

"Ah well," said Grandfather, "We are part of a very wonderful universe." He loved his grandchildren very much and he knew they wanted a story.

"I wonder why we're here at all?" Robert said hopefully. "Get into bed," said Grandfather, "and we'll talk about it." Jane and Robert jumped quickly into bed and waited with anticipation. "Since the very beginning of time people have wondered about the world around them, and they have asked themselves questions about it."

"Where does rain come from?" "Why does the sun travel across the sky?" "What happens to people when they die?" "Why are we here at all?"

"Stories were told to try to explain these things, and these stories are probably the beginnings of our great religions, but no one really knows."

"When people started to live together in groups they needed rules to help settle their quarrels and some of the stories helped them to do this."

Jane asked Grandfather whether people all believed the same things. "Not always," said Grandfather.

"Religions have grown up at different times in different places but some religions have similar stories. All religions expect their followers to help each other and care for people." He went on talking, more to himself than the children, about the temples, and mosques that he had seen on his travels, and the sacred holy books which his friends read. He also told of the different symbols which helped his friends to follow their religions and how some of

Christian baptism

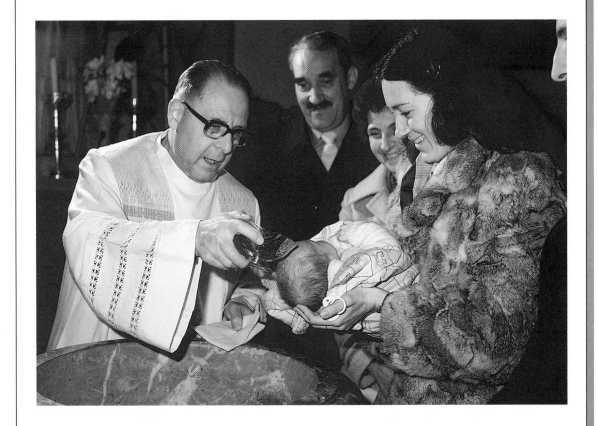

them had made pilgrimages to holy places. Then he talked about the different ways his friends prayed and how his Muslim friends prayed five times a day. This seemed to remind Grandfather that he had been talking for rather a long time and that Jane and Robert were almost asleep. "Well, I think it's time for you to say your prayers now and for me to say, 'Goodnight and God bless'." And after that Grandfather kissed them both gently, and creeping out shut the door.

If I can do some good today,
If I can serve along life's way,
If I can something helpful say,
Lord, show me how.

If I can right a human wrong,
If I can help to make one strong,
If I can cheer with smile or song,
Lord, show me how.

If I can aid one in distress,
If I can make a burden less,
If I can spread more happiness,
Lord, show me how.

From *Short Prayers for the Long Day*
by G. M. Harcourt

Things to do

▶ Start with collections of artefacts. Pupils working in pairs should pursue personal research into:
what the artefact is,
what it is used for,
where it is kept.

What does it tell us about the beliefs and practices of the people to whom it belongs?

▶ Encourage pupils in the class to bring along artefacts from their faith group and to talk about what they do in their religious practices.

▶ If your class is mono-faith, it is very worthwhile establishing links with another school and exchanging visits or correspondence so that children can share with others.

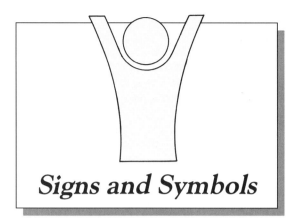

Signs and Symbols

Our everyday lives are guided by signs and symbols. There are so many we tend to follow them automatically without noticing them.

In many kinds of worship, at festivals and celebrations, symbolism plays an important part. Candles are lit as a sign of light coming into the world, special foods may be eaten or special clothes worn, all of these have a particular significance.

Talking points

▶ Discuss everyday objects which act as signs. For example: uniforms, colour, road signs, badges, coats of arms, flags.

▶ Discuss natural phenomena which act as signs, like sunsets, birds gathering, icicles, foot-prints, autumn leaves, spring blossom, cloud formations, position of the sun in the sky.

▶ Discuss the signs we give to others which tell of our mood or feelings. For example: smiles, tears, posture, gesture, acts of aggression, caring acts.

▶ Discuss the signs and symbols that are used in rituals, celebrations, festivals

and worship. For example: the use of water in Christian baptism, or a wedding ring.

▶ Discuss how deaf people depend on signs and symbols to understand what is happening in the world. For example: the green man on a pedestrian crossing, or the subtitles on some television programmes. Talk about sign language and lip reading.

The Red Cross

We often see a red cross on the sides of ambulances, or on the uniforms of nurses. Have you ever wondered why this symbol is used?

In the summer of 1859, there was a war in Italy. A young Swiss businessman called Henri Dunant was travelling through Northern Italy and witnessed the Battle of Solferino.

After the Battle he saw many dead soldiers and countless others who had the most terrible wounds. Injured men lay everywhere and there were very few doctors to help them. Henri was appalled that men should treat each other in this way and that there should be such useless bloodshed and slaughter. He stayed at Solferino and tried to organize some sort of help for the victims. The memory of this dreadful event stuck in his mind. He wrote a book telling the world what he had seen at Solferino and he tried to persuade people of the need for a medical organization which could be called upon in the time of war.

In 1864 he succeeded in founding the International Red Cross.

There was a meeting in Henri Dunant's home town of Geneva. At this meeting the

nations represented agreed on how prisoners of war should be treated, and that hospitals, ambulances and medical personnel should not be attacked. They decided that some sort of sign would be needed so soldiers would recognize the ambulances and hospitals. They chose a red cross on a white background – the Swiss flag in reverse.

The Red Cross Organization still uses this symbol today except in some Islamic countries which use a red crescent instead of a red cross. Membership has grown to 200 million in 131 countries. Its work has expanded to help relieve suffering caused by disasters such as floods, earthquakes and famine.

In 1901 Henri Dunant shared the first Nobel Peace Prize for his work in founding the Red Cross Organization, and a special day is set aside each year when people remember the founding of this organization. The 8 May is World Red Cross Day.

The lotus flower

If you were to visit the lands of Thailand, Burma or Sri Lanka you would see many Buddhist temples. At certain times of day (and especially on Poya days which are the days of the full moon), a large horn is usually blown to tell people that it is time for 'Puja'. This is a time when people come along to make offerings at the temple.

Amongst the people who attend the temple there are the old and the young. Tiny babies are taken along by their mothers. For many of these babies it is their first journey outside of their own home. Many school children are taken along by their teachers and everyone takes a gift. Very often these are inexpensive

Find out about these symbols

A Hindu prayer

O God,
Let your light of love
Shine in this world of darkness,
So that all people may see their way
As they journey through this world,
And find the true path
That leads to the world beyond.

From *Dear God* by Rowland Purton

Things to do

▶ Find out all you can about the food eaten by a Jewish family at the Passover Feast. If you know any Jewish people ask them to talk to you about this.

▶ Find out all you can about the Christian Eucharist or Holy Communion.

▶ Find out how a Sikh family worships in their Temple or Gurdwara.

▶ Find out all you can about how a Muslim worships

▶ Arrange a visit to a local Church, a Mosque, a Hindu Temple and a Gurdwara.

▶ Arrange a short walk around the neighbourhood and look out for signs of any kinds. Think about looking up (smoke trails, aircraft trails, cloud formations etc), looking down (marks on the pavement, hydrants etc) and looking around. Make drawings of the signs you encounter.

gifts, often just a little posy of flowers from the wayside. The most popular gift is lotus flowers or even just their petals.

The lotus flower is of special significance to Buddhists because it reminds them of the teachings of Buddha. Even quite young children can explain why the lotus flower was chosen.

This is what they tell you:

"At first the lotus flower is a small tight bud which has its roots in mud. It is like a baby which has just begun life on earth.

Then as it begins to grow it rises through the water. At this stage it is like a child at school. Just as by going to school children become enlightened, so the lotus bud reaches upwards and searches for the light.

Once it is above the water is petals start to open under the rays of the sun. It has become perfect. The lotus flower is like someone who has learnt how to live successfully with all creatures."

In Buddhist countries dancing takes place at special festival times and the dancers make signs with their hands which also remind the audiences of the lotus flower and its meaning.

(The sign of the lotus flower is also used in Indian art and is sometimes seen on the Shri-Yantra, a sign used by Hindus.)

A Right to Equality

Most people in Britain live in homes which have a roof, clean water and a lavatory. If they travel on public transport they can choose any vacant seat. All children in this country have a right to education and if they are sick medical attention will be available. We often take these things for granted but they are not available to all children in all countries.

Talking points

▶ How would you feel if you arrived home tonight and your parents told you that because your family surname begins with a certain letter, for example: B or M, you were no longer allowed to live in that house and must move all your belongings to a tent on the moors outside of the town?

▶ Discuss what we mean by discrimination. For example: should all people with brown eyes receive more wages than people with blue eyes for the same work? Is it fair to discriminate on these grounds, or any grounds?

▶ Should mother be the one who always washes the dishes? Should father be the one who always changes a fuse? Should women be allowed to drive buses?

▶ Should women earn more money than men? Should only boys be allowed to attend school?

▶ Do all people in Britain have equal rights today? What sort of rights do we have (voting, freedom of worship, education)?

▶ Are there any laws concerning equal rights (laws against discrimination on the grounds of sex, race etc)?

What is apartheid?

South Africa is a beautiful country with many natural resources, but it is a troubled country where people live in fear. Although there are many more black people than white people, it is the white people who control South Africa.

In 1948, the white people made laws that separated the black people from the white people. This policy is known in South Africa and around the world as apartheid. Most white Africans live comfortably under apartheid, but most black Africans live in overcrowded houses with no tap water, in poor areas where the streets are unlit and where the schools are very poor. Black Africans cannot choose where they want to live. They have to live in special areas called homelands. Over three million black people have been forced to move to the homelands. Families are split up and many frail and sick old people have no one to care for them.

Black people often travel great distances to work but there are benches on which they must not sit, and buses on which they are not allowed to travel, even in the taxi queue they must stand separately and use a second class taxi. Some beaches are reserved for white people only and the black people are not allowed to bathe there. At work, black workers are supervised by white, the black people do the humblest jobs and are paid at lower rates.

Because the South African government has this policy of apartheid it is very unpopular in the world outside. Some countries refuse to trade with South Africa and South Africa is constantly under pressure to liberalize its laws.

The black people within South Africa have become more and more angry at the injustice that they suffer, and this has caused them to rebel. The rebellions have often been put down by the use of force, and many people have been put in prison frequently for long periods without a trial.

Apartheid is only one example of a system where people are treated unjustly. Throughout the world there are serious violations of human rights. Oppressed people suffer under their own leaders or under those of another country. We cannot hope for a peaceful world until everyone works together to end discrimination of any kind.

A prayer

O God, we pray for oppressed people in many parts of the world. We pray for those who live in fear of their rulers and for those who are unjustly imprisoned. We ask you to comfort them in times of sadness and loneliness and to bless all those who are working to help them and their families.

Anonymous

The 'Homelands' of South Africa

South Africa produces enough food to meet 112% of the optimum daily energy requirement of everyone in the country, and yet malnutrition rates (89% among children in the Ciskei) are among the highest in Africa and the infant mortality rate for blacks is more than five times that of whites.

1. Bophuthatswana
2. Lebowa
3. Kwandebele
4. Gazankulu
5. Venda
6. Kangwane
7. Qwa Qwa
8. Kwazulu
9. Transkei
10. Ciskei

Oxfam, 1986

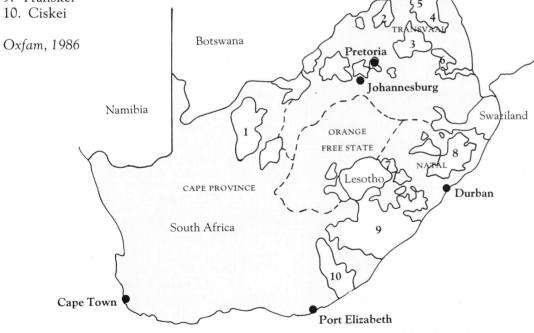

Xhosa kraals in Ciskeii

Things to do

► Make a list of the basic needs of all human beings, for example: food, water, shelter.

► Oxfam works amongst the people in the homelands of South Africa. Write to Oxfam and ask for information about their help projects in South Africa and in other parts of the world. The address is: Oxfam, 274 Banbury Road, Oxford, OX2 7DZ.

► Organize a 'sponsored spell'. Send your proceeds to an organization which works to achieve human rights.

► Find out all you can about Mahatma Gandhi. What methods did Gandhi use to achieve his aims of fighting injustice?

► South Africa is not the only unjust government. Find out about other countries where people are not treated equally.

► Make a poster with the caption '??? Human Rights ???' Find pictures and relevant newspaper cuttings to surround the caption. Cut letters for your caption from coloured pages in magazines. Try to use colour and unusual techniques to make your poster more effective.

► Find out about Abraham Lincoln and the cotton plantations of Southern United States, Martin Luther King, Mahatma Gandhi in India, Mrs Pankhurst, the Suffragettes and votes for women.

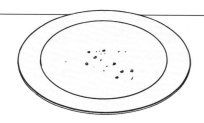

Freedom from Hunger

One basic human right is not to be hungry, yet all over the world there are people going without food. Although it is in the poor countries of the Third World that most people are suffering from malnutrition, even in the rich countries there are some people who are too poor to buy the food they need.

Talking points

▶ Discuss what it means to feel hungry. Discuss what it means to be hungry day after day and to be too weak to fight disease.

▶ Talk about famine and emergency food aid. Some famines are very dramatic and can happen unexpectedly but they account for only a small proportion of the hunger in the world.

▶ Discuss the long term poverty that causes most hunger.

▶ Discuss the organizations that try to change the situation like Oxfam, Save The Children Fund and the United Nations Food and Agriculture Organization.

There is no more

The crops are all dead.
The land is burned dry.
There is no more water.

The farmer is defeated.
The family go hungry.
There is no more home.

Walking for miles.
Nowhere to go.
There is no more home.

They arrive at the camp.
Half dead and tired.
There is no more hope.

A world split in two.
The rich and the poor.
There are no more equals.

Richard McKenzie and Chris Barrett

The Rainbow People

In the beginning the world was very still and quiet. The ground seemed to be covered with dull coloured rocks and stones. But if you took a closer look you could see that they were not stones but were tiny people who were not moving at all. One day a wind blew over the land. It warmed the people and filled them with life and with love. They began to move . . . to look at each other . . . to speak to each other . . . to care about each other.

As they explored their world they found coloured ribbons lying on the ground. They were excited and ran about collecting them up. Some chose blue, some red, some green, some yellow. They enjoyed tying the ribbons round each other and laughing at the bright colours.

Suddenly another wind blew. This time it made them shiver with cold. They looked at each other, realized they looked different . . . and stopped trusting each other.

The reds gathered together and ran into a corner.

The blues gathered together and ran into a corner.

The greens gathered together and ran into a corner.

The yellows gathered together and ran into a corner.

They forget that they had been friends and had cared for each other. The other colours just seemed strange and different. They built walls to separate themselves and keep the others out.

But they found that:

The reds had water but no food.

The blues had food but no water.

The greens had twigs to make fire but no shelter.

The yellows had shelter but nothing to keep them warm.

Suddenly a stranger appeared and stood in the centre of the land. He looked at the people and the walls separating them in amazement, and said loudly, "Come on out everybody. What are you afraid of? Let's talk to each other." The people peeped out at him and slowly came out of their corners into the centre. The stranger said, "Now just tell one another what you have to give, and what you need to be given." The blues said, "We have plenty of food to give but we need water. The reds said, "We have plenty of water to give but we need food." The greens said, "We have plenty of wood for fire but we need shelter." The yellows said, "We have plenty of shelter but we need warmth."

The stranger said, "Why don't you put together what you have and share it? Then you can all have enough to eat, drink, keep warm and have shelter."

They talked and the feeling of love returned. They remembered that they had been friends. They knocked down the walls and welcomed each other as old friends. When they realized that the colours had divided they wanted to throw them away. But they knew that they would miss the richness of the bright colours. So instead they mixed the colours to make a beautiful rainbow ribbon. They called themselves the Rainbow People. The rainbow ribbon became their symbol of peace.

Carolyn Askar

This story is particularly suitable for a class to present as a drama for assembly.

The Banana Game

The idea of the Banana Game is to demonstrate that what is convenient for some people can be unjust for others. It may be performed as a role play activity within the classroom or as a play for assembly.

You will need a bunch of bananas, a box, and 100 pence in money or tokens. The players have the following roles and sit in this order in a semi-circle:

Shopper
Retailer
Transporter
Exporter
Docker
Packer
Ripener
Shipper
Insurer
Grower

The bananas are passed from person to person starting from the grower and ending with the shopper. Each person, in turn, explains their part in the process. The shopper then puts the 100 pence into the box and passes it back around the semi-circle. The players remove their share of the 100 pence in the folowing proportions:

Retailer	32p
Transporter, Exporter, Docker, Packer	26p between them
Ripener	19p
Shipper, Insurer	11½p between them
Grower	11½

A discussion follows on how fair everyone feels these prices are.

Steve Pratchett for Christian Aid.

A prayer of an African Christian

O Lord, our meal is steaming before us
and it smells very good.
The water is clear and fresh,
we are happy and satisfied.
But now we must think of our sisters
and brothers all over the world
who have nothing to eat
and only a little to drink.
Please, please, let them have enough to eat
and enough to drink.
That is most important.
But give them also
what they need every day
in order to get through in this life.
Just as you have given enough to eat and drink
to the people of Israel in the desert
please give it also to our hungry and thirsty brothers,
now and at anytime.

Michael Hollings and Etta Gullick

Things to do

▶ Try writing your own poem about the foods that a hungry person in your country would see and smell around them. Describe the feelings of a person who is unable to share in the foods for sale in the shops, markets and restaurants which they see others using.

▶ Play the Banana Game.

▶ Write the story of a tee-shirt. Tell the story from the growing of the cotton to the purchase of the finished article in a shop in Britain. Write other stories for a cup of tea and a cup of coffee.

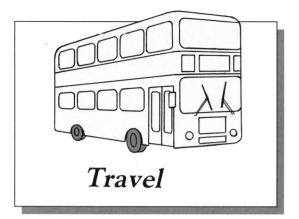

Travel

Children in Britain today are accustomed to fast travel: cars speed along the motorways; aeroplanes drone through the air; high speed trains whizz along electrified tracks. The speed of travel today has made the world seem a smaller place, but travel has its own dangers as well as giving insight into the ways other people live.

Talking points

▶ Ask the children to recount any travel experiences which they may have had, countries they have visited, what they saw or did.

▶ Discuss travel through the ages; travel on foot; the use of animals. For example: donkey and camel, horses, coaches, bicycles such as the penny-farthing, the first motor cars, simple sailing craft in early times, the coracle and the canoe, wind-powered sailing vessels, steam-powered liners, the first aircraft, the development of the jet engine etc.

▶ Discuss travel long ago: poor roads, highwaymen, toll-gates and turnpikes. Talk about how sailors relied on the stars and the compass. There were no facilities such as wireless, radio communication or radar.

▶ Discuss with the children how people make pilgrimages to the Holy Land, Mecca, Lourdes, Canterbury, Jerusalem, and the Rivers Jordan and Ganges. Tell the children about John Bunyan and *The Pilgrim's Progess* and how John Bunyan saw life as a journey.

▶ Discuss different modes of travel today and the inventions which have made such travel possible. Talk about the fact that because travel is so much easier the world seems a 'smaller' place. This creates a need for better understanding of people and their customs and cultures.

▶ Discuss tourism. What benefits do countries receive from having tourists? What disadvantages are there for these countries? (Seasonal work, money from abroad, sale of local crafts, eradicates pre-conceived ideas, intrusion into culture of the people, noise and disturbance, poor attitudes to other people.)

Travellers

Come, let us go a-roaming!
The world is all our own,
And half its paths are still untrod,
And half its joys unknown.
The way that leads to winter
Will lead to summer too,
For all roads end in other roads
Where we may start anew.

Arthur St John Adcock

This bridge

This bridge will only take you halfway there
To those mysterious lands you love to see
Through gypsy camps and swirling Arab fairs
And moonlit woods where unicorns run free.
So come and walk a while with me and share
The twisting trails and wondrous worlds I've known.
But this bridge will only take you halfway there –
The last few steps you have to take alone.

Shel Silverstein

Tourism

You could organize a debate on the advantages and disadvantages of tourism.

Appoint someone as chairperson. A group of eight children could dress as people from a country developing its tourist industry. Each could make a statement to provoke others into discussion. For example:

"I am glad that the tourists come to my country, it gives me employment in the hotel."

Then an opposite view:
"You only work for part of the year, and why should you be subservient to tourists, they don't think about you in winter?"

"I live in a small village and I am glad when I see the tourists because they buy my embroidered tablecloths."

"You spend a great deal of your time embroidering for very little money."

"I think it is a good thing for tourists to come as we can all share our music, folklore and dances with them."

"I regard that as an intrusion into my culture. We can sing and dance without the tourists."

Make a travel collage

You can use postcards, pictures from magazines or travel brochures to make a collage of different places around the world.

► Find out the main countries which rely on tourism today.

► Visit a travel bureau then set up a travel bureau in the classroom. Collect travel brochures and make advertisements. Make passports, tickets, book holidays, find out about the countries you wish to visit before you go. Work out the distance you will travel. Find the time of your flights outward and return. How many hours will you actually be travelling? Are there any time differences in countries along the route? Find out about the International Date Line. What sort of weather will you expect when you arrive? Will you need any special treatment before you go?

► Make a special topic book on *Our Roads Today*. Find out about road signs, speed limits, traffic lights, towns served by different motorways, cats-eyes. Include a traffic census taken in your neighbourhood. Find out about road builders, for example, Telford, McAdam, and bridge builders like Isambard K. Brunel.

► Make a wall frieze or scrap-books showing the development of travel through the ages, on land, by sea and in the air. Make a colourful collage from pictures you find in travel brochures. Compare these pictures with others you see showing the lifestyles of people in other countries.

► Make drawings showing new ways of travel in the future.

"I think that tourism promotes a better understanding amongst people of different countries, about their culture and religions."

"It may do that, but every summer we have to put up with noise and bustle, and look at all the rubbish they leave."

The last statement would be:

"I think tourism is good because it helps people realize the inequalities which exist and prompts them to help us."

The last counter-statement is then:

"Tourists don't always see us as we really are, and even if they know this, do you think they will help us?"

Allow an opportunity for points to be raised by children in the audience before the chairperson does a summary. A vote is then taken on the merits or otherwise of tourism.

The Land

Human beings depend on the land for their livelihood. They need land on which to build their homes and to provide most of their food. We often take our food for granted, but a good harvest depends on suitable weather conditions and also on people sowing, cultivating and reaping the crops. In Britain we often grumble about the weather but rain at certain times is needed for a good harvest. Much of our food is imported so we depend on people in other countries and on people who transport the food from one country to another.

Talking points

▶ Discuss 'The Breakfast Table' and the places that the food comes from. For example: tea, coffee, cornflakes, rice-crispies, marmalade, etc. Talk about the people of other countries and how we depend on them for some of our food.

▶ Discuss the crops of other countries. For example: cotton, rice, bananas, pineapples. Talk about how these crops are cultivated and harvested and then transported through merchants to other countries.

▶ Discuss climates in other countries and how people depend on the weather. For example: monsoons, floods in Bangladesh and Sudan, drought in Ethiopia, Sudan, India and the United States.

The little cloud

This story is suitable for dramatization.

It had been a long dry summer but suddenly a black cloud appeared in the sky. The cloud passed over the following groups of people: a mother who had just hung out her washing; a painter who was painting lines on the roadway; a family having a picnic on the beach; a school holding a Sports Day; some workmen mending a roof; the guests at a garden party. In different ways each of the groups told the little cloud to go away, that it was not welcome. Finally the cloud came to rest over a field where a farmer was driving his tractor. He welcomed the cloud and called to it not to pass by without allowing its precious raindrops to water his crops. The raindrops began to fall and the farmer then knew that his crops would not fail and sang a song of thanks as he drove along in his tractor.

Praise the Lord for times and seasons,
Cloud and sunshine wind and rain;
Spring to melt the snows of winter
Till the waters flow again;
Grass upon the mountain pastures,
Golden valleys thick with grain.

(Music: *Come and Praise* BBC 1978. Tune: *Laus et honor* by Gordon Hartless. Words: Timothy Dudley-Smith.)

The Iroquois Green Corn Festival

People around the world give thanks for their harvest. Here is the Iroquois prayer for harvest time:

We return thanks to our mother, the earth, which sustains us.
We return thanks to the rivers, streams and lakes, which supply us with water and food.
We return thanks to all herbs, weeds and bushes which furnish us with medicines for the cure of our diseases.
We return thanks to the corn, and to her sisters, the beans and squashes, which give us life.
We return thanks to the bushes and trees, which provide us with fruit.
We return thanks to the animals which provide us with meat and skins.
We return thanks to the wind, which, moving the air, has banished diseases.
We return thanks to the moon and stars, which have given us their light when the sun was gone.
We return our thanks to our grandfathers, the thunderers, that they have protected their grandchildren from witches and reptiles and have given us their rain.
We return thanks to the sun, that he looked upon us with a beneficent eye, and given us heat and light.
Lastly, we return our thanks to the Great Spirit, in whom is embodied all goodness, and who directs all things for the good of his children.

From *Let's Celebrate* by Caroline Parry

Make a Harvest Time display

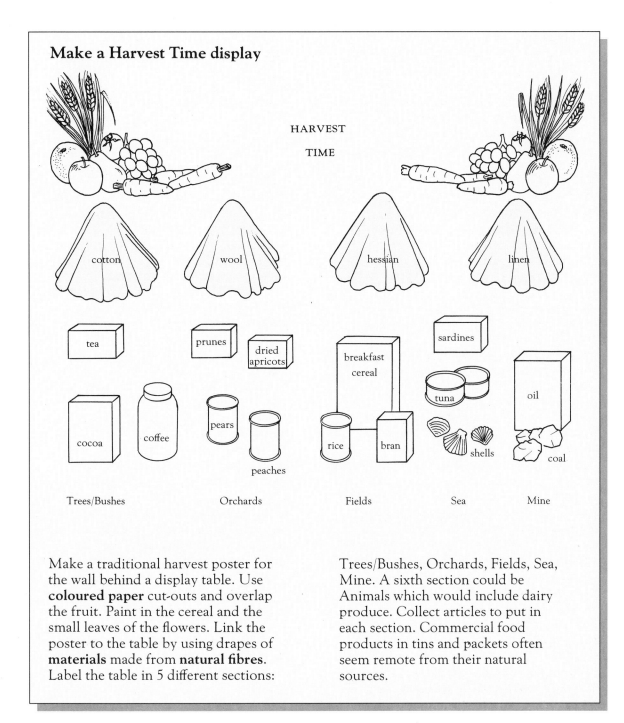

HARVEST

TIME

cotton   wool   hessian   linen

tea   prunes   dried apricots   sardines   oil

cocoa   coffee   pears   breakfast cereal   tuna   bran

rice   bran   shells   coal

peaches

Trees/Bushes   Orchards   Fields   Sea   Mine

Make a traditional harvest poster for the wall behind a display table. Use **coloured paper** cut-outs and overlap the fruit. Paint in the cereal and the small leaves of the flowers. Link the poster to the table by using drapes of **materials** made from **natural fibres**. Label the table in 5 different sections:

Trees/Bushes, Orchards, Fields, Sea, Mine. A sixth section could be Animals which would include dairy produce. Collect articles to put in each section. Commercial food products in tins and packets often seem remote from their natural sources.

A harvest prayer

O God, Creator of the world,
We thank you and praise you for the harvests
of the field, orchard, sea, forest and
mine.
Help those of us who have plenty to remember
others who have little.
Make us good sharers with each other and
with all.

Anonymous

Things to do

▶ Find out about harvests in Britain before mechanization. The number of people employed in the fields at harvest time, the use of sickle and scythe, horses and carts, women gleaning and young children helping, the long hours in the fields and eventually the last load and the merry-making.

▶ The Hopi tribe of Amerindians live in Arizona, USA. They have a special harvest home dance in which they carry green stalks and leaves. They offer these to their friends and neighbours. Work in small groups to device a series of movements that would be suitable for a harvest home dance.

▶ Use art straws and plait them to make corn dollies. Find out about the origins of corn dollies and the superstitions connected with them.

▶ Find a recipe for making bread. Can you make a sheaf loaf.

The Sky

From early times people have wondered at the mystery and beauty of the stars.

The moon and stars feature in most religions. Christians are familiar with the star of Bethlehem which led the three wise men from the east to the stable at Bethlehem at the time of the birth of Jesus. The sighting of a new moon heralds the beginning of the festival of Eid-ul-Fitr for Muslims, for the Buddhist the days of the full moon are special days known as Poya days when special visits are made to the temples. The Chinese hold a special Moon Festival in Autumn time whilst the Japanese hold a star festival called Tanabata. Jewish people include amongst their religions signs the Star of David. The star has always been regarded as a sign of hope.

Talking points

▶ Talk about the things we can see in the sky. For example: cloud formations, vapour trails, sun, moon and stars.

▶ Talk about the patterns which the stars make in the sky. Have the children noticed the shapes of the different constellations?

▶ Talk about how astronauts must feel when they travel in space for the first time.

▶ Talk about the importance of the moon to people before gas and electric lighting. Harvesting by moonlight and hunting by the light of the moon. Hence the harvest moon and the hunter's moon.

▶ Discuss the different festivals of various faiths in which the sun, moon or stars play a part.

One small step

Children today think that it is quite a normal event for astronauts to fly in space, but the first time a human being stepped on to the moon, people around the world watched on their television screens, spellbound. It was 20 July 1969.

The three astronauts, Neil Armstrong, Buzz Aldrin and Michael Collins, had lifted off from Cape Canaveral in the spacecraft Apollo 11. Their mission was to land on the moon. Nobody had been to the moon before. Nobody knew what might happen. As they neared the moon Neil Armstrong and Buzz Aldrin installed themselves in the lunar module. This was a landing craft that would take them down to the surface of the moon and, later, reunite them with the command module which was to stay in moon orbit.

The lunar module had been named *Eagle*, and on board there were anxious moments. "Would the fuel last out?" "Would everything go to plan?" "What would the surface of the moon be like?" "What if *Eagle* was damaged on landing?"

Viewers on earth watched tensely as *Eagle* sank down on to the Sea of Tranquillity, a large flat plain on the moon's surface. Everything went to plan.

When the astronauts realized that they had landed safely the first thing they did was to give thanks to God for a successful landing at the end of a dangerous journey into the unknown.

Both men were Christians and so they held a special service of Holy Communion. This is a service in which Christians take bread and wine to remind them how Jesus died and came alive again. The two men had taken with them little plastic packages containing the bread and wine.

Prayers over, Neil Armstrong opened the door, went down the ladder and stepped out on to the surface of the moon. As he left the first footprint on the dusty lunar surface, his blurred voice was transmitted back to Houston and from there across the world. "That's one small step for man, one giant leap for mankind."

Space flight is a tremendous technological achievement that demands huge amounts of money and incredible dedication. Much has happened since 1969. There have been great successes and horrifying failures. Holidays on the moon remain just as unlikely now as they were then. As Walter Shirra, another astronaut, said, people should do what they can to make the earth a better place because earth is where they are going to stay.

Tanabata

Tanabata is a Japanese star festival which was traditionally held on the seventh day of the seventh moon on the lunar calendar. Nowadays it is often celebrated on the seventh of July, the seventh month of our own calendar, because the festival is celebrated not only in Japan, but also in many countries around the world, where Japanese people have made their homes.

The festival is celebrated with demonstrations of judo, karate, origami, flower arranging and also Japanese dancing. Some people gaze up at the stars and make a wish whilst others write their wishes or prayers on strips of paper and hang these on to trees. Tanabata is a wonderfully colourful festival and it has its own delightful story:

There is a lovely star named Shokujo (Vega), she was a weaver-princess and the daughter of the King star. Shokujo fell in love with the herdboy star who was named Kengyu (Altair). Kengyu came to earth where he met Shokujo and her sisters who were all weavers for the gods. Shokujo and Kenygu were so happy on earth that they neglected their work and this made the gods angry because their herds were uncared for and the gods had no new clothes.

The gods decided that Shokujo and Kengyu should be separated. So Shokujo was sent to one side of the Milky Way river and Kengyu to the other. The separation made Shokujo so unhappy that she cried continually until her father eventually relented and said that he would allow them to meet on one day each year.

Each year as Vega and Altair draw near together the people say that Shokujo is crossing over the Milky Way on a bridge made by a flock of little birds to meet her lover, and if you listen very carefully the laughter of Shokujo can be heard.

Cape Canaveral

Things to do

▶ Keep diaries of the shape of the moon. Record the waxing or waning each evening and whether the moon seemed large or small, whether it was high in the sky or near the horizon. Keep a class wall chart.

▶ How is the Star of David formed? What shape is used?

▶ Make a chart showing the key dates in the history of voyages into space. Show the names of astronauts involved and the spacecraft in which they flew. Which nationalities have flown in space? When did the first woman enter space?

▶ Change your classroom into a booking hall for missions to other planets. Draw the planets and give some information about each one. Make timetables and write documents about what it might be advisable for passengers to take with them. For example: "You will need an oxygen mask."

The Sea

The sea covers two thirds of the earth's surface and in some places is several miles deep. It is vast, can be dangerous, and is an influential factor in the world's weather system. We get many things from the sea. Fishing has provided people with a livelihood and has kept others from starvation. In recent times rocks under the sea have yielded a rich harvest of oil and gas. All people who work with the sea are always aware of its dangers. It has claimed many lives over the years.

Talking points

▶ Discuss the rich harvests we reap from the sea. Fish, oil, gas, shellfish, prawns and shrimps, whalebone, sea-weeds, salt, codliver oil.

▶ Talk about different kinds of fishing: trawling, drifting, factory ships. Talk about traditional ways of fishing, and about the followers of Jesus who fished in the Sea of Galilee.

▶ Discuss the dangers of the sea and those who help fisherfolk such as lighthouse keepers, lifeboat personnel, helicopter pilots, air-sea rescue.

▶ Discuss the pollution of the sea and the effect of oil slicks on sea creatures and seabirds.

▶ Discuss how people can overfish areas and cause an imbalance in sea life. Talk about the reasons for limits on fishing areas.

▶ Discuss seal culling and whaling and the efforts of such organizations as Greenpeace to stop the overkilling of these creatures.

▶ Discuss how the fish reaches the fish and chip shop.

▶ Talk about the value of fish as food, for example, protein value. Talk about chips and fish as carbohydrate, fat, and protein.

Sea festivals

Just as harvest festivals are celebrated in most countries, so 'Fish Festivals' or 'Sea Festivals' take place in many seaside towns around the world. These festivals usually follow ceremonies to bless the fishing fleet.

Lobster suppers are a common feature of life in fishing towns and villages throughout the summer. In Canada on the 8 August, a community which originated in Sweden holds a traditional feast of crayfish. Paper lanterns are hung up outdoors for the party, everyone uses brightly coloured paper tablecloths and napkins on these days, because eating the crayfish with fingers is very messy. In Canada there is also the Oyster-shucking Championship, the Northern Pike Festival, the Salmon Festivals and many more. The festivals go on throughout the Summer.

I listen and I listen

In the morning early
I go down to the sea
And see the mist on the shore
I listen, and I listen.
When I go to the rocks
I go looking for shells
And feel the sand beneath my feet;
I listen, and I listen.
When the stormy day comes
Waves crash on the cliffs
And the wind whistles through my hair
I listen, and I listen.
And at night when I sleep
And the sea is calm
The gentle waves lap the shore;
I listen, and I listen.
I sometimes think that God
Is talking to me
When I hear the sound of the sea;
I listen, and I listen.
I listen, and I listen.

Hazel Charlton

The Fisherman's Birthday

My name is Rico. I live on the island of Grenada which is surrounded by the Caribbean Sea. Usually the days are sunny and warm and the sunlight on the waves makes the sea sparkle. It often looks so inviting but I have always been aware of how dangerous the sea can be.

My birthday falls on 29 June and I always have a happy time because on our island this date is a special festival which we call Fisherman's Birthday. The date was chosen because it is a special date when our church celebrates the feast of St Peter, one of the twelve apostles of Jesus. Peter was a fisherman.

Make a lighthouse

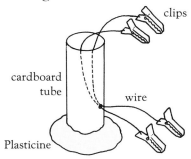

1. Cut a small hole near the bottom of the **tube**. Pass two wires through the hole and attach **clips** at each end. Stand the tube in **Plasticine**.

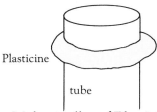

2. Make a collar of **Plasticine** around the top of the tube and place a circle of **card** around the tube to form a platform for the **bulb holder** and the **bulb**.

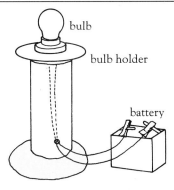

3. Connect the wires to the bulb holder at one end and to the battery at the other to form a circuit. Place an **aerosol cap** over the bulb.

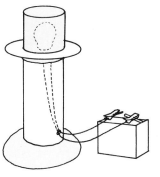

4. How can you make the light flash?

Very early in the morning I wake up and dress in my best tee-shirt. I usually have a new one for this special day. My brothers and I make our way to the church and see many of our friends attending Mass. After the church service all the people make their way to the shore and there the boats are blessed. The fishermen are there with their nets stretched out and the priest blesses them and their nets. Afterwards we usually visit out friends and neighbours all of whom offer us specially prepared food, and then the celebrations really begin.

There is special boat racing and music and dancing in the streets. It is a real carnival atmosphere with lots of fun, jokes and laughter. The older people sit and watch, they take this festival a little more seriously. They know that the people of our island rely on the sea for much of their food and they know also how dangerous the life of a fisherman can be. Fisherman's Birthday for them is a festival of thanksgiving for the harvest of the sea and also a time to thank God for the safety of the fishermen during the past year.

The prayer of the fishermen

Protect us, O God, this day
Our craft is so small
And the Ocean so wide.

Anonymous

Things to do

▶ Look at the globe and notice how much of the earth's surface is covered by the sea. Make a list of the great seas and oceans.

▶ Find out all you can about life on the seashore. Make a display with sand, pebbles, shells, nets, seaweed etc. Use drapes in different 'sea' colours as the background. Select a few interesting books about the sea to be part of your display.

▶ Find out all you can about tides. Why do we have tides? How are they caused? What do we mean by high tide, neap-tide, Spring tide?

▶ The jellyfish has a very interesting life story. Find out all about it. Make drawings with notes of the different stages of its life.

▶ Arrange a visit to the seaside where there is a lifeboat house. Try to find out when the lifeboat went out last and how many lives it has saved.

▶ Visit a fish market and ask the fishmonger to tell you all about the different fish on sale.

Endangered Earth

As we walk around our towns and cities we often see scraps of paper, potato crisps packets, lolly sticks, empty cans, broken bottles lying around. Sometimes we may even see old mattresses, bicycles or even old cars which have been dumped there. All this is evidence that there are many careless people in our world, but some people are becoming very concerned about the ways in which human beings are spoiling the earth. Through carelessness we have already lost many species of plants, trees and animals. Once a species dies out we can never get it back again.

Talking points

▶ Discuss the immediate environment of the school and its tidiness or otherwise; the types of litter which accumulate and from where these originate.

▶ Talk about life at the time of the Great Plague, the rotting and decaying rubbish attracting rats, the spread of disease.

▶ Talk about people who go out for picnics in the countryside or to the beaches and leave litter such as plastic bags, broken bottles, tin cans which can prove fatal to animals.

▶ Discuss the saying "As dead as a dodo".

▶ Talk about and show pictures of pre-historic animals. Discuss the reasons why scientists think some of these became extinct.

▶ Discuss how people have hunted animals for clothing and food and how greed has led people to want too much. Talk about how people have over-hunted and overfished.

▶ Discuss food-chains and independence-chains and how we upset one small part we cause a dangerous imbalance. For example: overfishing of krill (a shrimp-like creature which forms the basis of the food chain in Antarctica).

▶ Talk about wildlife in danger such as the golden eagle, toads and frogs, giant pandas, white rhinos in Africa, the tiger, many species of trees in developing countries, plants, whales and seals.

▶ Talk about the spread of populations throughout the world and how the building of homes and roads has encroached on the natural environment of some animals, for example, elephants. Discuss the setting up of Wildlife parks where animals are protected.

▶ Talk about organizations such as Greenpeace, Friends of the Earth, World Wide Fund for Nature.

The song of the whale

Heaving mountain in the sea,
Whale, I hear you
Grieving.
Great whale, crying for your life,
Crying for your kind, I knew
How we would use
Your dying.
Lipstick for our painted faces,
Polish for our shoes.
Tumbling mountain in the sea,
Whale, I heard you
Calling.
Bird-high notes, keening, soaring:
At their edge a tiny drum
Like a heartbeat.
We would make you
Dumb.
In the forest of the sea,
Whale, I heard you
Singing,
Singing to your kind.
We'll never let you be.
Instead of life we choose
Lipstick for our painted faces,
Polish for our shoes.

Kit Wright

A strange harvest in Manila

In some countries of the world, cities are expanding rapidly, but around the new buildings, shanty towns grow up almost overnight because people move from the countryside to the cities looking for work. In these places homes are no more than shelters built from all kinds of materials which are available.

In the Philippine Islands, a shanty town has grown up around the capital city of

Manila, and in one very poor area there is a place which is known as Smoky Mountain. This is not a mountain in the true sense of the word, it is a huge rubbish tip, where all kinds of refuse is dumped. Paper of all kinds, tins, bottles, broken glass, plastic, corrugated asbestos, bones and decaying food are all piled up there.

Smoky Mountain is a dreadful smelling place, where flies thrive and the dangers of broken glass and sharp metal are always present alongside the high risk of disease. But every day poor people make their way to Smoky Mountain. Men, women and children, sometimes whole families. Why does anyone go there?

The families go to scavenge amongst the rubbish. Some collect paper, others glass and others aluminium. This scavenging is harvesting for these people, but it is not done in the fields and orchards but on this foul tip known as Smoky Mountain.

The commodities they harvest are then sold for very little money to people who resell, at a much higher price, to firms who recycle rubbish.

Grey seal

Things to do

▶ Arrange to go on a local nature trail. Make a note of all the plants, birds and animals which you see. Be sure to look up, look down and look around you. Take a tape recorder with you and record the sounds you hear.

▶ Organize a 'Litter Campaign' in your school. Each class could be responsible for a particular part of the school grounds. Have a competition for the best 'Anti-Litter' poster.

▶ Make a frieze of animals that have become extinct. Add a caption such as "Who decided that I would never see any of these animals?"

▶ Find out more about some of the creatures which are in danger. Write to World Wide Fund for Nature.

▶ Read the story of Johnny Appleseed and then try to dramatize this.

▶ Plant seeds from different kinds of fruit in plant pots in your classroom. Try red apple, green apple, melon, acorn, conker. Keep a record each time you water the seeds and measure their different rates of growth. What are the best conditions for growth?

▶ What do all plants need to stay alive?

▶ Find a cross-section of a branch or tree trunk. Count the rings.

▶ It is a traditional American folk tale and can be found in Together Today by Robert Fisher, Bell & Hyman, 1983.

Pollution and Conservation

All religions have their own stories about how the world was created. Some also have stories of how a beautiful world was spoilt when people began to live here on earth. We often hear people talking about pollution and conservation. By pollution we mean 'spoiling things'. People pollute the earth's surface, pollute the air and the water and upset the natural balance of nature and living things suffer. Sometimes we over-use resources and cause damage which cannot be repaired. Recently studies in prevention and protection of our earth have helped to repair some damage, this work of repair and protection is known as conservation. Sadly some damage cannot be repaired, in these cases people have spoilt the beautiful world for ever.

Talking points

▶ Discuss the importance of fresh drinking water, the release of harmful and waste substance into rivers and streams and the pollution caused by this.

▶ Discuss the use of insecticides and fertilizers and how these can be washed from the fields into streams killing or affecting small water plants and algae and later fish.

▶ Discuss human and industrial waste; oil slicks, and the dangers to sea birds, polluted beaches, radio-active waste and human waste products such as untreated sewage.

▶ Discuss discarded household rubbish. For example: plastic bags, old furniture, sweet papers and crisp packets.

▶ Talk about breathing in clean air, the burning of fuels for warmth but these give off gases which pollute. The need for laws to keep air clean, for example, smokeless zones.

▶ Talk about traffic and exhaust fumes, firms adding lead to petrol and this being harmful. Spraying crops from a helicopter puts unwanted insecticides in the air.

▶ Discuss the ozone layer and the protection it offers. Talk about how it might be damaged and the resultant danger to plants, animals and people.

▶ Talk about how fumes in the air cause acid rain with the resultant dangers to trees and crops. Discuss the value of trees and plants to humanity.

▶ Discuss the explosion at Chernobyl nuclear power plant in 1986 and why this was a danger to Britain. Talk about the different kinds of power stations, coal, oil-fired, nuclear, hydroelectric plants. Discuss nuclear and alternative energy.

Leave them a flower

I speak on behalf of the next generation,
My sons and my daughters, their children to
*   come.*
What will you leave them for their recreation?
An oil slick, a pylon, an industrial slum?

Leave them a flower, some grass and a
*   hedgerow,*
A hill and a valley, a view to the sea.
These things are not yours to destroy as you
*   want to,*
A gift given once for eternity.

You plunder, you pillage, you tear and you
*   tunnel,*
Trees lying toppled, roots finger the sky.
Building a land for machines and computers.
In the name of progress the farms have to die.

Leave them a flower etc . . .

Fish in an ocean polluted and poisoned,
The sand on the beaches is stinking and black.
You with your tankers, your banks and
*   investments*
Say "never worry, the birds will come back."

Leave them a flower etc . . .

When the last flower has dropped its last
*   petal,*
When the last concrete is finally laid,
The moon will shine cold on a nightmarish
*   landscape,*
Your gift to our children, the world which
*   you've made.*

Leave them a flower etc . . .

Wally Whyton

The Bossy Young Tree

"Fallen leaves," said the tree,
"Are merely debris.
Do ask the wind
To blow them away."
"Before a year can pass
They will rot into me,
So don't be an ass,"
Said the grass.
"Bah!" said the tree,
"They are still debris,
So do ask the wind
To blow them away."
"Don't be so vicious,
They are quite nutritious,
As you will soon see
When they rot into me."
"They're keeping you warm,"
   said the tree,
"And you want them to stay
Because they're covering you
Like a double duvet."
"They're keeping me damp,"

said the grass,
"And I'm bound to get cramp
But I think they should stay
And rot the natural way."
"I insist," said the tree,
"I do not want debris
Littering the ground
In front of me."
"It's ecologically sound
To have leaves on the ground.
With them you'll thrive,
But without won't survive.
"Are you sure?" said the tree
"Yes," said the grass.
"Then let it pass," said the tree,
"I was being an ass."
"Did you call?" said the wind.
"Oh no," said the tree,
"I was merely admiring
this lovely debris."

Brian Patten

Things to do

▶ Arrange visits to your local water authority, sewage works or power station.

▶ Think about and then draw a number of food chains to show how people can be affected by pollution. For example: soil, worm, hen, human, or algae, small fish, large fish, human.

▶ Ask your butcher to obtain for you a pair of cow's or sheep's lungs with the 'windpipe' still attached. Examine these very carefully. Compare these with a picture of your own lungs. Do we always breathe clean air?

▶ Forests provide people with different kinds of timber. Find out what you can about different trees and their various uses. What important part do trees play in protecting our environment? Do we consider Autumn leaves to be 'litter'? Do these leaves serve any purpose?

▶ Find out the names of some of the prehistoric animals, also find out why these became extinct. Draw pictures of prehistoric animals and make a classroom frieze.

▶ Find out about lead-free petrol and the kinds of cars that can use it.

▶ Make a survey of ozone-friendly aerosols.

Conservation at Work

In some ways human beings seem determined to spoil the earth, but there are people who work very hard to try to save it. It seems likely that conservation will play a very important part in the lives of the children who are today in school and they need to be aware of the ways in which they can help.

Talking points

▶ Discuss the work of organizations like Friends of the Earth, the Wild Life Fund, and Greenpeace.

▶ Discuss the kind of laws that protect the environment. For example: the limits on the poisons that power stations and industry are allowed to release into the atmosphere and rivers; the banning of DDT as an insecticide.

▶ Discuss the ways in which ordinary people can help to protect the environment. The various societies that protect wildlife. The lobbyists who ensure that crossing points for animals are built into motorways and pipelines.

▶ Discuss the search for ways of efficiently using renewable energy sources rather than burning fossil fuels. Talk about the efforts to build a viable electric car.

St Vincent's parrots

Out in the Caribbean sea are many islands. Not so very long ago it was easy to catch sight of the bright plumage of parrots as they flew from tree to tree in the wooded mountain areas. The islands of Puerto Rico and St Vincent in particular had large varied parrot populations.

These colourful birds are now seldom seen for in St Vincent the magnificent parrot has come close to extinction. This is very sad and has come about because people have hunted this brightly coloured bird. There have always been ready buyers amongst pet collectors for this intelligent creature. People have also cleared away forested areas and have destroyed the birds' natural habitat.

A marine biologist called Bill Miller went to St Vincent in 1969, and became increasingly worried about the disappearing parrots. He realized that if something was not done to protect the species the parrot would be no more than a memory before very long. He went out into the dense forests that cover St Vincent's mountains and collected a number of young birds. He began a breeding programme and all was progressing well until Bill fell very ill.

A year later, Bill was sufficiently recovered to get back to his task. He was now living in Barbados, and the people of St Vincent allowed Bill to take ten of his fourteen young birds to Barbados so that he could restart the project. In Barbados the project began with a male bird whom Bill called Vincent and a female called Monty. Vincent and Monty began producing young birds who grew up to maturity. One of the offspring of Vincent and Monty was very tame indeed and was always known as Baby Chick. The project was successful and Bill gradually expanded his wildlife conservation activities to include other birds and mammals and reptiles of special significance to the Caribbean.

In 1984 Bill Miller opened his Wild Life Preserve to the public. A Nature Education Centre was built so that visitors could learn more about the conservation project and the creatures there because Bill said, "People who learn to love and respect animals make better citizens."

Bill has worked hard, his persistence has paid off and the colourful St Vincent parrot is no longer in danger of disappearing altogether.

The Turtle Puzzle

The turtle is a creature which is in danger of becoming extinct. Do you know the secret that the turtle carries on his back?

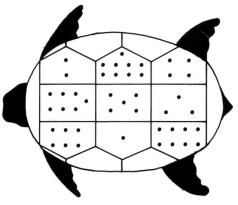

Add his spots in different directions. Find out more about magic squares.

Greenpeace stakes a claim to Antarctic

Richard House, on board M.V. *Greenpeace* in the South Atlantic, reports on a mission to save the world's last great wilderness.

"Greenpeace believes commercial pressures and the prospect of mineral riches are eroding the lofty principles of the 1969 Antarctic Treaty, under which the continent, which occupies 10 per cent of the earth's surface, would be preserved for pure science until at least 1991 . . . A Belgian Biologist points out that, whenever there has been a conflict betwen the environment and human beings, the environment has lost out . . . Antarctica is so fragile, a human footprint in a mossbed will remain visible for more than a decade. Seal colonies are only now recovering from the ravages of the 1820s, when sealers would even burn live penguins as fuel to extract blubber from slaughtered elephant seals . . . Greenpeace wants to extend the Treaty to exclude all commercial activity, and to ban the hunting quotas which in 1986 allowed the Soviet Union to kill 4,800 seals. The quotas still permit big catches of krill, the shrimp-like creature that forms the basis of the Antarctic food-chain."   *The Independent, 5 April 1988*

Conservation work

Marwell Zoo in Hampshire concentrates its effort into preserving endangered species.

Things to do

▶ Write to the World Wide Fund for Nature, Friends of the Earth and Greenpeace asking for information on the work they do.

▶ Borrow an incubator and hatch eggs in the classroom. These need great care but you will be well rewarded when your chicks hatch.

▶ Collect seeds from different trees. For example: oak, chestnut, beech sycamore and try to grow the seeds in your classroom.

▶ Collect newspaper cuttings on the effects of international pollution. For example: British pollution affecting Scandinavia, Italian toxic waste dumped in Britain, out-of-control Russian satellites scattering bits as they fall back to earth.

▶ Pretend you are a television reporter. Make a report on the state of your own environment. Mention any litter, signs of vandalism and graffiti that you have noticed. Make suggestions as to what will happen if this state of affairs continues.

Science and Technology

Science is the knowledge gained by the careful study and observation of the natural and physical world. Technology is a process of invention that combines this knowledge with art and design to produce things that people find useful and that make their lives more comfortable. This process of invention is fundamental to modern society and it brings with it a change which can be beneficial for some people but impossible for others to cope with. We need teamwork, cooperation and understanding to ensure that our world will be a pleasant and comfortable place for *all* members of future generations.

Talking points

▶ Talk about the things we use in our homes and which add to our comfort but which often we take for granted. For example: upholstered furniture, gas fires, electric light, washing machines, fridges, vacuum cleaners.

▶ Talk about the invention of smaller articles such as the zip fastener and the safety pin.

▶ Discuss what life was like before the invention of things that use electricity. For example: no radios, television, telephone, washing machines in homes, milking machinery and bottling machinery on the farms, computers and electronic tills in shops and offices.

The microscope

Anton Leeuwenhoek was Dutch.
He sold pincushions, cloth, and such.
The waiting townsfolk fumed and fussed
As Anton's dry goods gathered dust.

He worked, instead of tending store,
At grinding special lenses for
A microscope. Some of the things
He looked at were:
          mosquitos' wings,
the hairs of sheep, the legs of lice,
the skin of people, dogs, and mice;
ox eyes, spiders' spinning gear,
fishes, scales, little smear
of his own blood,

          and best of all,
the unknown, busy, very small
bugs that swim and bump and hop
inside a simple water drop

Impossible! Most Dutchmen said.
This Anton's crazy in the head.
We ought to ship him off to Spain.
He says he's seen a housefly's brain.

He says the water that we drink
Is full of bugs. He's mad, we think.

They called him dumkopf, which means dope.
That's how we got the microscope.

Maxine Kumin

Marie Curie

Marya Sklodowska was born in Poland in 1867. As a little girl she was always asking questions about everyday things. She was always curious to know why things behaved in a certain way. As she grew older she asked questions such as: "Why is iron magnetic and copper not?"; "What happens when solids melt?"; or "Why do some liquids flow more easily than others?" And she was always reading.

Marya left Poland when she was 24 years old to study in France at the Sorbonne in Paris. She worked very hard and qualified as a physicist. She also changed her name to Marie. In 1894 she met Pierre Curie who was a brilliant physicist nine years older than Marie. They were married in 1895.

Marie decided to work on the 'uranium rays' that had recently been discovered by another French scientist Henri Becquerel. Pierre found her a small room in the basement of the School of Physics and Chemistry where he worked and Marie began her research. She soon realized that there must be a powerful unknown material mixed with the uranium that was causing most of the radiation. Pierre helped Marie to try to make a pure sample of this material from the uranium ore pitchblende.

The Curies worked together for long hours in a bleak shed in the Rue Lhomond. Their lives were hard and they had barely enough money to live on. Finally nearly four years later they produced a pure sample of radium – a beautiful new element that glowed with a blue light in the dark. This light was caused by radioactivity. In 1903 Marie and Pierre shared the Nobel Prize for Physics with Henri Becquerel for their work on radioactivity. The money from the prize made life easier and more comfortable. Then in 1906 disaster struck. Pierre Curie was hit by a heavy horse-drawn cart in a Paris street and killed instantly.

Life without Pierre seemed impossible to Marie but she had her two daughters and her father-in-law to provide for and she was persuaded to take over Pierre's professorship at the Sorbonne – the first woman to ever hold a professorship there. She became the centre of much unwelcome publicity; all Marie wanted was to be left in peace to carry on her scientific work. In 1911 she was awarded the Nobel prize again. This time for chemistry and her part in the discovery of radium.

A few years later the Sorbonne and the

Institut Pasteur combined to build Marie her very own institute – the Radium Institute in the Rue Pierre Curie. Here Marie continued to work from the end of the First World War in 1918 until she died in 1934. She died of leukaemia brought on by her long exposure to radiation.

Marie and Pierre's main interest in life was scientific investigation. They never profited from their work and gave away freely the information on how to isolate radium to all who asked for it. Today radiotherapy is used to treat patients suffering from a variety of diseases and many owe their lives to the treatment. Radioactivity, however, also has its harmful side and many people besides Marie Curie have died from the effects.

Making wheels

1. Strip a strip of corrugated paper. Apply gum to the corrugated side.

2. Using a nail wind the corrugated strip round. Remove the nail.

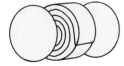

3. Cut two circles of card just smaller than your wheel. Stick one circle to each side to prevent unwinding.

4. Cut a strip of paper as wide as the wheel and long enough to go right round. Glue round the wheel.

5. Make several wheels of different sizes. Nail the wheels to wood or polystyrene.

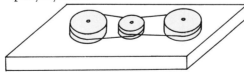

6. Join wheels with rubber bands. Can you move all the wheels by just moving one?

Things to do

► Find out about some ancient inventions. For example: kilns used for making building bricks; spindles used in the ancient cities of Harappa and Mohenjo-Daro in Pakistan; cuneiform writing developed in Sumaria; and the inventions of the Mayas of Southern Mexico who had an accurate calendar in 250 CE.

► Visit your local museum and look out for inventions by people who lived in your own locality.

► Make a classroom wall frieze showing a time scale and the names of different inventors and inventions.

► Ask your local hospital if it is possible for them to allow you to see some old X-ray photographs. Examine these carefully. Make drawings of skeletons in black and white.

► Make a list of all the words you can think of connected with light. For example: shadows, reflections, traffic lights, firelight, candles, gas-light, sunlight, moonlight, electricity, neon signs, lighthouse.

► Construct a lighthouse from junk materials, using batteries and bulbs to make your model work.

► Organize the class into groups for a 'Great Egg Race'. Give the groups the problem of transporting an egg 3 metres using only a box, cotton bobbins, elastic bands, string and drinking straws etc.

War and Peace

When we pick up a newspaper or turn on the television we often hear about fighting and war which causes trouble in the world. War usually begins for the same reasons that children's quarrels begin. That is greed, envy, unfair play, or unkind acts. War results in fear, injury, death, hatred and homelessness, and brings untold sorrow to many people

Talking points

▶ Use newspaper cuttings to discuss current troubles in the world. Talk with the children about any wars that they have heard about in the past.

▶ Talk about Remembrance Sunday – why we commemorate this day every year – the Flanders Poppy.

▶ United Nations Day is held on 24 October each year. Discuss the role of the United Nations as a peace-keeping body.

▶ Talk about the symbols which are associated with peace, for example, the olive branch and the dove. Why were these particular symbols selected?

▶ Discuss the words which the angels used to the shepherds on the hillside at Bethlehem, "Peace on earth – Goodwill to men".

▶ Talk about different kinds of greetings. For example, the Jewish greeting "Shalom" – Peace be with you.

▶ Discuss the work of the National Blood Transfusion Service and the need for blood donors. Show how people help others in this way.

The Nobel Peace Prize

Alfred Nobel was born in Stockholm in Sweden on 21 October 1833. Alfred's father was an engineer and Alfred himself became a very ingenious inventor. He was particularly interested in explosives and in 1866 invented dynamite. This was an instant success for blasting rock to make roads and for mining. Alfred took out patents in Britain and the United States which meant nobody else could use his process to make dynamite. He invented an even better explosive called gelignite in 1875.

The inventions made Alfred very rich. He was a peaceful man and he hoped that when people saw the power of his explosives they would never want to fight a war again, but quite the opposite was true. People wanted his explosives to make weapons and Nobel went on to develop military explosives with great success. His money was wisely invested and he amassed a great fortune.

Alfred decided that when he died he would like his fortune to help to make the world a better place. He arranged that most of his money would be used to give a prize each year to people who had helped others in the world. He decided to give prizes for Literature, Medicine, Physics and Chemistry and there was also to be a special prize for the person or organization that had done the most for Peace in the world.

Every year, on the 10 December, the anniversary of Alfred Nobel's death, these prizes are awarded by the Nobel Foundation. Amongst the winners of the Peace Prize are: Henri Dunant who founded the Red Cross; Martin Luther King who worked for equal rights for all people in the United States; Mother Teresa whose work started with the poor of Calcutta in India, but has now extended to many other countries; and Archbishop Desmond Tutu who works for human rights in South Africa.

The Red Cross won the Peace Prize in 1917, 1944 and 1963. Amnesty International, a world wide organization which works to defend human rights won the prize in 1977, the United Nations High Commissioner for Refugees won the prize in 1954 and 1981, and the United Nations peace-keeping forces in 1988.

If a Peace Prize were given in your school, would you have a chance of winning it?

A prayer for peace

O God, remove from our world all hatred, bitterness and prejudice. Show us where we are wrong, and inspire in each one of us a love of beauty, tolerance and justice. Give us peace among nations, peace in our homes and peace in our hearts.

Anonymous

Make a Peace Mobile

1. Take a **hoop** and fix **wires** diagonally across it.

2. Cut a strip of **green crepe paper** and about 20 green leaves with long stems.

3. Bind the hoop and work in the leaves.

4. Cut out several circles 15 cm in diameter from **card** to represent the world. Draw laurel leaves on them.

5. Cut out several dove shapes and wings from card

6. Slit the dove as shown. Fold the wings to pass through the slit.

7. Suspend the shapes at different heights to balance the mobile.

Hiawatha

An extract

"Oh my children! my poor children!
Listen to the words of wisdom,
Listen to the words of warning,
From the lips of the Great Spirit,
From the Master of Life who made you!
I have given you lands to hunt in,
I have given you streams to fish in,
I have given you bear and bison,
I have given you roe and reindeer,
I have given you brant and beaver,
Filled the marshes full of wild-fowl,
Filled the rivers full of fishes;
Why then are you not contented?
Why then will you hunt each other?
I am weary of your quarrels,
Weary of your wars and bloodshed,
Weary of your prayers for vengeance,
Of your wranglings and dissensions;
All your strength is in your union,
All your danger is in discord;
Herefore be at peace henceforward,
And as Brothers live together."

Henry Wadsworth Longfellow

Things to do

▶ Use newspaper cuttings to make a scrap-book about *Trouble in our World*.

▶ Organize a Peace Prize in school – an award to be given after three or four weeks. Children and teachers voting separately. Will the same children be chosen?

▶ Make a Peace Mobile for your classroom.

Our World

The aim of this topic is to draw together the many strands of thought which have been introduced earlier in the book.

We can think about our world in different ways. We can see it as a wonderful world or a beautiful world, but our world cannot be a wonderful or beautiful world whilst there is poverty, pollution, crime, war and injustice. When we see these things we seen an ugly and sad world.

All the people of the world are members of one large family. Just as members of a family are interdependent so are the people of the world. When we look at the world like this we see an interdependent world.

Animals and plants also share our world, all living things are interdependent and we therefore must care for them also. Is our world a caring world? Let us try to look at the world in different ways.

Talking points

▶ *A Wonderful World*
Talk about the world as one planet in the large universe. Discuss the wonder of the universe, the planets in our solar system keeping to their own orbits as they travel endlessly around the sun.

Talk about the wonders of creation. How do birds know when to migrate? How do they know how and when to build nests? Why do salmon return to certain streams to spawn? How do they find their way? Talk about the return of the seasons, the regularity of the tides. The wonderful way in which bees communicate.

▶ *A Beautiful World*
Discuss the things that we think of as beautiful. For example: a raindrop on a flower petal; the irridescence on a bird's wing; the glitter of a diamond; the new green leaves in springtime; the symmetrical markings on the coats of animals; the colour of a sunset; the clear water of a stream flowing over stones; the spray from the sea dashing on to rocks; beauty in music, ballet, art, architecture. The list is endless.

▶ *An Interdependent World*
Discuss the animal and plant life that shares our world. Talk about algae, mosses, ferns, flowers, trees, fish, amphibians, reptiles, birds, animals, people.

Discuss food chains and their importance to the survival of certain species. What would happen if the grass did not grow? Talk about recent awareness of the importance of interdependence, and conservation projects.

Discuss how people have used animals for food, transport, clothing, provision of materials for shelter and to help with everyday work. For example: drawing water from wells.

Talk about the different races of people who live in our world, the places where they live. Talk about multi-cultural and a multi-religious world. Discuss changes which have taken place in Britain in recent years.

Discuss the interdependence of people throughout the world. The growing of crops like tea, coffee, rubber, jute, bananas, oranges, cotton. The need for raw materials and oil for industries. Manufacture, marketing and transportation of goods around the world.

▶ *A Divided World*
Talk about a Rich World and a Poor World. Can we divide the world into rich and poor? (In rich countries there are poor people and vice versa.) What do we mean by the Third World? Where is the Third World? Talk about the parts of the world where people suffer from a low standard of living, high rate of population growth and general economic and technological dependence on the rich world, such as the poorer countries of Asia, Africa, Latin America, China and parts of the Middle East. Rich countries include the countries of North America and Europe, the USSR, Japan, Australia and New Zealand. These countries are sometimes known as industrialized or developed countries. Is it fair that the world should be divided into rich and poor.

Discuss the fact that although the rich countries contain 25 per cent of the world's population they consume about 66 per cent of the world's food. The livestock in the rich countries consume 30 per cent of the world's grain and 10 kilos of grain produce only one kilo of steak.

▶ *An Ugly World*
Discuss pollution of rivers, streams, air. Noise levels, litter in our towns and cities, graffiti in our neighbourhoods etc.

Talk about other things which prevent our world from being beautiful. For example: crime, injustice, hatred, inequality, hunger, discrimination, envy, jealousy, pride, greed, war.

▶ *One World*
How can we help to make a fairer world? Should we expect all people to be like us? Do we need to change? Do people want the world to change? Is the idea of a just and peaceful world where there is no hunger or strife only a dream?

Should we send aid to other countries, and how should this be used? Discuss Bob Geldof, his talents in encouraging others to help others, Live Aid and Sports Aid etc.

Should we pay higher prices so that people in poor countries can have more money for the raw materials they provide? How could we be sure that the grower would get the money? Should people try to travel to other countries to find out more about how others live? Should they spend their money there?

Could world change start with individuals changing their ideas about how they should live?

Children have rights

The *Declaration of the Rights of the Child* was unanimously adopted by the General Assembly of the United Nations on 20 November 1959. Ten principles establish the rights that all children are entitled to:

1. Equality, regardless of race, religion, nationality or sex.
2. Special protection for full physical, intellectual, moral, spiritual and social development.
3. A name and nationality.
4. Adequate nutrition, housing and medical services.
5. Special care, if handicapped.
6. Love, understanding and protection.
7. Free education, play and recreation.
8. Be among the first to receive relief in times of disaster.
9. Protection against all forms of neglect, cruelty and exploitation.
10. Protection from any form of discrimination, and the right to be brought up in a spirit of universal brotherhood, peace and tolerance.

Things to do

▶ Make scrap-books of children living in other countries so that the children come to terms with reality (avoid national costumes which are now rarely worn as a matter of course).

▶ Make a collection of dolls, commodities, artefacts and stamps from around the world.

▶ Group work:

Homes around the World;
Food around the World;
Working around the World;
Transport around the World.

Bring these together to make a large display.

▶ Hold an International Party. Prepare food using recipes from different lands.

▶ UNICEF and Oxfam produce pamphlets of children's games from around the world. Write off for these and play the games.

▶ World Children's Day is held on the 15 June each year. Find out all you can about Children's Festivals throughout the world.

▶ Write a poem about the world. It could be about a *Beautiful World*, *Ugly World*, *Divided World*.

▶ Make a list of all the things which we could do now to make the world a better place to live in for everyone in the future.

Further Resources

This page contains a list, by topic, of additional ideas to follow up. These include songs, poems, hymns, stories and useful addresses.

page 80
Can you be sure that the rain will fall?, *Come and Praise*, BBC Publications, 1978.
Join with us to sing God's praises, *Come and Praise*, BBC Publications, 1978.
Water of life, *Come and Praise*, BBC Publications, 1978.
Let's talk about, Why are people hungry?, Ruth Versfeld, Franklin Watts, 1987.
Rich world, poor world, Debates series, Olivia Bennett, Macdonald, 1985.

page 82
One more step along the world I go, *Come and Praise*, BBC Publications, 1978.
Oh! The world is big, *Tinder-box*, A & C Black, 1983.

page 86
The ballad of the sad astronaut, Judith Nicholls, *Spaceways*, OUP, 1986.

page 88
Fingal's Cave (music for listening).
Molly Mallone, traditional folksong.

page 92
Pollution and Wild Life, Survival series, Franklin Watts, 1987.
Pollution and the Environment, Debates series, Macdonald, 1985.
Pollution and Conservation, Topics series, Wayland, 1985.

World Wide Fund for Nature
11–13 Ockford Road
Godalming
Surrey GU7 1QU

Greenpeace
36 Graham Street
London N1 8LL

Friends of the Earth
377 City Road
London EC1 1NA

Royal Society for Nature Conservation
The Green
Nettleham
Lincoln LN2 2NR

page 100
I went to the cabbages one day, *Tinder-box*, A & C Black, 1983.
People and Customs, Macmillan, 1979.
Children Around the World, Macmillan, 1982.
Different Peoples, Macdonald, 1982.
The United Nations, Victoria Schofield, Wayland, 1979.
The Third World, Christopher Barlow, Batsford, 1979.

The Centre for World Development
    Education
Regent's College
Inner Circle
Regents Park, London NW1 4NS

RELIGIONS OF THE WORLD

Buddhism

Background

History Buddhism began in India about 500 years BCE with a teacher who came to be called the Buddha. It lost momentum in India but spread to China, Sri Lanka, Burma, Japan, Korea, Vietnam, Laos, Thailand, Kampuchea and Nepal.

Buddhism has spread to the West in recent years. Partly due to migration and partly due to the adoption of certain aspects of Buddhist philosophy, there are large groups of Buddhists in many countries. Buddhism emphasizes meditation as a means of reaching enlightenment. There are 60,000 Buddhists in Britain and 200,000 in the USA. Estimates of the total number of Buddhists in the world today vary from 200 million upwards.

In India community life developed into an order of monks adopting saffron robes and shaven heads.

Basic beliefs Buddhists believe that being open minded brings peacefulness and meditation brings enlightenment. Through these, people can feel at one with all living beings.

Some Buddhists do not believe in a creator god and do not worship gods. They seek enlightenment through following the eightfold path and with the help of monks. All Buddhists hold a belief in a life of harmony with nature. Each individual must make his/her own sensible choices.

Buddhism is based on 4 Noble Truths:
1. Suffering is part of life.
2. Suffering is caused by selfishness.
3. Suffering will end if selfishness is destroyed. Many Buddhists reject worldly things.
4. The way to destroy selfishness is by the eightfold path which leads to a state of bliss called Nirvana.

THE EIGHTFOLD PATH

> *Understanding*
> *Thinking clearly*
> *True speech*
> *True action*
> *Work*
> *Effort*
> *Mindfulness*
> *Contemplation*

Enlightened Buddhists can escape the cycle of rebirth and death that all people go through over and over again. Instead Nirvana can be attained. This means they can be free from desire, hatred and ignorance. It is these things that cause all pain and sorrow. Buddhism teaches that there is no soul so monks do not acknowledge birth or death in a religious way, though most lay people do have customs for these rites of passage which are usually connected to the traditions of their countries.

Prayers Buddhists do not pray to God –

The Buddha

but meditate on the Buddha 'within themselves'. They visit the temples and make offerings to the Buddha to show they are grateful for his teachings. They do not pray but honour the Buddha. Many use these five vows in front of the Buddha's image every day.

1. Not to harm any living thing.
2. Not to take what is not given.
3. Not to mis-use your senses.
4. Not to speak wrongly.
5. Not to use drugs or drink alcohol.

On Poya days Buddhists try to visit a temple in order to meditate. Poya days are the days of the full moon, the new moon and the quarter days.

Mantras Certain sounds or words are repeated to produce good 'vibrations' within a person. These are used to help people concentrate during meditation.

Prayer wheels These bronze cylinders are sometimes used, they are inscribed with 'Om mani padme hum' – 'the truth in the heart of the teaching'.

Clothes The Buddhist monk wears saffron or yellow robes and has a shaven head. His only possessions are his robes, razor, bowl, needle, and water-strainer. Buddhists who are not monks generally wear the ordinary clothes of their country or the traditional clothes of the country of origin. On full moon days, many Buddhists wear simple white clothes when they visit the temple.

Books The teachings of the Buddha are written down in the Tripitaka – 'three baskets'. These three books are divided into thirty one sections and deal with the various aspects of the Buddha's teaching. The books are written in verse and each contains hundreds of stories about the Buddha's life, each with a moral. Monks use these stories in their sermons.

Food Diet, like all aspects of life, is a matter of personal choice and there are no forbidden foods. Most families eat the foods from their country or country of origin. Some Buddhists are strict vegetarians eating no meat, fish or eggs.

Symbols The eight-spoked wheel symbolizes the eightfold path.

Festivals

There are many Buddhist festivals. The following selection is of interest to primary age children but the list is by no means comprehensive. The intention was also to select festivals from different geographical locations. At all Buddhist festivals it is the custom to give alms to the monks. The giver earns merit and is helped to a better re-birth.

Wesak (May – night of the full moon) This is the most important festival in the Buddhist calendar. This three day festival celebrates the birth, enlightenment and death of Buddha. All the great events in Buddha's life occured on the same day in different years. Huge numbers of Buddhist groups around the world have their own customs at this time but always a large puja (service) is held. This festival is not a feast day so there are no special foods. Sometimes birds, fish or turtles that have been captured are released to show love and compassion. Vietnamese Buddhists in particular do this. Flowers and lanterns are used to decorate homes and temples and are placed in front of Buddhist statues. In the evening there are processions with candles, flowers and incense sticks, then

Meditation

people settle down for an all-night session of the Buddha's teaching. In Thailand houses are cleaned and decorated with garlands of flowers. The temples are dusted with clean sand from the river banks and all the statues and books are cleaned. The largest of the statues is brought outside where a procession moves around it carrying lights and sprinkling scented water on to it. People sprinkle water on one another, on the statues of the Buddha and on monks who visit homes.

Dhammacakka (Usually the full moon day in July) This celebrates the day when the Buddha first preached. This first sermon taught the basic truths of Buddhism – 'Setting in motion the Wheel of Truth'. Through the fellowship of the monks Buddhism has spread and been passed on. This festival is the day before the Buddhist fast Pansa. People visit the monasteries and listen to the monks' teachings then processions set off to go three times around the temples. Gifts of food and special Pansa candles are given to the monks. During Pansa monks stay at the monasteries and do not travel as usual. Instead they study and meditate. The fast lasts for the length of the rainy season, which begins at this time.

Kathin At the end of the rainy season the monks are given new robes at a special ceremony. The community make the robes especially for this festival.

Festival of the Tooth (Perahera – July/August full moon). In Sri Lanka in the city of Kandy, there is a huge temple containing the tooth of the Buddha. It is kept in several caskets, each one inside another. A special procession is held and the casket containing the tooth is carried in a pagoda by a large elephant called Raja, and known as the Malagawi Tusker. There are very many other large elephants in the procession, all beautifully decorated, some are covered with magnificent cloths and others are painted. The drivers (mahouts) are also finely dressed. There are dancers, whipcrackers, torchbearers and musicians followed by still more elephants. The festival lasts for several nights and the procession grows bigger each night with fireworks after dark.

Songkran (*Thailand – April*) Several days during April, everyone gathers on a riverbank carrying fishes in jars to put into the water. As April is very hot in Thailand the ponds dry out and the fish would die. All the people have new clothes and celebrations take place. Water festival also takes place with people splashing and throwing water on each other. There is also a boat race at this time.

Ploughing Festival (*Thailand – May half-moon*) A gold plough is pulled by two white oxen followed by four girls scattering rice seeds. They are dressed in white with gold and silver baskets.

Around mid-July many Buddhist groups have festivals where the spirits of dead ancestors are honoured. Japanese Buddhists call this Obon, they believe spirits visit the family and lanterns are lit to guide them. Vietnamese call this Vu Lan. They hold ceremonies in the temple for the dead spirits. Chinese Buddhists call this Cung Ko Hon (the Feast of the Lonesome Souls). People lay out food and burn pictures of money and gifts for the spirits.

Buddhist temple in Wimbledon, London

The childhood of Buddha

Prince Siddhartha Gautama was born 2,500 years ago at Lumbini. His parents King Suddhodana and Queen Maya were the rulers of a beautiful area that lies at the foot of the Himalayan Mountains.

Always recognized as very gifted and intelligent, the prince was loved and over-protected by his father who did all in his power to give the prince a wonderful life which he thought would prepare him to become king when he himself died.

Fearing the predictions that his son would reject becoming the future ruler, the king showered his son with every kind of new and wonderful toy, beautiful clothing and exquisite food. He thought that this ideal life would stop the prince from wanting to find out about the world outside the palace and so he would not be tempted to leave. He hoped that the wise old teacher Asita, who earlier had seen signs on the young prince that predicted a life spent teaching, would be proved wrong. The king was desperate to stop Siddhartha from leaving home and becoming a teacher, so he was never allowed to see or hear any of the suffering or unpleasantness in the world beyond the palace.

We know that he did find out about life outside and that he left the life of a prince behind to eventually become the Buddha. His life as a child and young man, surrounded by beauty, and his gifts of wisdom and cleverness have their own stories.

These stories can be enjoyed by Primary age children, and lend themselves to drama, creative writing and art activities. The swan is one of the stories.

The swan

Prince Siddhartha lay on the neat lawn with his face up to the sky. A quiet nap in the shade of the tree was just what he needed after such a delicious lunch. In the beauty of the palace garden he could take it easy and decide what he would like to do for the rest of the day. Should he listen to music? Watch some dancing? Anything he wanted to do his father was only too pleased to arrange for him. The hardest thing the prince ever had to do was decide what to do next. "Life is good," he sighed.

As the breeze cooled his skin he watched the leaves of the tree dance against the blue of the sky. He thought that he might stay in that quiet peaceful part of the garden all afternoon. He liked to spend time alone but best of all, he liked to play with the animals and birds that lived in the garden. None of them was afraid of him. They knew this kind and gentle boy wasn't like the others who sometimes chased them and could be very rough.

The prince's sleepy eyes gazed as a flock of swans glided across the clear sky, but the scene turned to horror as an arrow, gleaming in the sunlight, spun upwards hitting its mark surely and swiftly. Helplessly he watched as the leading swan fell like a stone from the sky to land in the prince's garden.

Siddhartha dashed over to where the injured and terrified swan lay on the neat turf. "I'm not going to hurt you," he said, gently scooping up the swan into his arms. "Let's see what we can do with this cruel arrow."

The swan seemed to know by the tone of his voice that no more harm would come to it whilst the prince was there. Though its wing was very painful the swan trusted the prince would know what to do. Gently he took hold of the arrow keeping the swan firmly on his knee with the other hand. A smooth twist and a sharp pull brought the arrow clear of the wing. The swan's pain began to ease although a lot of blood was oozing out of the wound. "I've got something that will make this feel better," the prince said, pulling a small bottle of lotion from his pocket. "This wing will soon be fine," the prince's soft voice sang to the trusting swan, as he smoothed in the lotion with gentle fingers. Siddhartha had won the trust and confidence of the bird and their friendship was growing when a sudden rustling of leaves and whooping of victory broke the silence in the garden. "You'll never guess what," Devadatta called running breathlessly through the nearby trees. "The leader of the flock of swans, I got it! First shot!" Siddhartha saw the gleam of pleasure in his cousin's eye as he got near to him. "Oh! No," thought the prince, "How could he? Now there is going to be trouble." Keeping a firm hold of the swan he stood up and turned round to face his cousin, "This is the swan, I'll bet." A stony faced Siddhartha confronted Devadatta with the blood soaked bird. "Hey! That's mine, I shot that swan, so hand it over."

The prince stood his ground, he had no intention of giving his friend up to someone who was likely to harm it even more.

Tempers grew, Siddhartha kept hold of the swan even when his cousin challenged him to a fight for it. Thinking that there must be another way of sorting out the problem, the prince suggested they went along to the palace court, "It's what grown-ups do when they can't agree over things," he persuaded. Reluctantly, his cousin agreed, "Well, at least others will see my point of view, I shot the swan in the first place, everyone will agree it must be mine," he called to Siddhartha as he marched ahead towards the palace.

In the courtroom some of the judges thought the whole thing was a waste of their valuable time, "Two boys with a silly squabble," they snorted. "We've better things to do than discuss who owns a swan."

"Hold on a minute!" said one wise old judge. "These children will one day be rulers of this country, they should learn about justice. A proper trial is called for here. Let's get ready to hear the two points of view and give them a proper verdict."

Each boy was given a chance to convince the court that the bird should be theirs. "I shot the bird, it should be mine," Devadatta insisted. "I found the bird, it should be mine," Siddhartha argued.

The court spent a long time considering the dispute; some agreed with one boy, some with the other. Then a strange old man stood up in the court and spoke in front of all the judges. They all took notice of what he said as he seemed to have an understanding that all respected. "Life is the most precious thing of all," he said to the agreement of everyone. "So it seems to me that the swan should go to the boy who gave the swan life and not to the boy who tried to take its life away. Siddhartha valued the swan's life so he should have the swan."

Put in that way nobody could disagree with the decision and the prince kept the swan. The king, the judges and his cousin watched as the prince took the swan back to the garden. Later, they saw him caring for the bird until it was well enough to be set free again.

Mr Ratnayake's visit

Mr Ratnayake has come round to our house again tonight. Last time he came it was to advise my Mum and Dad when the best time would be for my sister Karuna and her boyfriend Ashoka to get engaged. Now we want his advice about the best day for the wedding, so he's in the front room with Karuna, Ashoka and both pairs of Mums and Dads.

Our family are Buddhists. Mum and Dad came here from Sri Lanka twenty years ago. We always think that it's a good idea to ask an astrologer about the best time to hold important events.

We're all very excited about the wedding, it seems ages since we first thought about Karuna getting married. She spent a lot of time talking with Mum and Dad about who to choose. My little sister Ruvini and I thought it was great when she finally said that it had all been arranged. Ashoka's parents and our parents agreed that the engagement plans could get underway.

Karuna and Ashoka have been going to the same college and we secretly hoped they would get married. They seemed to laugh a lot when they were together. Ashoka likes us too, he took us all to the zoo just before the engagement and it was great fun, he's like one of the family already.

I've asked Karuna where the wedding will be. She would like it at the Woodcrest Hotel on the edge of town. I hope it is there because it's very posh and has big gardens so that we children can play outside whilst the grown-ups talk. Sitting about at weddings can get a bit boring, so we can play some games outside if the weather is nice. I wonder if Mr Ratnayake

can tell if it will be good weather, I wish I was in the front room with them so that I could hear.

Last year my cousin Sunil got married. They have a big house in the country, so they had the wedding at home. We were all invited over to stay for the week, that's how long the celebrations lasted. I've never seen so much food in all my life. My favourite dish, rice cakes, every day. My other aunt and uncle came from Sri Lanka for that wedding, Mum and Dad enjoyed it so much they didn't want that week to end. I think that's what made them want to start planning Karuna's marriage.

I hope that I can have a new suit for the wedding. I think Ruvini is going to wear the sari that Uncle Nihal and Auntie Padma brought her from Sri Lanka last year. The blouse was too big then so she's been saving it. Mum will probably want to make Karuna's wedding dress but knowing Karuna she'll want to buy one, from one of the big London shops. She's not too keen on Mum's taste, she says it's not modern enough. Dad will have to step in as usual, he can always talk Mum round.

If the wedding is at the Woodcrest we will have to take all the things over there to build the poruwa. Dad and his friends will build the platform that Karuna and Ashoka will stand on when they give each other their wedding rings. Then I expect the thumbs of their right hands will be tied together by Uncle Nihal. I like that part of our tradition. I also like the chanting from our scriptures that goes on whilst the ceremony is taking place. If it goes on too long though that's when we get bored and we might slip out into the garden for a while. As long as we're back in time for the food.

Mum and Dad bought me my own

Buddhist wedding in Thailand

camera for my birthday. I'll have chance to use it at the wedding. It will be good to have pictures of Karuna and Ashoka in their poruwa. It will be so beautifully decorated with white flowers. I can see it all now . . .

Hey! Here they come. My sister's first through the front room door. "Well, when's it going to be?" "Secret," she says. "Don't think I'll tell you."

"Don't be mean, Karuna. I've been sitting here waiting all night. Mr Ratnayake will tell me, Won't you?" I plead as all the family appear.

"OK," says Karuna, "It's going to be on the first Wednesday in June at eleven o'clock."

"Yippee! A day off school, I can hardly believe my luck."

Karuna and Ashoka are taking Ruvini and me out to celebrate, with French fries and Cola. Mr Ratnayake and the Mums and Dads can have some peace and quiet to finish off their plans over a cup of tea. We'll leave them to it.

A Buddhist 'prayer'

All I Can

I will do all the good I can,
In all the ways I can,
In all the places I can,
At all the times I can,
As long as ever I can,
Thank You, Lord Buddha.

Lord Buddha is with me.

Anonymous

The King's dream

At thirty five years of age Buddha achieved Nirvana, the state of peacefulness for which he had searched many years. He decided that he would travel around India teaching others the things he had discovered.

Like teachers of many other faiths Buddha realized that difficult ideas can be taught to people through stories. Many of his teachings about love and caring were spread by imaginative tales such as this one.

"Get me the tallest most magnificent tree in the forest," ordered the proud King. "I'm going to have built for myself the biggest and best palace that the world has ever seen."

When the King gave an order everyone jumped to it immediately, he was not a patient man, he angered easily. The Chief Minister in turn quickly ordered a team of servants to go with him right away out into the forest to find that tree.

The tall majestic tree was quickly spotted by the search party. It stood metres above all the others. "Let's get back to the palace", instructed the Chief Minister. "It's going to be dark soon, we'll tell the King that we have found the tree and we shall come back tomorrow with our axes to chop it down. It will be a full day's work to chop it down and get it back to the palace. The King will understand." The kindly Chief Minister was always apologetic, he lived in perpetual fear of the King's violent temper.

"An early night for everyone," commanded the King, almost cheerfully when he had been told the plans for the following day. "We'll make a start as soon as the sun rises." He went off to his splendid royal bed quite happily and was soon sound asleep.

Instead of his usual dream of even bigger palaces and even more wealth, the King had a strange dream that night. The magnificent tree that the King was intending to have cut down appeared in the dream. From it came a Spirit which pleaded with the King to leave the tree alone. "It is my home, without the tree I will die." But the King ignored the crying and pleading of the Spirit. He wanted that tree for his palace and no other would do. The Spirit could see that the King would not change his mind, he was proud, stubborn and selfish.

"Well if you won't change your mind about cutting down the tree, perhaps I can beg you to cut it down a little at a time, starting at the top," pleaded the Spirit. "But why?" the King asked, now feeling confused. "Won't that be even worse for you? The woodcutters will chop many more times, and that will hurt you even more. Won't it be less painful if they just cut the whole thing down from the bottom?"

The Tree Spirit explained to the King that the tree was not just home to him but to hundreds of birds, small animals and insects as well.

"If you cut my tree down from the bottom it will crash to the ground, destroying all in its pathway. Think of all the creatures which will be killed and all the others that will lose their homes. Please will you cut my home down in the way I ask, so that less damage will be done to the others, please spare them!" the Tree Spirit begged.

The next morning as soon as the sun rose the Chief Minister woke the King, eager to get on with the work they had planned. He was shocked to find the King sitting up in bed with his head in his shaking hands, looking bewildered and confused. "Whatever is the matter?" The Chief Minister was concerned. He had never seen the King looking anything but proud and sure of himself. For the first time ever the usually arrogant King confided in the Chief Minister that he had changed his mind. Then he described his dream and thought in silence for a while.

"I can't do it," he finally announced. "That Spirit was prepared to suffer over and over so that the creatures of the forest would not be hurt, yet I could be so selfish, I would have done that awful thing for my fine new palace. I'd never given a thought to what would happen to all those creatures. I feel terrible, I've realized that I only ever think about myself."

"Most of us are like that," the kindly Chief Minister reassured him. "Your dream has helped you to realize and now's your chance to do something about it."

Slowly the King began to feel better and he wondered how to start making changes in his life. "I've got a wonderful idea. Come along," he grinned. He put his arm around the Chief Minister and they stepped into the main hall. "Today is a holiday," he announced to the working party, who were surprised. They had all turned up with their axes and ropes ready for a hard day's work. "Leave those behind," the King ordered. "We're off to the forest to decorate that tree, it's going to be left standing. It will always remind us to be just and kind. Ready everyone? Let's celebrate."

Soon word of the King's dream spread to all the people of the kingdom. They were only too pleased at the King's change of heart. The magnificent tree would be honoured.

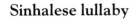

Sinhalese lullaby

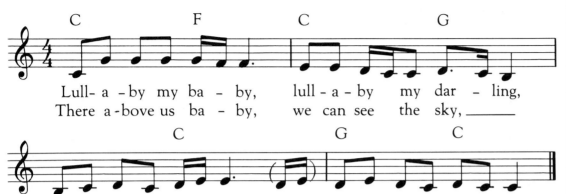

Lull- a - by my ba - by, lull - a - by my dar - ling,
There a -bove us ba - by, we can see the sky, ____

Lull- a - by my ba - by, lull - a - by my dar - ling.
There a - way be- yond us is ___ sun-light in the gar - den.

Lullaby my baby, lullaby my darling,
Lullaby my baby, lullaby my darling,
There above us baby, we can see the
  sky,
There away beyond us is sunlight in
  the garden.

Lullaby my baby, lullaby my darling,
Lullaby my baby, lullaby my darling.
Where my little one has your mother
  gone?
She goes to the pond where blue lilies
  grow.

Lullaby my baby, lullaby my darling,
Lullaby my baby, lullaby my darling.
When at night my son, clouds come
  o'er the moon,
Then it's time my son, to sleep and
  cease to cry.

traditional

Recipe for Kiri-bath

(Sri Lankan rice squares – A New Year dish)

Half a cup of white rice
One and a half cups of water
Half a cup of flaked coconut
Two tablespoons of sugar

Wash the rice and place in a saucepan.
Pour the water into the pan.
Cover with a lid and bring to the boil.
Turn down the heat to very low and
  simmer until the rice is soft. (About ten
  minutes.)
Drain the rice, saving the water.
Measure out about one cup of left over
  water.
Top up with more cold water if necessary.
Put all this water back into the pan with
  the rice, add the coconut and sugar.
Gently cook the mixture stirring all the
  time until the water has gone.
Turn the mixture into a 20 cm square cake
  tin. Smooth down and allow to cool.
Put the tin into the fridge for at least one
  hour to chill.
When firm, cut into squares. Cover with
  honey or jam.

Follow-up activities

Design an eight-spoked wheel pattern.

Display the eightfold pathway on the wheel
with children's creative writing of their
own views of each pathway (I could try
to . . .)

Collage (using fabric, beads, foil, glitter etc)
of the elephant procession at the Kandy
Perahera.

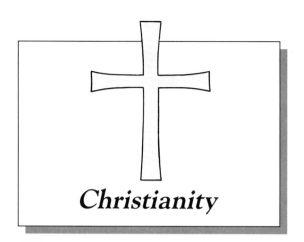

Christianity

Background

History Christianity began with Jesus who was a Jew. The first Christians continued to practise Jewish customs and used the synagogue for worship. Later, certain customs were changed. For example, they changed the Sabbath from between dusk on Friday and dusk on Saturday, to the Sunday. There are many different branches of Christanity, such as Orthodox, Roman Catholic, Protestant. There are Christian communities in almost every country of the world. It has the largest following of all world religions.

The birth of Jesus Christ was an important date for Christians so they mark dates from this. Most countries of the world have adopted this calendar. The letters BC mean Before Christ and AD, from the Latin *Anno Domini*, means after the birth of Christ. Some people have begun to use CE instead which means 'Common Era' whilst BCE means Before Common Era.

Basic beliefs Christians believe in one God; the Creator of all things who is present everywhere.

All believe Jesus is the Son of God and died for the human race, that he rose from the dead and is 'alive' today. The belief that Jesus was both God and human is central to the Christian faith.

Christians hold a belief in the Holy Trinity. This means that they recognize God as a Creator and Father, God in the form of Jesus and his teachings, and God as Spirit. The Holy Spirit is God alive today in the hearts of Christians. Christians believe that through Jesus they will have life after death.

Jesus Christ's teachings are a guide for the lives of Christians, who try to live as he lived. Many Christians also believe that God's authority is revealed in the Bible. It is a source of truth and a guide for all behaviour.

Place of worship Places of worship vary greatly. Christians may worship in cathedrals, chapels, mission halls or in their homes. Some buildings are very beautiful and ornate, others emphasize simplicity.

There are certain special places of worship and pilgrimage, these include Rome, Canterbury and Lourdes.

Prophets/leaders Christians and Jews share a belief in the teachings of the Old Testament prophets. Christians believe that Jesus was divine. During the early ministry he chose twelve disciples who eventually became the first leaders and teachers of his doctrine, many of these later became known as Saints. Saints are people who can be admired for their faith and actions. They are canonized after their death. Martyrs are people who have died for their beliefs, they too, are honoured by Christians.

Ministers, vicars, rectors, and priests are responsible for the spiritual guidance of Christian communities, and lead formal worship. There is an hierarchy of leadership in some churches which includes bishops and archbishops. The Pope is the Head of the Roman Catholic Church. The spiritual leader of the Church of England is the Archbishop of Canterbury.

Prayers Christians make time in their everyday lives to pray alone. They also join with other Christians to pray in churches and chapels. Church services are held on Sundays and other festal days but some churches have daily services, especially Roman Catholic churches. Sunday is the day set aside for worship. Services include Holy Mass, Eucharist or Holy Communion (or Lord's Supper), Matins and Evensong. There is a great deal of variety in choice of worship. Some Christians pray when they get up, before and after meals, before going to bed. The Lord's Prayer is used at most church services. Rosary beads are used by some Christians to assist them in prayer.

Clothes Particular clothes are associated with religious communities. Many monks and nuns wear habits which vary according to their specific orders. Clergy wear cassock and surplice together sometimes with mitres, cloaks and scarfs. Some Christians cover their heads when entering places of worship.

Baptism Baptism usually takes place during infancy but believers can be baptized at any age. It marks the entry into Christian life. Baptism involves the use of water. Water is a symbol of the washing away of sins. In some denominations the person seeking baptism is also given the sign of the cross on the forehead.

Books The Christian Bible contains two parts, the Old Testament, and the New Testament. The New Testament was written later than the Old Testament and contains books written in the years following the death of Jesus. The Gospels of the New Testament are a record of Jesus' life and teachings. The Bible has been translated into many different languages and there are different versions of it.

Food There are no particular rules about food. There are special festival foods in many countries around the world.

Christians come together to celebrate Holy Communion – 'sharing' the memory of Jesus' death and resurrection. Bread and wine are shared at this service. Its distribution and the interpretation of its meaning all vary within different groups.

Symbols There are many pictorial symbols, for example the crucifix. The dove with an olive branch represents peace, while an anchor and a fish represent hope and certainty. Early Christians used X (chi) and P (rho), the first two letters of the Greek word for Christ, as a symbol. Bread and wine are the symbols of the Sacraments.

Festivals

Easter Easter Sunday is the first Sunday after the first full moon after the 21 March. It is the most important Christian festival.

Lent This is a forty day period of fasting which immediately precedes Easter. There are many pre-Lent festivals.

Shrove Tuesday This is the last day before the fasting season of Lent. There is a tradition of making pancakes to use up forbidden foods before Lent. Some places hold pancake races. There is a race between women in Buckinghamshire and Kansas. The time is recorded and telephoned across the Atlantic!

Mardi Gras (*Fat Tuesday*) In New Orleans there are processions of gaily coloured floats, marchers, dancers with fabulous costumes. A time of carnival.

Carnival Carnival means literally 'farewell to the flesh'. In Trinidad the Roman Catholic pre-Lent festival is the largest of all the carnivals and people travel from the other Caribbean islands to take part in three days of feasting before the 40 days of Lent. Slaves brought from Africa in the 18th century added African musical elements to the already existing festival. The three main days are Dimanche Gras (Carnival Sunday) people arrive in the capital and other parts of Trinidad to meet with friends and hold parties; Jour Ouvert (Carnival Monday) a morning 'jump up' marks the beginning of street dancing to steel bands; Mardi Gras (Carnival Tuesday) is the climax with a parade of Masqueraders which ends in a park. These follow more than three weeks of pre-Carnival events.

Once Lent begins it is a time of self-denial and penitence. It reminds Christians of Jesus' forty days in the wilderness fighting temptation.

The last week of Lent is known as Holy Week. It begins with Palm Sunday. Church services are held when crosses of palm leaves are given to the congregation.

Maundy Thursday Christians remember that on this day Jesus ate the last supper and washed the feet of his disciples – it became the custom in England for the King/Queen to wash the feet of the poor as Jesus did. Now 'Maundy money' is given to a number of people, as many coins as the years in the monarch's age.

Christian symbols

Good Friday This is a sad day in the Christian year, it is the day when Christians remember the death of Jesus. In some countries the crucifixion of Christ is re-enacted.

Easter Sunday This is the most important day of the Christian year when Christians celebrate Jesus as risen Lord. The giving of Easter eggs is a customary symbol of birth and new life. It is a time of rejoicing and looking forward to the future. All confirmed Christians are expected to attend Holy Communion on this day.

Ascension Day This is celebrated forty days after Easter Sunday. It is the day when Jesus was taken into heaven and appeared to the apostles on earth for the last time. Most churches have special services on this day.

Whitsun (Pentecost) This takes place seven weeks after Easter Sunday. Christians believe that the Holy Spirit came to give the disciples help in spreading the word of God.

It used to be the custom to admit new members into the Christian Church at this time. They wore white hence 'Whit'. In some areas it is still the custom to hold a procession of witness around the parish boundaries, with banners, flowers and special clothes.

Harvest Festival There is no definite date but this festival is usually held in August or September in European countries. In Australia and New Zealand it is held in February or March. It is a time of celebration, thanking God for food and crops. Churches are decorated with produce. Those situated around ports will include fish.

There are many different customs regarding harvest festivals around the world, for example, the Festival of Trays in Portugal. Harvest trays are made containing 30 bread rolls, flowers and streamers and a crown of flowers with a cross to decorate it. The trays are carried through the streets to the church to be blessed. The rolls are given to the poor with meat and wine.

Advent This is the four week period before Christmas. It is a time of preparation and expectation. Its importance varies amongst different Christian communities and special services are held on the Sundays during Advent.

Christmas This is the second most important festival. It celebrates the birth of Jesus. Nobody really knows when Jesus was born. Most countries have chosen the date of 25 December as the day to celebrate. This date in December was chosen to coincide with the pre-Christian Roman Sun festival. On Christmas Eve a service is held outside the Church of the Nativity in Bethlehem and cribs are set up in many churches throughout the world. Midnight services are held in some churches. Twelve days after Christmas comes Epiphany.

Epiphany This means 'showing forth'. Christians remember how Jesus was shown to the Magi (wise men from the east who had brought gifts to the baby). It is held on 6 January. At one time this was the date of Christmas day itself, now it is known as the twelfth night of the Christmas Festival and in many parts of the world is a time of fun and games and present giving.

Candlemas (2 February) Candles are blessed and given to worshippers in some churches Jesus is thought of as 'The Light of the World'.

World harvest

Push the trolley with the basket
Down between the rows of shelves,
See the tins and jars and packets,
This is how we serve ourselves.

First we sail to distant prairies,
Maize is ripening in the sun
Ready for our bowls of cornflakes
When another day's begun.

Let's steer on to warm Jamaica
Pick bananas from the trees,
See the canes and get our sugar,
Then sail off across the seas.

Next stop – beef from Argentina,
Coffee beans – Brazil ahead!
Round the world we find New Zealand,
There's the butter for our bread.

Tinned sardines in Portugal, and
Juicy oranges from Spain,
Grapes from France and cheese from Holland,
Then we'll sail for home again.

Rosy apples in the orchards,
New laid eggs must not be missed,
Vegetables from Market gardens,
Now we've ticked off all our list.

Well our trolley's really loaded,
What a busy shopping day,
Seems we needed all the world, and
Now there's just the bill to pay.

Richard Graves and Cecily Taylor

Child for the world

Lying in a manger
Ox and ass beside
Man above the manger
Watching with his bride
A little boy lay on the straw
Sleeping in the hay
And angels sang a song for him
Born on Christmas day.

In the fall of winter
Out beside the stream
Lying in a wigwam
In the silver beam
The tribes around brought rabbit skins
And coloured beads to play
And angels sang a song for him
Born on Christmas day.

In the summer sunlight
Down below the hill
With palms above him
The seaweed sleeping still
A little boy lay in the sand
The seabirds watched him play
And angels sang a song for him
Born on Christmas day.

In the smoky city
In the foggy street
Mist around the houses
Water at your feet
'A boy is born at No.4',
I heard the milkman say,
And the angels sang a song for him
Born on Christmas day.

David Medd

Saints days

There are many Saints Days in the Christian calendar. Sometimes holidays are taken though mostly they are marked by services in the churches dedicated to that particular saint. There are customs associated with certain saints, for example,

St Patrick

St Valentine's and St Swithun's.

St David's Day (1 March) St David is the Patron Saint of Wales. During his lifetime he founded many churches and monasteries. Welsh people everywhere show their pride in their country by wearing daffodils.

St Patrick's Day (17 March) St Patrick is the Patron Saint of Ireland. His symbol is a three-leaved shamrock the symbol of the Trinity. In Chicago USA green dye is poured into the River Chicago. In New York a green line is painted down the middle of the street for St Patrick's Day Parade.

St George's Day (23 April) St George is the Patron Saint of England. The story is told of St George and the Dragon which depicts the triumph of good over evil. This day had been adopted as 'thinking day' by Scout and Guide Associations.

St Andrew's Day (30 November) St Andrew is the Patron Saint of Scotland. Andrew was a disciple of Jesus, a fisherman. His remains were said to have been brought to Scotland by monks and are believed to be buried under St Andrew's Cathedral. This day is a time of celebration for Scots all over the world.

All Saints Day (1 November) Many Saints who are not given a special day are remembered on this day.

All Souls' Day (2 November) On this day prayers are offered for souls of people who have died. In many countries flowers are laid on family graves and prayers are said for the departed.

115

Prayer of St Teresa of Avila

Christ has no body now on earth but yours;
No hands but yours; no feet but yours:
Yours are the eyes through which his love
*   looks out to the world:*
Yours are the feet with which he goes about
*   doing good:*
Yours are the hands with which he blesses men
*   now.*

Liam's first communion

Liam's Dad should have been home early Saturday evening. He'd telephoned last night to say that his ferry crossing had been cancelled, the sea was too rough. He was going to sleep in the cab of his lorry and then he'd be on the first ship for Dublin in the morning.

Mum let Liam speak to his Dad himself, she could see how anxious he was getting hovering by the telephone.

"You will try to make it, Daddy," he sounded desperate, "my first communion just wouldn't be the same without you there."

"Sure," his Dad's voice was so clear that it was hard to imagine he was across the Irish Sea in Liverpool, "you know I'll do my best. I'm parked at the very front of the queue and my lorry will be the first on that boat just as soon as they give the OK to board. Let's pray that the storm will soon die down. Have an early night Liam, so you'll be fresh for your busy day tomorrow. See you soon."

After his bath Liam knelt by his bed, he said his usual prayers then asked God for a special favour, "Please please God, have the storm die away so that my Daddy can get safely back across the sea in time for Church tomorrow." Then he peered through the window to see if the rain had stopped and the wind had calmed. It hadn't.

When the alarm rang at 7.30 that Sunday morning, Liam didn't dare open his eyes in case he should look out across a stormy Dublin. He listened for the sound of rain on his window, when he heard none he opened his eyes. The sun was sending strong, bright rays through the gaps at the sides of his curtains. Liam jumped out of bed, flung open his curtains and stared out at the bright blue sky and the city flooded with sunlight.

"Oh it's a beautiful day,' he laughed as he dashed downstairs to where his Mum had already begun preparations for the afternoon's celebrations.

"When did the storm pass?"

"What time did the ferry sail?"

"What time will it dock?"

"Will Dad be on his way?"

"Will he make it?" Liam bubbled around the kitchen with his questions.

"Hang on a minute," she smiled, "I haven't a clue, but we'll all just keep on hoping that he makes it. Meanwhile there's a lot to get on with, come on you can help."

Before they set off for Church Liam helped John and Kathy, his brother and sister, to count out the twenty four knives, forks and spoons and the napkins that they'd need later for the family get-together. Mum was getting stacks of bread rolls from the freezer. "Will fifty be enough?" she wondered, "Oh one more won't be wasted with Aunty Marie's gang coming over, they're always hungry. Now John will you get the barbeque out of the garage and put it down at the bottom of the garden? Kathy will you get the charcoal out? Thanks kids you're a great help especially when your Dad's away." By ten o'clock they were all in their best clothes ready to set off for Church. Liam's face was glum.

"Daddy never made it after all," Liam couldn't hide his disappointment as they walked up the path to St Mary's Church.

Even meeting up with his classmates didn't cheer him up, he couldn't share their excitement. He stood very close to his Mum, he could tell that she was sad too, but she could always put a brave face on, Liam couldn't.

"You're family's third from the front, Liam," Mr Donnelly, his class teacher, led the way to their bench.

John, Kathy, Mum and Liam joined Grandma and Grandad who always arrived early wherever they went. Liam sat at the end of the row, he would be first to get up. As he looked along the bench it seemed empty without Dad.

When mass began Liam found it hard to concentrate. He'd thought about this moment for so long, he'd enjoyed preparing for his first communion at school and looked forward to it being his own special day.

Mum nudged him out of his daydream, "Off you go lad, it's time for you to receive your communion."

As he stood up and turned round to walk up to the communion rail, his eyes glanced down the aisle. He couldn't believe it, Daddy was dashing into the church, his hair ruffled, his clothes crumpled but his smile beamed out in spite of the tiredness.

Liam had a spring in his step as he walked to the front with his friends. Every now and then he glanced over his shoulder to see his Daddy smiling proudly back at him from the family bench.

The first communion

Liam's grin did not leave his face all the way through the photograph session. The whole class got together in front of the altar and Liam now felt just as happy as his friends. Later at the communion breakfast in the church hall, Liam tried to describe the feelings he had about taking his first communion, "But I don't think it would have been the same if you hadn't got there, Daddy." His father looked worn out as he had his tea and biscuits, so they left the other families to enjoy the party and set off

for home. Nobody minded really, they were all looking forward to the barbeque they would be having later that afternoon.

"It's a good job we planned it for two o'clock," Mum said, "it'll give Daddy a chance to recover and tidy himself up before the rest of the family arrive."

Mum turned the key in the front door and Daddy staggered into the house making straight for the stairs.

"A bath and an hour's kip," he said, "then I'll take on that barbeque and even

cope with Auntie Marie's family's enormous appetites." Half way up the stairs he turned to speak to Liam, "Hey I nearly forgot to give you this," he said handing a small package over the banister, "I bought it in England for you."

Liam carefully took off the wrapping, there inside was the most beautiful little white leather-bound Bible he had ever seen.

"Thanks Daddy. I'll always keep it by my bed to remind me of today."

The prodigal son

Jesus, like other religious teachers, used stories to help people to understand the basic ideas of his beliefs. Here is one of many to be found in the New Testament that can be adapted and made enjoyable and stimulating for young children. It is likely to generate a lot of discussion amongst children. It seems unfair when seen from the point of view of the character Thomas. Discussion of this in context of the Kingdom of Heaven is an essential follow-up to the story.

Simon leaned on the wall and looked out across his father's land.

"Just think what all this must be worth, Thomas," he said to his brother, "and one day it will all be ours."

"Oh not for a long time, Dad's in good shape. Nothing's going to happen to him for a long time, I hope." Thomas loved his father very much and couldn't bear the idea of him not being around.

"Anyway I'm bored hanging around here. There's nothing to do and nothing exciting ever happens. I'd like to get away from here and see a few places while I'm still young," Simon had decided to speak to his father about an idea he had.

"How about giving me my share of your money now instead of me having to wait until you die? I'd like money now to do what I want. Here it's tied up in the farm, what use is it to me?" Simon's words made his father stop and think.

After a while he agreed, "Why not?" he said, "I've a feeling that you've got a lot to learn. It'll do you good to see something of the world."

His father made all the arrangements and handed the money over to Simon when he was packed and ready to leave.

Thomas didn't know what to make of it all. He couldn't understand his brother wanting to up and go like that, and he couldn't understand his father just letting him. He felt very confused as he stood with his father waving Simon off.

Simon was soon having a great time in the big city. His money made him very popular, new friends gathered around to share his good times. Sadly good times cost money – the best hotels, delicious meals, the latest fashions in clothes.

Soon Simon had spent up. He hit very hard times, not only because he was no longer rich, but the country was going through a bad time too.

There were few jobs. There were so many unemployed that Simon was forced to take the only work available. He became a labourer on a pig farm. The pay was very low, not enough to live off, and he was often so hungry that he took the food that he was meant to give to the pigs.

He was desperate, although he knew that he had had his fair share of his father's money, the only thing he could think of to do was to go home. He could only hope that his father would understand how sorry he was for his stupidity and forgive him. Perhaps he would let Simon work for him – that was his best hope.

Simon kept his head down as he walked up the lane to his father's farm. He was embarrassed and ashamed of what he had become. He knew what a sight he looked.

He thought he must be imagining things when he glanced up to see his father running towards him, waving his arms about and grinning. He stood still and waited for his father to reach him. They hugged each other and cried for a long time. When he could get words out, his father ordered the labourers, who had stopped working nearby to watch what was going on, to take his poor son into the house.

"Find him some decent clothes and get him something to eat. Then we'll get a party going. You, Simon, could do with a bath," he chuckled.

As Simon followed the workers up to the house, Thomas, who had been watching from nearby, wasn't particularly pleased to see the welcome his father had given to his brother. He walked over to speak to him.

"I don't understand what's going on, Dad," he complained, "it doesn't seem fair to me. All this time Simon has been away spending all his money I've stayed here with you. Yet here you are planning great celebrations because he's come home. You've never had a party for me."

"But Thomas, please try and understand," his father began to explain gently, "You know that I love you and all I have is yours. Try to see that all the time Simon has been away I've worried about him. I thought he was lost, dead. Now here he is. We've got him back, he's found. Don't you think that it's only right that we should be celebrating?"

Thomas went away, he had a lot to think about. Later he had to agree, he started to feel glad that his brother was home again.

The original story is to be found in the New Testament, Luke 15 verses 11–32.

Crown of candles

In Sweden and in countries where many Swedish people live 13 December is a day given to the celebration of Saint Lucia, Queen of Light.

Ronya had hardly slept all night. She had set her alarm for 6 o'clock, just a bit earlier than usual, but she hadn't needed to. She was wide awake well before it was due to go off.

At quarter to 6 she could bear it no longer, she crept out of bed and carefully crossed the bedroom without turning on the light, so as not to wake her sister.

It had been Ingrid's turn to play the part of St Lucia last year, if she woke up now she would start bossing Ronya and telling her what to do. Ronya knew exactly what to do but her older sister always interfered, so it was better not to disturb her.

In the kitchen Ronya took a tray and set out four coffee cups. Next she filled the coffee jug with water, put in the filter then suddenly remembered about the Lucia buns. Her first job should have been to get them out and put them in the microwave oven to warm. Quickly she plugged the coffee jug into the socket and turned it on.

"Now I wonder how many minutes these buns will take?" Ronya opened the oven door, put in the buns and set the dial, "Oh I don't suppose it matters that much, I'll give them five minutes."

While the buns warmed Ronya put plates, knives, spoons, a jug of milk and a bowl of sugar on the tray. It was looking fairly full but she thought a small candle would make it pretty so she found a space, placed the candle in it and carefully lit it.

While the coffee jug started to bubble Ronya went into the living room where she'd put her white dress, red sash and crown of greenery the night before. It was all set out ready, and soon 'St Lucia' was in costume with just her crown to put on.

Ronya's Daddy had fixed up a clever little battery hidden behind a star, the candles round the crown were lit by tiny bulbs. Ronya just had to connect the wires to make a circuit and 'Hey Presto' the candles were glowing. She put it on her head. Ronya was really proud of herself as she admired the results in the hallway mirror. This was her first time at acting the part, she thought she made the perfect St Lucia. She was lost in admiration, looking at herself from every angle and trying the model poses she'd seen in the magazines. Then, suddenly another face appeared in the mirror over her shoulder.

"Ingrid, you shouldn't creep up on people like that," Ronya was surprised and embarrassed.

"Ha-ha, that's lit your cheeks up even more," teased her sister.

"Don't be so mean," scowled Ronya, "you only got up to make fun of me. Nobody did that to you last year when it was your turn."

"Sorry, I didn't really come down to spoil it for you. I just thought you might need a bit of help."

"Well I've managed thanks," Ronya sounded a bit smug. Then the microwave bell was ringing, the buns were done, "If you really want to you can help me take the things up to Mummy and Daddy's bedroom. You can carry the tray and I'll bring the plate of buns and the coffee jug."

Ronya led the way with Ingrid following carefully behind. When they reached the

St Lucia's day

The traditional St Lucia's day role for young Swedish girls is the Queen of Light.

top of the stairs they began to sing the traditional song for that day *Santa Lucia*. Ronya pushed the bedroom door open with her foot. Mummy and Daddy were already sitting up in bed waiting for the morning's treat. The night before Daddy had gone through the stages of making coffee and warming buns with Ronya so he was especially pleased that it all seemed to have gone so well.

"What sweet voices our girls have," Mummy was pleased with them too, "and how beautiful our little St Lucia is." Ronya beamed at their admiration. She told Ingrid to place the tray down on the bedside table.

"You sit down too, Ingrid," she ordered, handing out the mugs and plates to the three of them. Each was given a bun, they felt very hot. Then Ronya began to pour the coffee, she began with Mummy.

"Not very strong this coffee," Mummy kept her face straight, "do you think you might have forgotten something?"

Daddy and Ingrid burst out laughing, but Ronya's smile had disappeared as she saw the clear liquid stream from the jug.

"These delicious buns will be just as good with hot water," Mummy consoled Ronya, she could see how upset she was. She tried to bite into her bun, "Oh my teeth!" she gasped, the buns were rock hard.

"I only cooked them for five minutes," Ronya's face had dropped still further.

"Just one minute would have done, Ronya, don't you remember I told you that last night?" Daddy had tears of laughter running down his cheeks and Ingrid was rolling about the bed clutching her sides with laughter.

Ronya stood at the side of the bed, she felt a big lump in her throat. It had all gone

wrong. Then, suddenly, there was a 'pop', the bulb of her crown went out. That was the last straw.

Ronya howled, she couldn't keep it inside any longer. She felt she must be the silliest St Lucia ever. She threw down her crown and ran out of her parents' room. She flung herself down on her own bed.

Soon she felt arms wrapping around her, it was Ingrid. "I'm sorry I laughed Ronya, you tried so hard and I was mean."

Then Daddy was there, "Sorry about the candles, it was my fault, I forgot to check the bulbs this year. I promise I'll get some new ones in town and fix them up for tonight." Mummy joined them, "Ronya we're proud of how you had a try at doing all this by yourself. Ingrid is three years older than you and she needed my help to make the coffee last year. So don't be too angry, you did so well to try."

All the family hugged each other and soon Ronya was laughing too, "Just my luck those candles going out like that. I suppose I'd have laughed if it had been somebody else and not me."

"Right, let's get going," Daddy brought the uproar to order. "Mummy and I will be late for work and you two will be late

for school if we don't get a move on. You can wear the crown tonight for the neighbourhood procession, Ronya. I promise the candles won't do that again."

As they all started to get ready Ronya's voice called out, "Anyone know what's for breakfast?"

Recipe for Gingerbread Houses

St Lucia's Day treat

In Sweden it is traditional to make elaborate gingerbread houses. (You could make one by sticking different shaped biscuits on to a cereal packet using icing.) Here is a recipe for biscuits that you could use.

225 g self-raising flour
85 g margarine/butter
85 g brown sugar
85 g treacle or golden syrup
2 teaspoons of ground ginger

Mix together the margarine, sugar and syrup until soft and creamy.
Stir in the flour and ginger slowly.
Knead it together with your hands.
Roll out the dough on a floured board, it needs to be quite thick.
Use a template to cut around, in the shape of a house.
Put each house shape carefully on to a greased baking tray. Leave plenty of space in between.
Bake in a hot oven (200°C, 450°F or gas mark 6) for five to ten minutes.

When cool you can put on windows, doors and so on, using piped icing, making them as decorative as you can. Use small colourful sweets to make it even brighter.

Carnival in Trinidad

Romance in the tropic air
Here and there and everywhere
Everyone is on the go,
Pans to tune, costumes to sew;
Money lending
Wire bending
Metal sheeting
In the beating
Bleachers building
Coaches gilding
Miles of gold and silver braid
Heralding the masquerade.

Share our nation's festival,
Heritage of great and small,
Most exciting of them all;
Blaze of glory – Carnival.   (extract)

Carnival in Trinidad

A view from the Carnival procession in Port of Spain, Trinidad.

Recipe for Sugar Cakes

Carnival Dish

200 g grated (dessicated) coconut
300 g sugar
Half cup of milk
Pinch of ground ginger
(Food colouring if you want to make cakes bright).

Boil milk and sugar together stirring slowly to make sure sugar is dissolved.
Remove from heat.
Add coconut, ginger and colouring, stir together thoroughly.
Drop teaspoonfuls of mixture on to a greased tin, leave to cool.
Chill in fridge for one hour.

Follow-up activities

Visit a local parish church – find out about past and present.

Look at illuminated manuscripts – children make own designs on names.

Get examples of Rosary Beads – compare with other religions.

Design costumes for 'Mardi Gras' – organize a parade at school.

Investigate all different buildings for Christian worship in the area.

Christian children to bring Baptism certificates. Find out about Baptism or initiation ceremonies in other religions.

Sunday is the special day set aside for worship by Christians. Find out about the special days in other religions.

Find out more about traditional characters of Masquerade, for example, Pierrot Grenade, Jab Molassi, Midnight Robber.

Find examples of Creole patois.

Make a list of schools, hospitals, churches and other buildings in your area which are named after Saints.

Find out which children in class are named after saints. Find out about these saints and their qualities. When did they become saints?

Many saints have connections with animals, make a class book about these. For example, Francis and Anthony.

Hinduism

Background

History Hinduism is the third largest religion in the world. About 80% of the population of India are Hindus and there are large groups of Hindu communities in Pakistan, Sri Lanka, Nepal, Bali, Europe, Canada, USA and East Africa. It is an ancient religion and probably began before 2500 BCE. This is the time when the Indus Valley civilization was thriving – the city of Mohenjo-Daro was perhaps the great centre of religion. Now it is in Pakistan.

Basic beliefs Non-Hindus are often confused as to whether Hindus believe in one God or many gods. Hinduism embraces a spectrum of belief regarding this. Most groups hold that there is one God, Brahman, being the perfect Truth beyond human understanding, without shape or form and present everywhere. For most Hindus the many gods and goddesses are different ways of representing the divine. The many gods are ways of seeing the One.

It is because the Brahman is so difficult a concept that Hindus have other gods that are part of the Supreme God. These can be pictured and prayed to.

Of the many gods associated with Hinduism most groups choose either Shiva, Vishnu or one of the forms of the goddess Devi as their main deity. Devi is thought of by some as the central deity. In many Indian villages she is considered as the protector of mothers and children. She can take various forms such as Lakshmi, the goddess of good fortune, or Durga, the warrior. The family shrine will be dedicated to this chosen god. Some have human and some have animal form. Hindus generally agree that God is One and whilst some believe the other gods are similar in significance to the disciples or Saints of Christians, other Hindu groups do give greater importance to them.

Hindus believe that the spirit of God is in all living creatures, plant, animal and human.

Ahimsa This is a basic Hindu belief which means not harming other living things. Hindus share this belief with Buddhists and with Jains.

Samsara This is the belief in re-incarnation, the cycle of life and death which continues until the highest state Moksha is achieved. The soul may pass through various forms of life, human, bird and animal in this process. The things done during a life time determine the form of life that follows. The moral law of cause and effect that determines the future is known as Karma. Wrong actions will lead to rebirth into a lower order of life, while good ones will lead to rebirth into a higher one. Thus through a series of rebirths (Samsara) good Karma is gradually acquired which can lead to Moksha (salvation).

Each soul is trying to return to the Supreme One. Hindus have great respect for all living things. The form in which we return to earth depends on the type of life we have lived. Hindus believe Dharma, the duties to family and God provides further guidance for their lives, the duties to caste which it also involved is less important to many Hindus today. Dharma covers codes of honesty, justice, self-control and charity amongst other values.

Place of worship Hindu temples can be found the world over. In India many temples are designed not for group but for individual worship. Hindus usually have a shrine in their homes where they pray everyday – they worship as individuals, families or congregations. The shrine will have pictures and statues of the family's chosen gods or goddesses, with candles or lamps and incense sticks. Sometimes flowers decorate the shrine. Gathering at temples is more popular in some countries than others. (For example in the United Kingdom.) There are no special rules stating when or how often a person should attend. Some temples have no weekly congregational gatherings. A person can go to the temple weekly, monthly or never and still be a good Hindu, but temples are used at special times, for example, festivals and weddings. At the gateway of most temples are bells which worshippers ring when entering. Inside there are usually small shrines before one reaches the main one. The temple priest sits by this main shrine and he places a red mark, a tilak, on the forehead of the worshipper.

Benares is the Holiest City of the Hindu. It is situated on the River Ganges which is also considered holy. Cremations often take place on the banks of the river and the ashes of the dead are scattered on the water. Both are places of pilgrimage.

Leaders Brahmins are the priestly class of Hindus and many devote their lives to teaching and prayer. The priests will conduct ceremonies in the temple. A Guru is a religious teacher and spiritual guide. There are many Indian Gurus but the size of their following varies. Guru Maharishi has been particularly popular in the West in recent years.

Gandhi, one of India's greatest 20th century political and religious leaders, believed in non-cooperation rather than violence to achieve goals. The path he chose to achieve Moksha was of selfless service to society. Daily he read the Bhagavad Gita (see under *Books*) and urged others to do so. His methods for achieving change in India were in keeping with the belief in Ahimsa.

Puja (worship) This act of worship is usually performed at home and is a simple ceremony with oil lamps and incense sticks lit. Water is sprinkled over a statue of a deity and food offered – this is later eaten by the family. At the temple, prayers are said in front of the sacred flame. The priest performs the ceremony of Arti. This involves a tray with candles or an Arti dish which is moved slowly in front of a god. This is then brought round to everyone. Worshippers hold their hands over the candle flame then pass their hands over their foreheads and hair. An offering of money is made. Prashad (Holy Food) is sometimes eaten. Special Arti hymns are sung to show devotion to God and the sound 'Om' is chanted.

Clothes There are no rules for dress in Hinduism therefore there is great variety.

Hindu women usually wear a sari – 5.5 metres (6 yards) of material which is wrapped around the body. In different parts of India the sari is draped in various styles. A short blouse (choli) is worn with it. Jewellery is important and often given to a bride at her wedding, and handed down in the family. Hindu men wear a variety of styles according to their job and the region or country in which they live.

Books The Vedas are four collections of verses and hymns written in Sanskrit. Brahmanas are rules for ceremony, offering and sacrifice. Ramayana is the epic story of Rama and Sita. Bhagavad Gita is the teaching of Lord Krishna that action must not be for reward. It tells the story of war. The Upanishads are holy books concerning the basic beliefs about God and the individual soul. These were new ideas when they were written down 2,500 years ago.

Food Many Hindus are vegetarians. Whilst all life is sacred, cows are especially protected in India, for economic as well as religious reasons. Fasting is part of Hinduism. Hindus sometimes choose to fast for a day each week as part of their devotions. Others may choose to fast prior to a festival.

Greeting On meeting Hindus usually put their hands together to touch their foreheads – usually using the word 'Namaste'.

Symbols Om is part of most Hindu prayers. It is a symbol of good. Many Hindus wear it as a pendant, and most have a plaque or poster of it in their homes.

A shrine in a Hindu home

Festivals

Hinduism has a vast number of festivals some are particular to a region and some to a community. In some countries temples have at least one week-long festival in honour of the god to whom the temple is dedicated and these are happy occasions with much festivity, processions and bathing in the temple pool or river.

It is important to understand when discussing Hindu custom associated with festivals that most refer to some story in the Hindu scriptures. For each festival there can be a different focus on characters or stories depending on the particular region or country.

Hari Krishna

Unaccompanied

Ha – ri   Krish – na _____   Ha – ri   Krish – na _____
Ha – ri   Ra – ma _____   Ra – ma   Ra – ma _____

— Krish-na   Krish – na _____   Ha – ri   ha – ri. _____
— Ra – ma   Ra – ma _____   Ha – ri   ha – ri. _____

Hari Krishna, Hari Krishna,
Krishna Krishna, Hari hari.

Hari Rama, Rama, Rama,
Rama Rama, Hari hari.

traditional

Diwali (October/November) The Festival of Lights is one of the oldest Hindu festivals. It is a five day New Year Festival. Its theme varies in different parts of India. Oil lamps are lit and houses cleaned to welcome the Goddess Lakshmi.

Rangoli mats are designed and made and fireworks are set off to frighten away evil spirits. Lakshmi is said to visit the homes which are brightly lit bringing food and luck in the coming year. She is believed, by the children, to bring the toys, sweetmeats and new clothes given at this time. Like many other New Year festivals, Diwali celebrates the triumph of good over evil and light over darkness.

Even in the world of business and trade Diwali is an important time. Most businesses 'close their books' ready to make a new start. With the worship of Lakshmi it is hoped for good honest trade in the New Year. In Bengal the festival is called Kali Puja and people worship Kali instead of Lakshmi.

Holi (Time of full moon in March or end of February) This festival is held at the time of spring harvest. Images of the goddess Holika are made and burned on communal bonfires. These bonfires are sacred, the ashes are streaked on the forehead to bring good luck. There is a carnival atmosphere to the festival with processions in the streets and singing and dancing. In the streets people spray and splash each other with coloured water or bright powder and remember stories of the fun Lord Krishna had with milkmaids.

Sarasvati Puja (Springtime) Sarasvati, patron of learning, is believed to have invented the Sanskrit language. The goddess is worshipped along with all the holy books in the house. Prayers are especially offered by students about to take examinations, writers and composers.

Raksha Bandhan (August) Girls tie a rakhi (a red and gold thread) around the wrists of their brothers with a prayer for their protection. Brothers also promise to protect sisters. The custom has its roots in an ancient Hindu story of the god Vishnu giving this thread to Indra's wife to tie on her husband's wrist to protect him from the demon king, Bali.

Dashera – Durga Puja (Autumn festival lasting ten days) The last day of the festival is the most important day. The preceding 9 days are known as the Navaratra and are celebrated with dancing and the offering of sacrifices. Sometimes this festival is celebrated with processions, sometimes, in recognition of the importance of warriors, with fighting competitions or athletics. On the last day of the festival there is plenty of merry-making and a play is usually performed which tells of the adventures of Rama, and how with the help of the goddess Durga he was able to overcome Ravana, the demon king of Lanka, and return home rejoicing with his bride Sita. Sometimes the demon is shot with fiery arrows or maybe filled with fireworks. This is to demonstrate good triumphing over evil.

The story of Ganesh

The goddess Parvati was fed up. Day after day, week after week she prowled about the beautiful but lonely palace – waiting. "It's all I ever do," she moaned as she gazed through the window towards the mountain where her husband spent his time. "Shiva's never here. There he sits upon that mountain peak. I know he's happy up there praying, but what about me!"

It was true, Shiva spent his time in blissful meditation on the mountain, and it was also true that he hardly gave a thought to his wife back at the palace. Parvati desperately wanted a baby, it would be somebody to love and be with her, then she wouldn't be lonely. "Maybe Shiva would spend more time at home if we had a child," she thought. She became more and more angry thinking she would never have her wish, there would never be a baby. "Shiva just doesn't care." She stamped out of the palace gates, feeling angry yet not wanting the servants to see her in a rage.

Making her way along the mountain path she found a crag which sheltered her from view. She threw herself down on to the ground for a good cry. Wringing her hands in her sorrow and anger, she hardly noticed that her hands had gathered a lump of clay and that without realizing it, she had formed the clay into a human shape, the shape of a baby. Suddenly her anger vanished. Parvati worked on the details, she formed arms and legs, a tiny head – it needed a face. She worked with love and pleasure, modelling delicate eyes, a nose and a mouth.

When the clay baby was finished Parvati felt proud of her creation, but a model could not satisfy her. She looked at the child and willed it to live. "Be my baby, my real baby," her thoughts were strong and powerful, "You *will* come to life. You will live."

To her surprise the eyes of the child opened and sparkled up into hers, then a smile turned the lines of his lips into a happy curve. He wriggled a little in her arms, and she knew he was real. "My baby," she cooed at him and his giggle answered her.

Parvati's happiness cannot be described as she presented her son to everyone at the palace. He was surely a lovely, lively child, and soon everyone loved him. Ganesh, was the name Parvati chose for her special child.

As Ganesh grew his strength and power amazed everyone, most of all his mother who was very proud of him. In turn Ganesh loved his mother very much and wanted to care for her and protect her. He spent his time guarding the palace and became very fierce whenever danger threatened Parvati.

"I wish Shiva could see what a fine and good son we have," Parvati dreamed as she looked up from the palace window at the snow-capped mountain. "I know he would feel as proud as I do, and they'd get on really well together if only he'd come down from that mountain and meet Ganesh."

Not long after Parvati's daydream Lord Shiva did arrive home, but it did not turn out as Parvati had hoped. Ganesh and Shiva had never seen each other, so instead of a warm welcome Ganesh, guardian of his mother's palace, confronted this stranger stopping him from entering. Shiva, angry that this guard should dare to try and prevent him going into his own

Shiva　　**Parvati**

125

home, whisked out his sword and with one strong swish cut Ganesh's head clean off.

Running through the long corridor's of the palace grief-stricken Parvati feared the worse. When she reached the gates she crumpled to the ground where the head of Ganesh lay.

"He was my child," she wept uncontrollably. "He was protecting me, he loved me so much. Now you've killed him, my dear dear child. Oh, I can never forgive you Shiva."

"Please forgive me," pleaded Shiva. "I had no idea he was your child. I didn't stop to think. Give me the chance to put things right, I know just what to do."

He helped Parvati up from the ground and sent for a messenger. "Spread the word across all the universe that I must

Ganesh

have the head of the first living thing that can be found which has its face to the north," he instructed.

Although the request was a strange one, Shiva's words were always obeyed and the search began.

Parvati spent the following weeks mourning for her son. She lost weight and couldn't sleep, she looked at his headless body and cried, never wanting to go out of the palace or speak to anyone. Shiva tried to comfort her, he told her that everything would be alright, a head would be found and he could make Ganesh whole again. Days passed though, and Parvati just pined.

Then suddenly one day the palace gates crashed open. "We have it," panted the messenger, bursting in. "It's a magnificent head, and it was certainly facing north."

"Indra wasn't too pleased, but we managed to get it," his companion added pulling off the cloth from the head. "Well!" roared Lord Shiva in admiration, "You've done very well, it is a magnificent elephant's head."

With no trouble at all Lord Shiva took the beautiful beast's head to where Ganesh's body lay and placed it on the shoulders.

Ganesh stood up, he looked so wonderful to Parvati that she cried again, but this time her tears were of joy. She knew that her son would now have the kindness and wisdom of the elephant as well as the strength and power.

Shiva and Parvati were always proud of Ganesh and he was, and still is, loved by everyone.

Ganesh is one of the most popular of Hindu gods. He is believed to bring success and wealth and is thought to have great wisdom.

Sima's story

I have had a long lie-in this morning, it was one o'clock when I finally got into bed, and I was exhausted.

It had been a wonderful night though, dancing in front of the mayor, the huge hall was packed with people. The worst bit was knowing some of my school friends were out there watching.

The show was called *Eastern Night* and my Dad had helped to organize it. He's a member of the Hindu Society Committee and they had been planning the show for months. There had been so much to do. Our dance was just a small part of it. There was a fashion show, a band and lots of other performers. The Chinese Lion Dance was there, that was brilliant.

It had all begun for me over a year ago. My Auntie Shobena loves dancing. She is in the women's group of our Society. They learn traditional Indian dances, and are often invited to perform them at shows and parties. Well, Shobena and two of her friends, Nina and Jasheri, thought it would be a good idea to teach the dances to some of us younger ones. That way, we could be more involved in our festivals and celebrations. As well as learning the steps of the dance we spent a lot of time talking about the music we would dance to, and the costumes we would wear.

Auntie Shobena was really busy. As well as all the things she had to do for our dance, she was learning another with her friends. They like to change the dances they perform.

We'd begun last August before *Eastern Night* had ever been thought of. We were learning the dances of our Diwali celebrations which would be in November. It was great that Summer, planning for the

Traditional Hindu dancing

festival so far ahead. We could look forward to it without panic at the last minute, but poor Shobena had so much to do that even four months seemed short notice.

Auntie Shobena, Nina and Jashira laughed at us a lot, the six of us never seemed to be in step. I am the oldest so I had to stand at the front then the others could follow my steps. That was all very well, but I kept forgetting them, so by October the giggling had stopped and my Auntie was beginning to despair. "It's a good job our women's group know their dance, we might end up having to do it twice over, if these girls don't shape up."

The best part though was the costumes. Shobena and her friends made them. The long white dresses with short sleeves showed off the red and gold shawls, with bangles on our arms, bells on our ankles and flowers in our hair we felt like film stars.

"It's been such hard work these last two weeks that it's only thinking about the costumes that's kept me going," I moaned to the others at the last rehearsal before the Diwali celebrations and our first performance.

We had our real Diwali festival the week before. Our families don't like us to miss school so apart from opening our cards, saying our prayers and lighting the lamps on our little shrine in the front room, we'd not really celebrated very much. Auntie Shobena had taken the day off work and made a delicious meal for all the family in the evening. We had taken round presents for my little cousins and Dad had bought cakes and ice-cream. The real celebrations were the following Saturday. All the Hindus in town and other visitors besides, came to the school hall that our

Committee had hired for the night.

Hiren, my big brother, set up all the sound equipment. Rugs and carpets were laid out on the floor for the audience to sit on and incense sticks filled the air with beautiful perfume. I didn't see any of this because all the dancers were busy getting ready in the back room. It took us two hours to get dressed and put on our make-up. We hardly recognized each other when we were finished.

Uncle Mukan's voice was calling us out, it was our turn to dance and we were very excited. Most of the audience were friends and family, and we knew them, we always get together like this at Diwali. So we just enjoyed ourselves showing off our dance and beautiful costumes. My little cousin Amit sat on the front row, he was laughing and waving at me. Tiny Nisha who was only four stood up and tried to join in. The audience laughed, clapped and cheered when we had finished. It was really good.

Eastern Night was different though, the hall was very big and full of strangers. The two hours of getting ready was not excited giggling but nervous twittering. Would everything be alright? Would we forget the steps? Would my shawl stay in place? "Put more pins in," I begged Shobena who was even more nervous than me. She had her own dance to think about as well as ours.

When we were introduced I stepped out on the stage but my head did not seem in control of my feet and arms. I was glad of one thing, with the bright lights it was impossible to see the faces of the audience. I tried to tell myself that nobody was there and I just had to get on with it. Still, all the way through the dance I couldn't stop worrying. Those little ones were relying on me, if I did a wrong step they would all copy.

At last the music ended. I managed to smile as we put our hands together and touched our foreheads and bowed to the audience. The cheers were amazing. It had all been worthwhile.

Even though it was very late when we got home that night I asked my Dad if I could say one little prayer. I knelt down at our shrine, lit an incense stick, and just said "Thank you" to the statue of Shiva.

Goodbye to Grandad

Pravan had hoped that the doctor could help when he came in with his black bag and serious expression. Grandad had been ill for a very long time. When he caught 'flu last winter, he just seemed never to get better. Mum said that he was over eighty years old and the illness had left him very frail.

The weeks turned into months. Grandad went into hospital. They did some tests and sent him home with lots of different kinds of medicines, but he didn't seem to get back to his lively old self. He used to be such fun, at Holi he would always be the first to scatter the powder on the children then he would nip off pretty quickly before they could get him back. These last few months though Mum has asked us to be quiet in the house. "Try to keep the others quiet, Pravan," she had asked. "Grandad is sleeping, he needs as much peace and rest as he can get."

Pravan had spent a lot of time out playing or at his friend's house. Later on he'd come in and Grandad would be awake and smile his Namaste greeting, inviting Pravan to sit on his bed. Sometimes he would tell one of the old Indian tales which Pravan loved. He had grown up hearing Grandad's stories. They were shorter these

days. Grandad got tired quickly, but Pravan knew them so well that he would often add the ending himself. Grandad chuckled at how well he had remembered. Pravan had noticed that the stories had stopped now. Grandad couldn't sit up, he only drank and didn't want any food. Mum and Dad were worried, they knew Grandad wanted to be at home with all the family around him, so the doctor's suggestion of hospital last week was out of the question. He was a good doctor, he called everyday, but today Pravan was afraid that he couldn't help Grandad at all.

Pravan sat on the step hoping he was wrong but fearing inside that the doctor could do nothing. "You'd better come inside," Mum said gently as she opened the door, "I'm afraid Grandad is dying, he would like to see you to say goodbye."

Much as he loved his Grandad Pravan felt a shudder down his spine, he'd never seen anyone die but he had to go in. He knew it would make Grandad happy. He stepped into the room where Grandad lay, a gentle hug and kiss was all they had time for, before Grandad's eyes closed.

Later that night Pravan's Mum talked with him about Grandad's death. "You know that we believe that when we die we will be born again. Your Grandad led a good life so he will be reborn. He will not need the body he had so we will have it cremated. It is his soul that is important." Pravan still wanted to know what would happen so his Dad helped to explain. "Well the next few days won't be easy, we will all stay at home until the ceremony has taken place at the crematorium. It's going to be on Tuesday. We think you had better stay off school on Monday and on Tuesday too because now you're old enough to attend Grandad's cremation. When it's over we will have his ashes. Mum and I have been talking and we have decided that we will use our savings for me to fly to India with Grandad's ashes. I will scatter them on to the Ganges our sacred river. It's what Grandad would have wished. I will stay with my sister and brother in Delhi. We will scatter our father's ashes together."

By Monday night Pravan was still feeling bad about Grandad dying. It was so hard to talk about it. Mum noticed how sad Pravan looked. She took out the Bhagavad Gita as she often did, but this time she brought it to show Pravan. "This might help," she said, handing him the book open at a special page. Pravan read:

"For to one that is born death is certain; and to one that dies, birth is certain. Therefore, do not grieve over what is unavoidable."

Pravan thanked his Mum. It had helped.

The Ganges at Benares

Follow-up activities

There are many books available which tell the story of Ramayana in a form suitable for young children. These can be told/read at festival times. These stories lend themselves to dramatization.

Make a 'Bottom 10' and 'Top 10' of things you could come back as if reincarnation took place.

Draw up a day's menu that shows that you respect all living things. Use a collection of cookery books especially those containing menus for vegetarian dishes.

Find out about 'Festivals of Light' in other religions.

Make Rangoli patterns for Diwali using brightly coloured powder paints. Have a Rangoli design competition in the school playground. (Chalk on flags.)

Find out how to do a simple 'stick dance' – make sticks and decorate them for the dance. (If there is a local Indian Dance group invite them into school.)

Make a display of as many different forms of lighting as you can find, torches, bicycle lamps, candles, lanterns etc.

Make Divas (small cup-shaped light holders) from Plasticine or clay, use a small night light or make imitation flames from paper.

Make a large Holi splash painting. Put large pieces of paper together on the floor or on a large wall. Children can take turns in splashing very brightly coloured paint.

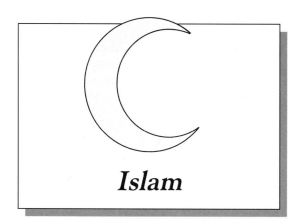

Islam

The word Islam means submission or peace.

Background

History Islam was founded by Allah and revealed to Mohammed who was born in Mecca in 570 CE. Mecca is the Holy City of Islam (A more correct transliteration of the Arabic is Makkah.) The religion has spread to cover the Middle East and North Africa, Iran, Afghanistan, India, Pakistan, Bangladesh and the southern USSR, China, Malaysia and Indonesia. There are communities of Muslims in most countries of the world today. About 85 per cent are Sunni Muslims and accept a code of behaviour based on Mohammed's examples as recorded in Hadith. About 15 per cent are Shi'ite and are guided more directly by the teachings of their Imams.

Basic beliefs To a Muslim, Islam is a complete way of life. Mohammed stated that the religion of Islam is upheld by 5 pillars: Shahada, Salat, Sawm, Zakat, Hajj.

Shahadah is the confession of faith. "There is no god but God and Mohammed is the prophet of God." Salat is prayer which is carried out five times daily. A timetable showing the times of prayer is kept in the homes of many Muslims. Sawm is fasting during the month of Ramadan when all healthy Muslims should not eat or drink from dawn to dusk. Zakat is the giving of alms to the poor. This is done in different ways. Hajj is pilgrimage. All Muslims should make a pilgrimage to Mecca, the Holy City, during their lifetime. Pictorial representation of Allah is forbidden and the strictest Muslims reject photographs and television pictures of any human or animal form.

Place of worship The place of worship is the Mosque (masjid). Mosques vary greatly throughout the world, some are very ornate, others are simple converted buildings. Muslims may pray anywhere. To a Muslim the prayer mat is his own place of prayer, wherever he may be at prayer time he can set down his mat to face Mecca. Some Mosques have a special place for women to pray but practice varies. In some cases it is more usual for women to pray at home. There is congregational prayer every day and especially at midday on Fridays. Wherever Muslims pray the same preparations are made. Shoes will be removed outside the Mosque, or at the door of a house used for prayer, and ablutions will be performed.

Prophets Muslims believe that God has sent many prophets to teach people. Most important are Adam, Noah, Abraham, Moses and Jesus. Although Muslims think of him as a prophet he is not considered divine, as he is by Christians. Mohammed (the words "Peace and blessings be upon him" are usually said by Muslims after his name) was the last prophet. His birth and death are important festivals. Muslims do not have a priesthood. Islam has a long tradition of recognized theological scholars.

Prayers Prayer is central to Muslim worship and is always performed facing Mecca. Adhan is the call to prayer. This was always called by the use of the human voice but today loudspeakers and cassettes are sometimes used. The muezzin calls the faithful to prayer at set times. Clocks which show the times of prayer can be seen in Mosques. Ritual ablutions, known as Wazu, are always carried out before prayer.

Bismillah is a supplication "I begin in the name of Allah, the beneficent, the merciful". It is said during washing using running water. First hands to wrist, then mouth and nostrils, then face, forearms, scalp, ears and finally feet are washed. "Cleanliness is half the faith." It is also said at meal times. Muslims use a Muslim Rosary which is made up of 99 beads. Each bead represents a different name for Allah.

Adhan, the Call to Prayer, is also said into the right ear of a baby as soon as it is born so that it should know its duty.

"God is most great (4 times)
I witness that there is no god but God (twice)
I witness that Mohammed is the Messenger of
  God (twice)
Come to Prayer (twice)
Come to Salvation (twice)
Prayer is better than sleep (twice at dawn)
God is most great (twice)
There is no god but God".

Clothes People must remove their shoes before entering a Mosque. Muslim dress should be decent and modest – burka/ purdah, covering the face, legs and arms, though this varies with community custom. Muslims usually cover their heads when praying.

Books The most important book to Muslims is the Qur'an meaning written in heaven and revealed to Mohammed. Because this is a holy book Muslims always provide a special covering for the Qur'an. The book is usually placed in a special place in Muslim homes usually higher than any other book because of its importance.

The Hadith is a collection of sayings spoken by Mohammed.

Greeting Muslims use an embrace or handshake with a greeting: "Asalaam o Alakum" reply "O Alakum Asalaam".

Food Muslims are forbidden to eat pork. Animals killed for meat must be killed in a ritual way. This is called Halal meat. Muslims are not allowed to drink alcohol.

Symbols Islam has no particular religious symbols but the star and crescent moon are sometimes used. The name of Allah (God) written in beautiful calligraphy is considered a suitable symbol by many Muslims and is displayed in the home.

Festivals

Dates of festivals are determined by the lunar calendar and move throughout the seasons. Calendars are available from Community Relations Councils. Festivals move backwards about 10 days each year against the Gregorian calendar.

Ramadan (the ninth month of the Muslim year) All healthy Muslims fast between sunrise and sunset for one month in order to experience self-denial, and for rich people to experience poverty. The 27th night of Ramadan is Lailat-ul-Qadr (the night of power) which commemorates the first revelation from Allah to Mohammed through Archangel Gabriel (Jibril). Muslims stay awake all night reciting the Qur'an and saying prayers.

Eid-ul-Fitr (first day of the month of Shawwal) This is often known as small Eid. It marks the end of Ramadan. It is a very happy time when families and friends

Muslim prayer

send cards, visit each other and share special food. Most people, especially children enjoy wearing new clothes and gifts of money are given to the children. Special early morning prayers are held at the Mosques.

Eid-ul-Adha (month of Dhul-Hijjah) This is known as great Eid. It is a world wide festival which falls seventy days after Ramadan. It comes at the end of Hajj (pilgrimage to Mecca). This festival commemorates the sacrifice of a ram in place of the son of Ibrahim. At this festival an animal, usually a lamb or goat is killed. The meat is shared equally between the family, the family's friends and the poor.

Lailat-ul-Ishwal Mi'raj (27th of month of Rajab) On this day Muslims remember the journey of Mohammed from the Ka'ba in Mecca to Jerusalem.

Meelad-ul-Nabi (12th of the month of Rabi ul-Awwal) The Prophet's birthday is celebrated with readings telling of his birth and the events of his life.

Day of Hijrah (1st day of the month of Muharram) The first day of the Islamic year celebrates the first emigration of Muslims from Mecca to Medina in 622 CE. The Islamic calendar dates from this journey which is known as the Hijrah.

A prayer

O Lord, I beg of You all the good of this day and all the days thereafter and I seek Your protection from all the evil of this day and the days to come.

From Al-Higbul-A'zam

The revelation to Mohammed

Mohammed was born in the city of Mecca in 570 CE. He was born into a noble tribe of Arabia, and was brought up by his grandfather and then his uncle, as his father died before he was born and his mother when he was only 6 years old.

When he grew up he found work with the merchant caravans of Mecca, travelling many hundreds of miles. Soon he became known as Al-Amin, which means the trustworthy.

His wife was a wealthy widow, Khadija, who was previously his employer. Although he was very clever and good at business, he did not devote his life to becoming rich, instead he chose to meditate. In his thoughts he always puzzled about why the people of the city treated each other so badly and why they worshipped many idols.

Each year when the month of Ramadan came around Mohammed went up into the hills to meditate and to fast in a cave on Mount Hira.

It was during Ramadan in 610 CE that Jibril appeared to Mohammed whilst he sat meditating in the cave. He was terrified and thought he must be going mad.

Mohammed was afraid and set off running for home as soon as he thought that the angel had gone, but the angel called after him, "I am Jibril and *you* are the Messenger of Allah". Mohammed stopped in his tracks, the angel had appeared huge and towering in the sky in front of him, he felt that there was no getting away but still he kept running until he was safe with his wife at home.

Khadija was worried when she saw the state Mohammed was in. He was breathless and trembling with fright. She wrapped him up and listened whilst he described what had happened up on the mountain. Listening to his story, Khadija had a feeling that what had happened to Mohammed was important, and she reassured him enough for him to return to the cave.

Over the following months Mohammed had many experiences in the cave, where Allah's words were revealed to him, and the laws of Islam came into being. The first law that there is no god but God was the most important one. Then came Allah's commands for the way people should live their lives.

It was another three years before Mohammed began to tell other people apart from his wife and close family, about the messages he had received from God. At first many people in Mecca took no notice of what he was saying. Then they realized that he was becoming a danger to them, he questioned their wealth and power and their beliefs in their gods. Mohammed now had enemies but he continued to speak out and he gained more and more followers. His life was full of dangers and adventure and there are many stories about how, despite all this, Islam continued to spread.

The Prophet Mohammed taught that all small creatures and animals are the creation of Allah and must be treated with care and kindness. He told stories about being kind to all living creatures, so that his followers would understand God's message. Here is one of his stories, but many more stories from the life and teachings of Mohammed can be found in the children's books published by the Islamic Foundation.

A careless fire

Once during a long journey, when Mohammed and his followers had set up camp for the night, Mohammed was making his usual tour of the site to make sure that all was well, when he noticed a fire. He walked over to the fire where a group of his companions were huddled up trying to keep warm.

As they talked Mohammed noticed that nearby was an ant hill and round it the ants scurried about their business. He looked closer and saw that some of the ants, as they worked away, were getting too close to the fire and were so busy that they did not notice the danger they were in. The Prophet felt worried, he could not bear to see any of God's creatures coming so close to being harmed.

He suddenly stopped talking, but then asked which of the companions had made the fire. One man explained, "It was me, we were so cold that I had to do something to keep us warm." "Let's put it out quickly," Mohammed cried. "But why?" asked the man beating out the flames with his blanket. As the flames died down the group looked closely at where the fire had been. Then they noticed the ants and just how near they had been to the fire. The man who had made the fire realized why Mohammed had acted so strangely in ordering the fire to be put out.

He told Mohammed that in future he would always remember to check carefully that no creatures are nearby before making a fire. The Prophet reminded him that God forbids that anyone should harm his creatures. The man knew he would always remember how close he had come to harming the tiny ants by being careless when building his fire that night.

A Saturday visitor

Mrs Hall set off driving into town to do her shopping one Saturday morning. She would have liked to have a lie-in for once, she'd had a hard week at school. Her class had been very busy and excited making cards and decorations for the Eid party which they were going to have in school very soon. She had enjoyed it, even though she had been exhausted by the Friday afternoon.

Still, the shopping had to be done and it was a warm sunny Spring day. She felt quite cheerful as she drove along London Road heading for the shops, waving to one or two children as she passed the end of the road where her school was. Quite a few of the children in her class lived in the area. Suddenly she remembered Irfan lived along here. "Oh! I promised Irfan months ago that I would visit his new baby sister, and I've never got round to it," she thought. She stopped her car in front of number 47. As she knocked on the door she was looking forward to seeing the baby though it was hardly *new* anymore.

Mrs Aslam opened the door, a smile lighting up her face when she saw who her visitor was. "I'm sorry its taken so long to get round to seeing the baby," Mrs Hall apologized. "You're very welcome anyway, I'm afraid Irfan has gone to town with his Dad and his sister Saiqa, but they won't be long. Please come in and sit down." Mrs Aslam led the way into the lounge. "Now you hold little Salma, she has just woken up, while I go and make some tea."

Salma gurgled happily at Mrs Hall, she liked the faces she was pulling and the sounds she was making. Mrs Aslam was soon back putting a tray of tea down on the coffee table in front of Irfan's teacher.

Eid-ul-Fitr

"There's only one cup," Mrs Hall said in surprise. "Aren't you going to join me?"

"Well, you see, it's Ramadan, and I'm doing Rosa, that means I won't be having anything to eat or drink until after it has gone dark. You enjoy your tea and have a biscuit too." Mrs Aslam was not sure whether Mrs Hall knew about fasting during that month, but the teacher told her that the children in her class had talked about it a lot. She asked Mrs Aslam how many Rosa's she had done and if she knew when Ramadan would be over, and if Eid-ul-Fitr would be here. Irfan's Mum explained that it would be about five more days but nobody is quite sure until the new moon is seen. Then a message will come from the Mosque.

Suddenly the front door burst open and Irfan and Saiqa shot into the lounge. "I knew you were here Mrs Hall when I saw your car. I didn't think that you'd

133

remembered about coming to see my baby," Irfan said, puffing with excitement. Saiqa, who was four, giggled half hiding behind her brother. "I've had a lovely time but I'm afraid I'll have to go," his teacher said. She stood up and passed the baby back to its Mum. "Before you go can we show you what we've bought in town." Irfan and Saiqa opened up the carriers they were holding. "Do you like our new shoes, Mrs Hall? They're for Eid." Saiqa asked in a tiny shy voice. Mrs Hall told them both that she thought their shoes were lovely and she hoped they would wear them for the Eid party at school. As she left the children's mother asked if she would like to come again at Eid. "We'd like you to come after school and have some of our special Eid food."

"I'll be there," called Mrs Hall as she climbed back into her car. She drove off into town wondering how Mrs Aslam could look so happy and yet she must be feeling hungry. She was sure that she could not manage a month of fasting.

Ramadan

Ramadan, that special month,
Is a hard time for us all.
Grown ups fast while it is light,
And eat when darkness falls.

Allah will help us to be strong,
And show we love and care,
Rich and poor are all the same,
Hungry feelings we all share.

Ramadan reminds me now
That many do not have
The things I have that help me grow
So, Allah, Help me give.

The Hajj

It was a wet Friday morning and Mubeena rushed into school with a letter stuffed in her pocket so that it wouldn't get soggy and wet. "It's about Monday," she said, handing over the letter to her teacher. "Mum and Dad would like me to have the day off. Will it be alright Mrs Owen?"

"Let me see what the letter says," the teacher said, opening it up. After a moment she looked at Mubeena. "I think so, it's very exciting. It's just a shame about the day. Our class are going on our trip to the airport that day, so you'll miss it!"

Mubeena's usual smile faded – she'd forgotten the class trip to the airport was next Monday. The same day that she was going to wave Grandmother and Dad off. Weeks ago her Mum and Dad had said that she could go to the airport with them when Grandmother and Dad flew off to Saudi Arabia. They had planned for a long time to go and perform Hajj at Mecca. Monday was the day they would leave.

Mubeena sat very quiet at school all day and could not get interested in anything. Mrs Owen asked if she would like to paint but Mubeena shook her head. "How about the computer?" Mubeena shrugged her

shoulders. "What would you like to do?" her teacher asked. "Well," said Mubeena, "I'd like to talk about which you think I should do. I want to go on our class trip, but I also want to see Dad and Grandma off too. Please help me decide, Mrs Owen."

"Do you think your Dad and Grandma would be upset if you didn't go? Do you think you will be sorry if you choose to come with us when you'll not see Dad and Grandma for a while?" The teacher gave her something to think about.

By the end of the day Mubeena's smile had come back and she bounced up to Mrs Owen. "I've decided," she announced, "I'm going to wave Grandma and Dad off instead of coming on the trip. That way I'll not worry so much about them going off all that way. I'll be with you and my school friends every day, but I'll not be seeing them for over six weeks." Once she'd decided Mubeena felt much happier and skipped home with her friends.

Monday was all rush in Mubeena's house, the packed cases were pushed into the taxi boot, Dad's camera was nearly left behind but he remembered it and dashed back into the house to get it.

Mubeena hugged Dad and gave Grandma the biggest kiss and hug she

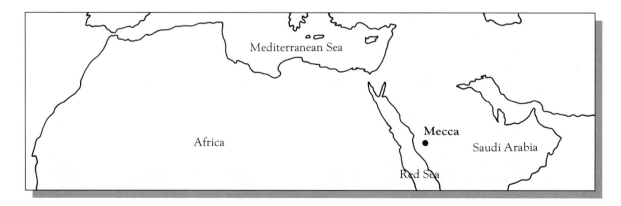

could as the two went through the customs barrier and had to leave Mum and Mubeena behind. Mum asked if there was somewhere where they could go and watch the plane for Saudi Arabia take off. A steward pointed the way to the window. From there it was possible to see down on to the runway. The plane was being filled up with the luggage. Mubeena rushed along the hallway towards the window and who should she bump into but Mrs Owen, Class 3 following on behind two by two in a long crocodile.

"Why didn't we guess?" laughed the teacher. "I didn't ask you which airport your Dad and Grandma would be flying from. It is the same one we chose for our trip." Mubeena jumped up and down as her Mum walked over to shake hands with Mrs Owen.

"All that worrying on Friday, we should have realized that you could do both: come on the trip *and* wave your Dad and Grandma off on Hajj."

"Show us which plane they're going on Mubeena," Saima, her best friend said. All the class dashed over to the huge window. There was room for all of them to stand up to the glass and watch. Soon the doors of the aeroplane were closed and the engines were roaring. Then the plane was slowly moving out towards the runway.

Class 3 were the quietest they had ever been as they watched the plane going faster and faster along, then up it went. Soon it was high up and disappearing into the clouds. The whole class cheered, then turning round Mubeena saw a tear run down her Mum's cheek, and went over to give her a hug.

"Never mind, Mum, they'll soon be back and I bet nobody has ever had such a send off before."

The Islamic calendar

The Islamic year is 354 days long. Islamic months begin with each new moon. Because the Islamic year is ten days shorter than the solar year the times of the festivals change and eventually are celebrated during all the seasons.

Muharram	30 days
Safar	29 days
Rabi-ul-Awwal	30 days
Rabi-ul-Akhir	29 days
Jamadi-ul-Awwal	30 days
Jamadi-ul-Akhir	29 days

Rajab	30 days
Sha'aban	29 days
Ramadan	30 days
Shawwal	29 days
Dhul-Qa'adah	30 days
Dhul-Hijjah	29 or 30 days

You can make a movable dual festival calendar using a large circle of card and a small circle of card both divided into 12 parts. Fasten together through the centres with a brass paper fastener.

On the outside circle write the main Christian festivals month by month, and do the same for the Islamic festivals on the inner circle.

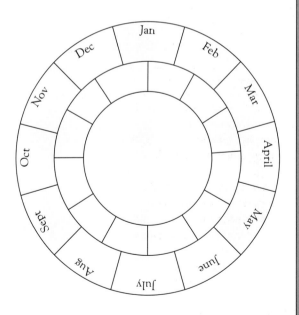

135

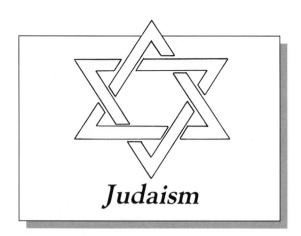

Judaism

Background

History Judaism was founded about 2000 BCE in the Middle East. Throughout their 4,000 year history Jewish people have established, lost and re-established a Hebrew nation in Palestine. In 1948, the State of Israel was set up as an independent Jewish state. Many Jews came to settle there from all over the world but many others have remained as citizens in the countries where they had long been established.

Basic beliefs Jews believe there is one God and they have a duty to keep this Covenant. Some Jews believe that a Messiah will come one day and unite all people under God. Loving God means loving your neighbour. Jewish people provide charitable help not just for people of their own faith but others too. As God's chosen people, Jews believe they have great obligations in the world. Orthodox Jews believe that the Jewish laws and teachings of the Torah must be followed today just as they were laid down in the time of Moses. Progressive Jews (these can be either Reform, Conservative, or Liberal Jews) believe that some of the Torah's teachings could be adapted to make them more relevant to life in the modern world. Orthodox Jews worship in different ways at the synagogue. Men and women worship separately in Orthodox synagogues, but sit together in Progressive, where women also take an equal part in religious life. Orthodox Jews do not permit women to become rabbis. All over the world Orthodox Jews conduct their services in Hebrew, Progressive use both Hebrew and their local language.

Places of worship Worship for Jewish people mostly takes place in the home. Communal worship takes place in the Synagogue which also serves as a place of study and as a place for social gatherings. The central feature of the Synagogue is the Ark, this contains the scrolls of the Torah. There is an embroidered curtain in front of the Ark, and a light known as the Ner Tamid that is always kept burning. There is a raised platform in the centre of the synagogue or at the end near the Ark with a reading desk or table from which the prayer leader directs the congregation in worship. The seating in the synagogue is arranged so that everyone can see the Ark and so that the procession of the Torah can pass through.

The city of Jerusalem is the most important place of pilgrimage to Jews. Zion was originally the name of one of the hills on which Jerusalem was built. 'Zion' symbolizes the place of peace and the fulfilment of Jewish dreams of a nation. The Western Wall of the Temple in the Old City is a particularly important place for prayer.

Books The Torah is the most important collection of Jewish scriptures. It is one of three parts that make up Tenakh, the 39 books of the Hebrew Bible. The Torah contains the first five books. It sets out the 613 Commandments, laws to protect human rights, and the duties of a Jew. The whole of the Torah is read out over the course of a year. Together with the reading from the Torah there is always a reading from one of the two other sections.

The Neviim (the second section of the Hebrew Bible) tells the history of the earliest Jewish settlements, the leaders and the people from about 1200 BCE. It also contains the sayings and writings of the prophets from 800 BCE. The third part of the Hebrew Bible is the Ketuvim, this contains the writings from later prophets and the psalms.

The Talmud is a collection of interpretations of the Bible, and instructions on the Jewish way of life. It is based on teachings handed down by word of mouth from the time of Moses. It is studied by those who wish to become rabbis and teachers.

The Siddur is a prayer book which contains prayers for different occasions – everyday, Sabbath and festival. It has prayers for solitary and congregational worship and reaffirms historic ties and group belonging.

Prophets and leaders Throughout the history of Judaism there have been many leaders. Their stories are documented in the Hebrew Bible.

Abraham was the first leader and 'patriarch' of Judaism. He is the father of 'monotheism' (faith in one God). He was the first to teach that there is only one God who created the world and that only God should be worshipped. Abraham's son, Isaac, was the second patriarch and his grandson, Jacob, was the third. God told Abraham to leave his home and take his family to Canaan where they would become a great nation if they obeyed his laws. During the centuries that followed the Jewish people with their leaders met with hostility forcing them to move many times. They were eventually led to freedom by Moses.

Moses is of great importance as a leader. He led the Hebrews out of captivity. He set up the Ark of the Covenant which housed the stone tablets inscribed with the 613 Commandments. He had been the person chosen by God to receive them and spread the laws contained in them. Moses' successor, Joshua, led the Israelites back to Canaan. There followed a long succession of leaders who were either judges, prophets or kings.

A rabbi is not a priest, but a teacher and community leader. All Jews can lead the services in the synagogue.

Prayers The Jewish sabbath is called Shabat and it begins at sunset on Friday and lasts until sunset on Saturday. During Shabat no work is done, that includes housework and study.

Both Orthodox and Progressive congregations have three daily services, though not necessarily in the synagogue. The Jewish day begins at sunset so the first service is known as Ma'ariv (dusk), the second is Shahrit (dawn), the third is Minha (afternoon). The prayers at Minha are considered the most valuable because it is very difficult to pray at that time of day. It is easier to put yourself in the right frame of mind for prayer either early morning or at night.

Symbols Outside most Jewish homes there is

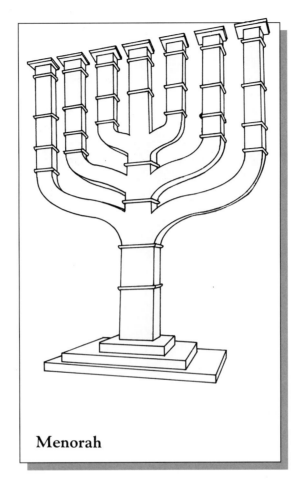

Menorah

a mezuzah. This is a small box that is attached to the right hand doorpost. It contains a parchment scroll with extracts from the Shema, a Jewish prayer. Some families also have mezuzahs on other door frames inside their houses.

The Star of David is the best known of Jewish symbols. It is made up of two interwoven triangles. It represents the shield used by King David. Another interpretation is that the centre represents the sabbath and the six corners represent the six working days.

The Menorah is a seven branched candelabrum. The original Menorah was made of gold and kept burning continually in the Temple in Jerusalem. Today it is the official symbol of Israel, but is, in fact, one of the oldest Jewish symbols. Either the Menorah or the Star of David, are displayed outside Synagogues.

Clothes Orthodox Jewish men wear a Kippah or Yamulkah – a small skullcap – at all times. A shawl, known as a Tallit, is also worn for prayers. Small leather boxes containing prayers on parchment are worn by men for weekday morning prayers. These Tefillin are worn on the forehead (near the mind) and the left upper arm (near the heart).

Food All food must be Kosher, that is prepared according to Jewish law. Animals have to be killed so that the blood drains away out of the body. It is done according to Shehita custom. Jews will only eat animals that have cloven hoofs and chew the cud, for example, cows and sheep. They may not eat pigs or rabbits. Shellfish and eels are forbidden, only fish with scales and fins can be eaten. Milk and meat products may not be prepared or eaten together. Separate utensils must be used for each.

A prayer for harvest

Bless this year for us, O our God, and bless every species of its fruits for our benefit. Bestow a blessing upon the face of the earth, and satisfy us with Thy goodness. O bless our years and make them good years; for Thine honour and glory.

Anonymous

137

Festivals

Purim (14th day of the Jewish month of Adar – February-March) Throughout their history, the Jews have been attacked by many enemies. Their survival is celebrated at Purim. The Book of Esther in the Bible is central to this festival. It tells the story of how, with God's help, Queen Esther saved the Jews from a plot against them by the evil Haman who was out to destroy them. On the evening of the start of festival day, and the following morning, the story is read out either in the home or at the Synagogue. During the story the children make a lot of noise with their voices or special rattles ('greggers'), each time the villain's name is mentioned. In some Jewish communities a huge model of Haman is made and paraded through the streets at a great carnival. As the model passes, the crowds hiss and boo, and at the end they cheer loudly when the model is finally burnt.

Pesach – Passover (15th day of Nisan, March-April) This festival celebrates the Exodus of the Israelites from slavery in Egypt which showed the Jews that they were God's chosen people. Seder is held on the first two nights of this eight day festival. Family and friends come together at home for a special meal. During this meal the Haggadah is read and sung aloud. This takes the form of four questions that are asked by the youngest person present, they are answered in the book. The foods eaten at the Seder meal are symbolic of the harsh treatment suffered by the Israelites during their slavery:
– bitter herbs represent the bitter feelings of the slaves;
– Matzot (unleavened bread) is a reminder that the Israelites had to leave Egypt in a great hurry, so there was no time for their bread to rise;
– charoset (a mixture of minced fruits moisened with wine) represents the mortar which the slaves used in building for their masters;
– 'Elijah's glass', a special glass of wine, is set at the Seder table. It expresses the hope that the prophet will return to the world to herald the arrival of the Messiah.

Pesach is a festival of deliverance and hope.

Shavuot (7 weeks after Pesach, May-June) The festival of Shavuot celebrates the receiving of the Torah at Mount Sinai. Long ago this festival was linked to the traditional Harvest Festival when people would offer part of their crop to thank God for a good harvest. Shavuot is a time of thanksgiving for both the food of the body and food for the spirit. Synagogues are decorated with flowers and plants. This reminds the people of pilgrims taking their first harvest fruits to the Temple.

Shavuot is a time when Jews affirm the high value of Hebrew education. In the past young children were taken to their first Hebrew class during Shavuot. Today some congregations have a 'graduation service'. Teenagers who have reached a level of education beyond what would be considered that of 'children', are honoured in various ways. Some young people read a passage from the Torah, others may lead the service. Families may also have a special meal to celebrate.

Rosh Hashanah and Yom Kippur (1st and 10th days of the Jewish month Tishri, September-October) Rosh Hashanah is the first day of the Jewish year. It celebrates the Creation and is also a day of Judgement. God is the judge of the world and weighs up the future of all people. This means it is a solemn time when people think about their faults and failures of the past year. A Shofar, ram's horn, is blown during the service in the Synagogue to call everyone to pray for forgiveness. It is the custom at home to eat pieces of bread and apple dipped in honey, this represents the hope for a 'sweet' New Year.

On the tenth day the time for repentance ends with Yom Kippur. This is a fast day which most people spend at the Synagogue. The special prayer, 'Kol Nidrei', opens the fast, asking pardon from God for vows made but not kept. This prepares Jews for the demands of a New Year. At the end of the day the Shofar is blown a final time.

Succot (during the Jewish month of Tishri, September-October) This 8 day festival celebrates the autumn harvest. It is the time when Jews remember the forty years that the Israelites spent wandering in the wilderness. Jewish families erect 'succahs' in their gardens. These represent the little huts Jews built to live in during their time in the desert. The roof of the succah is decorated with leaves and branches and is hung with flowers, fruit and other colourful decorations. During the week of Succot, families eat their meals in the succah, weather permitting. Each Synagogue builds a succah for the whole community. During the service at the Synagogue the worshippers carry branches in one hand and a citrus fruit in the other. These represent their worship of God with the whole of their being. The waving branches show that God is everywhere.

Simchat Torah is the day after the end of

Succot. It is a happy time, a celebration of the Torah. Most people attend the Synagogue where the last chapter of the Torah is read, followed by the first. This begins a new cycle and shows the continuity of that book. The Torah scrolls are carried round the Synagogue while children carry banners and sing songs.

Hanukah (25th day of the Jewish month of Kislev – December) Hanukah is the time when people remember the story of the regaining of the Temple in Jerusalem by the Jewish army over 2,000 years ago. The Jews cleansed the Temple but could find only a small amount of oil to light the Menorah which they needed for the rededication of the Temple to God. Miraculously the oil lasted for eight days when it was only expected to last for one.

This winter festival also lasts for eight days. On each day a special candle is lit. The usual Menorah, a seven branched candlestick, is replaced by an eight or nine branched one. Each evening another candle is lit until all eight are alight.

Parties are held with special food cooked in oil, it reminds people of the Temple oil. A special game is also played where a dreidel is spun. This is a small top with Hebrew letters on each edge. Depending on which edge the dreidel rests you take or give to the 'treat bank', usually sweets.

A Jewish prayer

The Lord bless you and keep you
The Lord make his face to shine upon you
And be gracious unto you.
The Lord turn his face unto you and give you peace.

Anonymous

The Jewish calendar

The Jewish calendar is based on both the movement of the moon and the movement of the sun. There are 12 months each of 30 or 29 days. To keep the months in harmony with the seasons an extra month is added 7 times in every 19 years. The Jewish year begins with Tishri.

Tishri	September–October
Heshvan	October–November
Kislev	November–December
Teveth	December–January
Shevat	January–February
Adar	February–March
Nisan	March–April
Ivar	April–May
Sivan	May–June
Tamuz	June–July
Av	July–August
Ellul	August–September

To calculate the Jewish year from the civil year you must add 3760. So, 1989 is 5749 on the Jewish calendar. To discover whether a particular Jewish year is a leap year, you must divide the Jewish year by 19. If the remainder is 3, 6, 8, 11, 14, 17 or there is no remainder, then it is a leap year and will have an extra month of Adar.

You can make a movable dual festival calendar using a large circle of card and a small circle of card both divided into 12 parts. Fasten together through the centres with a brass paper fastener.

On the outside circle write the main Christian festivals month by month, and do the same for the Jewish festivals on the inner circle.

Steven's special weekend

Steven didn't want to go to bed on Friday night. His head was spinning – half excited and half so nervous he felt sick.

"I'll never be able to sleep, Mum. Let me stay up a bit longer," he begged at ten o'clock.

"I was hoping for an early night, myself Steven," Mum yawned as she answered. "I've had a hard day, too, getting all the food ready for the parties tomorrow."

Mum and Steven stood beside the loaded kitchen table staring at the mountain of food. "This morning I didn't think it would all be ready in time. If we hadn't finished by the start of Shabbat, we never would have. No work can be done now until the first party's over tomorrow night."

Steven put his arm round his mother and kissed her cheek. "Thanks for everything, Mum, I know how hard you've worked for my Bar Mitzvah."

"Well it will be worth it tomorrow. Everyone is really looking forward to your special day. Now off you go to bed. You need a good night's sleep." She gently pushed him in the direction of the stairs.

Steven turned round and pulled a face. "I hope I manage to do my reading as well as I did it at my last class. A whole year of lessons at the Synagogue will be wasted if I get it wrong. My head feels empty. Say I lose my place, or I trip up, or my voice goes or ..."

"Look, Steven, you've worked very hard. Three nights a week at the Synagogue *and* Sunday afternoons – nothing will go wrong. It's just nerves. Everyone feels like this." His mother stood her ground at the foot of the stairs.

Steven remembered when his friend Paul was Bar Mitzvah last January, he had said it was a great time but a bit scary. "Just my luck to be the youngest in my class, 13 in July. All my school friends have already been Bar Mitzvah. I'm last and they'll all be there watching me. I bet they'll be thinking they're glad theirs is over with." Steven seemed to be thinking of all the worst things that could happen tomorrow and making himself even more nervous.

"If you think like that, Steven, you'll not enjoy your day at all." His Mum's voice was getting firmer. "That would be a pity. Your Dad always says that second to the day he married me, being Bar Mitzvah was the happiest day of his life. So go to bed and keep your mind on all the good things you know will happen to you this weekend." She gave him a final push up the stairs. "Goodnight! When you're ready for bed I'll send Dad up. He'll put your mind at rest."

While he cleaned his teeth and put on his pyjamas, Steven did as Mum said, he thought about the good things. Mum and Dad had already had lots of fun just planning. They'd taken hours over choosing the invitations and writing the guest list. Even longer choosing the outfits to wear. Steven had got a new suit – so had Dad. Ellen, his sister, and their Mum had taken weeks to choose their new dresses. Planning food for the parties had been fun for all of them. What had made Mum happiest of all, though, was when she got the phone call from Israel. Auntie Miriam had rung to say she would be flying over specially for his Bar Mitzvah. He thought about the look on Mum's face as she listened to the news.

Lying in bed Steven thought next about the parties – in *his* honour. He knew how lucky he was. Not every boy gets three parties. First there would be the Kidush after the service tomorrow afternoon. The food was already down at the Synagogue hall. The Kikhals and other 'nibbles' were laid out. There was just the wine to pour. Later on in the afternoon Mum's delicious mountain of food would be spread out in their dining room at home for their family and special friends. Then on Sunday there would be the party that Steven was especially looking forward to. Mum and Dad had booked some caterers to put on a spread at the Synagogue hall that night – 100 guests! They'd let him have the same disco as Paul had at his party. It was brilliant! "All this just for me," he beamed. Then there would be the presents. The family had asked him a while ago to draw up a list. "There's lots of things I'd like," he'd said showing them the list, "but if you're stuck I'm saving up to buy a computer. Money would be handy," he'd hinted.

Steven's eyes were closing. He snuggled down under the quilt. Pictures floated through his head of the things on his present list ... a skateboard ... a sportsbag ... "He's already nodded off," he heard his father whisper, "he can't be all that worried."

"Not too bad now," Steven said sleepily with one eye open. "Goodnight Dad."

"You know I felt just the same when it was my thirteenth birthday. I dreaded going up there with all the men and ..." Dad had got so carried away remembering his own Bar Mitzvah he hadn't noticed Steven was fast asleep.

Everyone was up very early the next morning. They all wanted to look their best and didn't want to rush. They were almost ready to leave the house when Auntie Miriam handed a small parcel to

Bar Mitzevah

Steven. "There'll be something else for you later, but this is from Uncle David in Israel, he was upset that he wouldn't be here." She watched as Steven put the Kippah on his head. The skullcap was beautifully embroidered with the the words 'Bar Mitzvah'.

There was a knock on the front door. It was Grandma and Grandad, they always called for the rest of the family on the way to the Synagogue. "Everybody ready?" called Grandma as she stepped into the hall.

The family stood for a minute and looked at Steven. They wanted to remember him exactly as he was. No photographs on Shabbat meant they must keep the pictures in their heads. Steven hardly said a word as they walked to the Synagogue. He felt very nervous. Paul had met up with them on the way but Steven wasn't really listening when his best friend told him everything would be fine.

To Steven the Synagogue looked especially full this Shabbat. He took a deep breath as he walked in. Ellen, Mum, Auntie Miriam and Grandma sat down in their usual place at the Synagogue. Grandma leaned over the balcony a little way to see Steven wearing the present that she and Grandad had bought him. Steven had put on the lovely white silk shawl for the first time. Mum winked at Steven as he took his place near the front with the other men. He could see how proud she was of him. "I'll not let her down," he thought, though he knew that from today on he would be judged for himself not his parents.

The service began. Steven looked around at all the family and friends gathered around. He had known them all his life, he must do his best. He heard the name

141

"Yitshak ben Yisrael" being called. Grandad went up to the Bimah and read a short passage, then he stood down to the side. "Yakov" was called next, this was only the second time his friend Paul had been called since he was Bar Mitzvah. His passage was quite long. Steven could feel his hands getting very sweaty, "At least my passage doesn't last that long," he told himself. "Nisan Dov ben Yitshak", his father's Hebrew name was called, he knew his turn would be very soon. Father's voice rang out so clearly, then he stood to the side while the next reader sung out what seemed like an endless passage. Then the call came that he had been waiting for: "Shimon Mendel ben Nisan Dov".

Steven stood up and walked to the Bimah at the call of his own Hebrew name. He took a deep breath, picked up the Yad and with it pointed to his passage on the Torah scroll. His voice sang out loud and sweetly as he concentrated hard on the passage he had practised for so long. Then it was over.

He stood to the side, he saw a shower of sparkling sweets in the air all around him. "I did it," he thought. His whole body relaxed. He heard the happy calls of "Mazeltov" as everyone congratulated him and his family. The giggling children dashed out of their places to pick up the sweets, he remembered how he used to love that part of Bar Mitzvah when he was little.

Steven's had been the last reading, two of his cousins came forward to dress the Torah in it's covers. Everyone was quiet while the holy scroll was paraded round the Synagogue and then put away in the Ark. As he walked back to his place he realized that now he was Bar Mitzvah he could be called up to read quite a lot. "It

wasn't so bad after all."

At the Kidush in the Synagogue hall after the service everyone told Steven how well he had done. When they had all shaken his hand and were busily tucking into the food, Mum made her way over to him. "Last night you had me worried," she laughed, "I hardly slept for imagining you falling off the Bimah or something. But you were wonderful. Even Auntie Miriam said she had never heard a more beautiful Bar Mitzvah voice. 'Now let's enjoy your special weekend. It's time to celebrate!''

A tree in Israel

The Hebrew New Year Festival for Trees (Rosh Hashanah L'ilanot) around the middle of January, is celebrated by Jews in many parts of the world. As well as planting trees in their own neighbourhoods, communities will collect money to be given for trees to be planted in Israel. The festival is important for the environment. It has helped reclaim land which was once desert.

Abigail sat at her desk in front of her bedroom window. She looked up from her writing and stared out across the snowy New York skyline. She loved the city, and though she often heard other people say it was a dirty, noisy, overcrowded place – she thought it was beautiful. In fact, watching that pink January afternoon sunset, she knew she wouldn't like to live anywhere else in the world. Picking up her pen again, Abigail carried on writing. It was an important letter. It was going to be sent by "air mail", and she was being extra careful with her writing and spelling.

The letter was to her cousin Sarah in Israel. They'd sent picture postcards to each other ever since they'd learned to sign

their names. When they were tiny Mom or Dad would do the writing and they would put their names on the bottom. Now they were both nine years old and could manage long letters by themselves. They swapped news about the family, and told each other what was going on at their schools. Abigail read Sarah's letters over and over, life on the Kibbutz was so different it amazed her!

One day she would like to go to Israel and have a holiday with Sarah. But for now she was happy in the cosy apartment with the bustling street down below. She wrote about the snow and how prettily it had settled on the trees in Central Park, bending their branches. Abigail wrote: ...

Talking of trees brings me to the main point of this letter. I'm asking you to do me a favour, Sarah. You know that even though I'm a city girl, I'm just crazy about trees and flowers. Well this year I want to do something really special and I need your help. A couple of days ago I pestered my friends to help me organize a cookie stall at our school's Parents afternoon. We baked stacks of different shaped cookies and decorated them really carefully. We cut the shape of a huge tree out of cardboard and pinned it to our classroom wall. We threaded thin string through holes in the cookies and tied them to the tree.

Oh, it looked really pretty!

We had lots more cookies on plates round about too. Everyone thought it was a great idea, and we'd sold out of cookies in 15 minutes. My friend John's Mom came by and bought ten dollars worth as soon as we'd opened. I guessed John would be having cookies for his snack for the rest of the week. I was right! Anyway the idea worked well and we raised lots of money. I'd told my friends what it was for right at the beginning. They'd been happy about it because we talk a lot about conservation and things in school.

So this is where you come in.

Mom took the money we'd earned. She went to the bank and had a money order made out and sent to your Mom in Israel. It should come pretty soon and this is what I'd like you to do – please please please!!!! Buy a neat little tree. I don't mind what kind you choose, and when it is the festival of New Year for Trees on the 15th Shevat, which is any day now, plant it on your Kibbutz in my name.

My friends don't mind. I've told them that I'll help them with another cookie stall later in the year and they can choose what to send the money for.

I hope this letter and the MONEY reach you in time!

> Write soon
> Shalom
> Love from Abigail

She folded up the letter and put it in the envelope. As she sealed it she looked up – it would be lovely to see that tree in Israel some day, she thought. Then she put on her jacket, gloves, hat and snowboots and headed for the gorgeous crisp snow on the side-walks. She'd enjoy taking that letter to the mailbox.

Tree planting ceremony

Trees are planted at the Hebrew New Year Festival of Rosh Hashanah L'ilanot.
This festival is celebrated around about the middle of January.

Haman's plan goes wrong

A story for Purim (The Festival of Lots)

"How can I thank you, Mordecai?" King Ahasuerus asked the man who had just saved his life.

Mordecai shook his head, there was nothing he needed just then. "Maybe something will crop up some time," he told the King, "for now it's good enough to know that you are safe and the plotters are no longer on the loose."

"Well I'll remember what you did and reward you some time in the future," the King announced jotting down the event in his note book. Then he turned and left the courtroom, he was a busy man. Soon he forgot his promise. King Ahasuerus had a lot on his mind. His wedding had taken place not very long before, the arrangements had taken much preparation and he was behind in his work. Though he did not realize it, he had married Mordecai's niece, Esther. They were Jewish and at that time the Jews had many enemies planning to kill them. The King and Esther would be in danger if it became known that she was a Jew, her uncle warned her to keep it secret. Being so busy the King did not notice how badly his Prime Minister, Haman, was treating the people of his country. Haman would walk through the city of Shushan with his followers threatening the people to make them bow down to him. Most people knelt down quickly when they heard his procession coming along, but not Mordecai.

"How dare you," snarled Haman. "Who do you think you are? Everyone bows down to me!"

"I was just wondering who you think

143

you are," Mordecai replied calmly. "I only bow before God, Prime Minister."

Haman was furious. "I'll get that man. It's the last time he'll show me up," he thought. His mind was working fast on a plan to get rid of the trouble-making Mordecai and all the other Jews too. He went to the King, "You don't realize, Your Majesty, what traitors these Jews are to you. They refuse to obey your orders and please themselves what they do."

"If this is true, then it's a very serious problem. I've been so busy I had no idea things were getting so dangerous. What do you think we should do about it, Prime Minister?" King Ahasuerus had great trust in Haman.

"I suggest that we get rid of all Jews in our country. We'll choose a day to do it by drawing lots. Give an order to the governors in all parts of the kingdom, that Jews in their area must be killed on that day." Ahasuerus was listening carefully but did not notice the evil gleam in Haman's eyes as he persuaded him. The lots were cast. The day was chosen.

Soon the news of what the King had ordered spread. Terrified Jews begged Mordecai to plead with the King. After all, they remembered, he still owed Mordecai a favour. "He's long since forgotten about that," Mordecai said. But he was determined to try and help his people. He arranged a secret meeting with his niece, Esther.

"I've heard about the plot, Uncle, and though I'm terribly worried about you and all our people, I just can't help," she was sobbing.

"You must Esther. You're our only hope. The King will listen to you." Mordecai tried to give her confidence.

"It's difficult. Not even I can see the King unless he commands it." Esther was still feeling helpless but at last agreed to try.

The next day she bravely faced her husband. "I have only come to give you an invitation. It would make me very happy if you and Haman would come and have dinner with me tomorrow night. There will be all your favourite dishes, and the very best wine. Please say you'll come."

"How can I resist?" smiled the King, "I'm sure Haman will be delighted too."

Later that night King Ahasuerus was reading through his note book, remembering all he had done since he became ruler, turning a page he came across a note he'd written a while ago. Suddenly be jumped up. "Oh, no!" he thought. "I'd forgotten all about this. My promise to Mordecai. I never rewarded him for saving my life." He called for his Prime Minister right away. "I know it's late but I need your advice, Haman. Tell me what you think I should do to reward someone for doing a good deed for me."

The Prime Minister's first thought was that the King must be talking about *him*, so he craftily suggested, "Well . . . You should let everyone in the country know about this wonderful person. Why not put him on your horse wearing your finest clothes and make all the people bow down before him." (Secretly that had always been Haman's greatest wish.)

The King thought that it was a great idea. "Right, tomorrow Mordecai will ride through the streets of the city and you can lead him to make sure everyone bows."

Mordecai! In his rage Haman was speechless. He knew that he had to do what the King had commanded but then, when the day came for killing the Jews – he would get his revenge. The next day he sulked as he carried out the King's wishes, but later enjoyed himself by preparing the gallows for Mordecai to be used on that allotted day. Later that evening he sat quietly at the table which Esther had prepared with a most beautiful meal, his head was still full of hatred. He could think of nothing else. The King hardly noticed how silent Haman was, he was far more worried about Esther – she ate nothing, hardly spoke, and seemed so sad.

"I can't bear to see you so unhappy," he told her. "If there's a problem maybe I could help?"

"There's something I must tell you," she announced sadly. "I don't think you realize what's going on. The Jews in your country love you, their King, and would never harm you. Yet, it has been ordered that they should be killed. I have to tell you, too, that I am a Jew. I will be killed. You have been tricked and Haman is the one who has tricked you. He is behind this wicked plan."

The King's face was solemn. Why hadn't he realized what Haman was up to? "I trusted you," he spoke gravely to his Prime Minister, "and this is what you do. I will punish you for this." "Guards, take him away!"

Quickly he sent out a new order to all his governors. The Jews should not be killed. Throughout that country, though, the Jews had many enemies who were glad of the excuse to attack them. They ignored the King's new order. When the allotted day arrived and many Jews were in danger of being killed the King sent words to encourage them to defend themselves. They did – and they won. Wicked Haman was punished and Mordecai became the new Prime Minister helping the King to rule more justly.

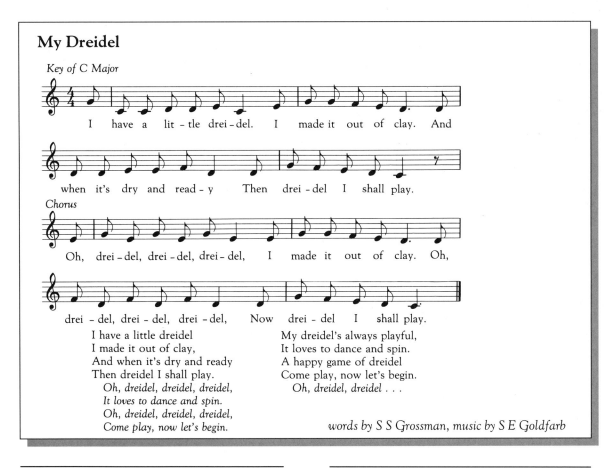

My Dreidel

Key of C Major

I have a lit-tle drei-del. I made it out of clay. And
when it's dry and read-y Then drei-del I shall play.

Chorus

Oh, drei-del, drei-del, drei-del, I made it out of clay. Oh,
drei-del, drei-del, drei-del, Now drei-del I shall play.

I have a little dreidel
I made it out of clay,
And when it's dry and ready
Then dreidel I shall play.
Oh, dreidel, dreidel, dreidel,
It loves to dance and spin.
Oh, dreidel, dreidel, dreidel,
Come play, now let's begin.

My dreidel's always playful,
It loves to dance and spin.
A happy game of dreidel
Come play, now let's begin.
Oh, dreidel, dreidel . . .

words by S S Grossman, music by S E Goldfarb

Recipe for Charoset

A traditional Passover dish

2 medium apples (peel and core first)
A handful of chopped dates
   (stones removed)
1 tablespoon of candied peel
Half a teacup of peeled almonds
Apple juice

Chop all the ingredients finely or mince
   them together.
Form into a paste using apple juice. Add
   cinnamon to taste.

Recipe for Latkes

A traditional Hanuka dish

4 potatoes
1 grated onion
1 tablespoon self-raising flour
2 eggs
salt and pepper

Grate the potatoes and drain well.
Stir in the grated onion, the flour, the eggs
   and the seasoning.
Fry tablespoons of the mixture in oil until
   brown on both sides. Serve hot.

Follow-up activities

Try to arrange a visit to a synagogue, or to
a Jewish museum.

Find out if any Jewish people live in the
community around your school. Ask if
they would be willing to talk to the
children and if they have any Jewish
artefacts they would be willing to show
them.

Try to find examples of the Hebrew script.
Discuss how some religions have a
'language', and how this remains common
in whichever country of the world the
worship takes place.

Locate Israel on a world map. Look on the
supermarket shelves to find any products
from Israel. Make a topic book on Israel
finding out about its history etc.

Find out about the Kibbutz movement.
Discuss everyday life in a Kibbutz.

There are festivals of light in many
religions. Make a display of light and how
it features in these festivals. Find as many
forms of light as you can.

Use your school or local library to find out
about the lives of well-known 20th century
Jews. For example: Albert Einstein, Golda
Meir, Anne Frank, Hannah Senesh, David
Ben-Gurion, Jonas Salk, Leonard
Bernstein, Yehudi Menuhin.

Discuss the way Shabat might affect some
Jewish children at school in Britain.

Find out more about what 'keeping a
kosher home' means.

Sikhism

Background

History Sikhism was founded by Guru Nanak in Punjab in north west India in the 15th century CE. He travelled preaching his beliefs and gathering followers throughout the subcontinent and visited both Muslim and Hindu holy places. He announced who was to succeed him as Guru when he died. This tradition of selection continued for all the following 9 Gurus. The word Sikh means disciple. During the 18th century there was much torture and cruelty, many believers were killed. The Sikhs were forced to become militaristic in order to survive.

Basic beliefs There is neither Muslim nor Hindu – all men and women are equal. There is only one God – present everywhere. To love God,you must first learn to love one another. Equality is demonstrated at the Golden Temple at Amritsar which has four doors, so that people of any caste or religion can enter from any side. The steps lead down into the temple so that everyone however humble must go still lower to meet with God. Some Sikhs believe we have many lives – animal, plant, mineral.

Sewa is another basic belief of Sikhs which means service to others. Guru Gobind Singh said that Sikhs should give one tenth of their income to others. There are also other ways of service. For example some Sikhs do voluntary work in hospitals or day care centres and some do translation work. Sewa can also involve talking to others about God, not to convert them but to encourage people to think about their own beliefs. All people should believe in and love God it does not matter whether you are a Hindu, a Muslim or follow any other religion. Some Sikhs will do Sewa by helping clean and maintain the Gurdwara or by looking after shoes whilst the owners are attending the service inside.

Khalsa is the special *brotherhood* of the Sikhs. For their act of faith Guru Gobind Rai named his followers Singh for all males, (which means 'lion'), and Kaur for all females, (which means 'princess'). He also changed his own name to Singh instead of Rai.

Place of worship A Sikh temple is known as a Gurdwara – 'God's House'. It can be purpose built or a simple converted house. No alcohol, tobacco or drugs can be taken inside. Each Gurdwara has a kitchen attached where a meal known as the langar is prepared and served. Inside the Gurdwara gifts of food or money are offered, Sikhs bow to the Holy Book before sitting down.

As well as the famous Golden Temple of Amritsar there are three other temples of special importance. They are at Patna, Nander and Anandpur.

Leaders Guru means teacher. After Nanak (the first Guru) came 9 other Gurus – the last one was assassinated in 1708 CE. The last Guru (Gobind Singh) announced that after him the Holy Book (Granth Sahib) would be the *teacher* and be called Guru.

Prayers Sikhs pray every day and they can pray while doing everyday activities but they should pray before sunrise. Japji Sahib, the morning prayer, has 38 verses. Some Sikhs recite them all, others just a few of them. Those with little time for prayer will repeat over and over 'Waheguru' (Wonderful Lord). Rahiras are the evening prayers of thanks. A service in the Gurdwara has a set content of hymns which are sung. Sikhs have no special day for worship. Worship usually takes place every day, especially the 'day of rest' of the particular country the Gurdwara is in.

Clothes The Patkha is a piece of cloth which young boys use to cover their hair until they learn to tie a turban. The turban has traditionally been worn in India but was adopted as a symbol of Sikhism by Guru Gobind Singh. Sikh women often wear shalwar and kemeez which is the traditional clothing in the Punjab region of India. Shoes are removed before entering the Gurdwara.

Books The Guru Granth Sahib, (the most Holy Book of the Sikhs), may be read in the Gurdwara by any man or woman. Some Gurdwaras have a full-time reader (a Granthi). When the Holy Book is read it is placed on a special platform and shaded by a canopy. A fan is waved over it as a sign of respect. Guru Granth Sahib is called Guru because it replaced human Gurus. On special occasions it is read from beginning to end, this takes about 48 hours.

Food At each service in the Gurdwara,

Karah Prasad is shared between members of the faith. A meal is served in the langar room, and anyone of any faith can share this. Sikhs have a special ceremonial drink called Amrit (this means nectar). The drink is made from sugar crystals dissolved in water and stirred with a sword. It is drunk at festival times, at the Khalsa initiation ceremonies and when a new baby is brought to the Gurdwara.

Sikhs will only eat meat from animals killed in a humane way, some choose to be vegetarians, no meat is eaten at the Gurdwara.

Symbols There are five symbols known as the 5 K's, because their names in Punjabi begin with K: Kesh is the uncut hair. It is a symbol of devotion to God and *men* usually cover it by a turban. Kanga is the comb which keeps the hair in place. It is an indication of cleanliness. Kara is the steel bracelet worn on the right wrist to symbolize the unity of the Sikhs. Kirpan is the sword that symbolizes the duty of Sikhs to defend truth and the weak. Kaccha are special short trousers worn by the Sikhs for ease of movement. A further Sikh symbol is the Khanda a double edged sword.

A Sikh prayer

"There is One God. His name is Eternal Truth. He is the maker of all things. He is without fear and without enmity. His image is timeless. He is not born; neither does he die to be born again. By the grace of the Guru he is made known to men."

Guru Nanak

The 5 K's

Kirpan

Kanga

Kara

Kesh

Kaccha

Festivals

There are two main kinds of Sikh festival. Those shared with Hindus are usually ancient Indian celebrations but with special significance to Sikhs. There are also Sikh celebrations to remember events in the lives of the Gurus. These festivals are known as Gurpurbs.

Guru Nanak's Birthday This festival is celebrated on the full moon day in November. It starts two days before with continuous reading of the Granth Sahib in the Gurdwara. The reading finishes on the morning of the full moon when the usual Sikh service takes place. When this is over lectures are given and stories of the Guru are told. The langar room is open all day and more and more people arrive at the Gurdwara as the day goes on. In India there are usually processions with the Granth Sahib carried at the head.

The Martyrdom of Guru Arjan Dev This festival is celebrated in the early summer time (May-June). It is a lively festival with a celebration, meal and a special drink of Shabil, which consists of milk, sugar and water (like a milkshake) is drunk throughout the third day. The two days prior to the festival are spent reading the Granth Sahib in the Gurdwara. Guru Arjan Dev was the first Sikh martyr. It was this Guru who had the hymns of all the other Gurus written down.

Baisakhi This festival is held in April – a time of harvest in India. It celebrates the founding of Khalsa, the brotherhood of Sikhs, by the 10th Guru Gobind Singh. He initiated the first five disciples to become the holy order of Khalsa, and began the wearing of the five K symbols. Harvest time is celebrated all over India, and has been from ancient times. It is especially important for Sikhs. Today this festival is both serious worship and fun. In the Gurdwara the Granth Sahib is read continuously for 48 hours before the festival. On Baisakhi Day prayers are said and new members often initiated. There are processions in the streets, food is shared and charity given.

Hola Mohalla This is the festival which is held at the same time as Hindus celebrate Holi. It is a three day festival originally a time for warrior training, with mock battles, wrestling, and horsemanship competitions. It is still celebrated in similar ways at Anandpur and other parts of the Punjab.

Diwali This festival is of less importance to Sikhs these days but is similar to the Hindu festival. It celebrates the release from prison of the 6th Guru, Hargobind. Sikhs share with Hindus the Festival of Light – they illuminate the Golden Temple and celebrate with lights and fireworks as well as prayer.

Prayer

O True God, What is there, which is not present in Your House?
Everything exists in Your House, One to whom you give, shall receive the same.
He will constantly go on singing Your praises and glories, and will fix Your Name in his heart.

From the Anand

Gurinder is named

Prem and Harjinder had taken turns this morning in the bath. Harjinder had jumped in and out in thirty seconds flat. Mum told her to get back in. "Today is important," she said. "Put some bubble bath in and have a good scrub." Then it was Prem's turn, after twenty minutes of splashes Mum came upstairs to make sure that he hadn't flooded the bathroom. "Come on, get out, Prem, we haven't got all day, the water must be stone cold by now," she said as she passed him the towel and pulled out the plug.

The twins put on their best clothes, it was the first time that they had worn these outfits because they had been specially bought for today. Harjinder liked the way her scarf matched her shalwar and kemeez, she wore a sweat-shirt and jeans most days but enjoyed feeling dressed up for special occasions. Prem stood in front of the mirror, "I'll never be able to do it," he said in a bad temper. "I've tried three times to fasten this turban and it just keeps slipping down over my eyes." "I'll go and ask Dad to come and give you another lesson," Harjinder offered. "It's got to be perfect today, if it slips over your eyes whilst we are at the Gurdwara you'll miss everything." His sister giggled as she dashed downstairs to bring Dad back up to help Prem.

Downstairs Dad had just finished bathing and dressing the baby. Harjinder thought her little brother looked so lovely in his new suit, wrapped up so snugly in a soft white shawl. Dad put the baby into the carrycot and called to Mum who was busy packing carrier bags in the kitchen. "Prem's having turban trouble again, I'm just going up to help him. The baby's ready

in the carrycot so we are just waiting for you and Prem – better hurry up!"

Dad dashed off upstairs to hear Prem's frustrated shouts coming from the bedroom and soon he had the job done.

Harjinder went to help Mum in the kitchen. She took the carrier bags that Mum had packed and put them into the car. There was one special parcel which was light and very carefully wrapped. Prem carried that one and put it gently down in the car boot. He knew that it was the special cloth that Mum and Dad were giving to the Gurdwara as a gift to celebrate the naming of their baby. Prem and Harjinder had seen it in the cupboard weeks ago, then Mum had explained that it was a cloth to cover the Holy Book. It is called a Romala and had been sent from the Punjab by their uncle when the baby was born. Mum had put it away in the cupboard ready for today.

At last they were all in the car. Before Dad switched on the engine he did a quick check, "Have we got everything?" he asked, "Vegetables, rice, ghee, sugar, flour? Romala? Prem, Harjinder, the baby?" He joked. Harjinder looked at the carrycot and made sure that the seatbelt was safely fastened around it.

The twins were laughing, "You would hardly notice him today. He's so quiet. Usually he's yelling loudly." "Do you think he knows it's his special day, and he's trying to be especially good?" asked Prem.

The journey to the Gurdwara passed quickly, Dad parked the car and friends helped to carry all the food inside. The twins had never felt so excited and nearly forgot to take off their shoes before they went into the temple. Mum carefully lifted the baby out of the carrycot and took him

A Sikh naming ceremony

into the temple, he was just beginning to wake. "Uh-Oh!" whispered Harjinder to Prem, "he's bound to start his howling the minute the prayers begin."

Everyone was ready, the gifts had been handed over, the baby had been welcomed, and the twins had sat themselves down as close behind Mum and Dad as they could get. They wanted to see everything that was going on. They felt important sitting so near to the Guru Granth Sahib.

The prayers began. The baby did not make one sound all the way through even when the drop of Amrit was put on his tongue with the sword. The twins were glad to see Mum drink the rest, it would take far too long for their baby to drink the whole dishful.

Now the next part was what they were really looking forward to, the choosing of the baby's name. Mum, Dad and the Granthi opened up the Guru Granth Sahib. The Granthi's finger pointed to the first letter on the left hand page. Prem couldn't make out what it was, and was getting impatient as the three grown-ups chattered on.

At last Dad stood up, "Our baby will be called Gurinder Singh," he announced with a smile. The twins hugged each other now they had a name for their little brother. Later, when they were with their friends in the langar eating their meal, they could hardly believe how good and quiet he had been in the temple. "Not one sound out of him all afternoon," said Harjinder. "Maybe he really did know it was his special day."

The faithful Khalsa

Every spring the festival of Baisakhi is celebrated in many parts of India and has been for centuries. To Sikhs it marks the beginning of the brotherhood of Khalsa.

In 1699 CE Guru Gobind Singh and his followers had come together to celebrate the harvest at Anandpur. A great crowd of them had gathered around a huge tent which had been set up on top of a hill.

Sikhs had been attacked for a long time because of their love of God and the Guru had decided that it was time to put a stop to this. He knew that in order to defend themselves Sikhs needed to have great courage and so he decided that there at Anandpur he would put his followers to the test.

In front of the tent he announced to the crowd, sword in hand, that he wanted a volunteer to come forward and die for the faith.

The crowd was silent, everyone was shocked at such a request. Could he be serious? Then after a pause one man went slowly forward towards the tent. Daya Ram was willing to die for God. Whilst the crowd watched in silence the two men walked steadily into the tent.

Moments later the crowd recoiled in horror to see the Guru reappear holding high his sword covered with blood. As silence returned he repeated his request, asking for a second volunteer to come forward and give his life for God. Surely no-one would agree to go into that tent and die so horribly, but after just a few moments a man stepped forward out of the crowd to follow Gobind Singh into that tent.

The silent crowd heard for a second time the swish of the sword blade and watched as the Guru stepped from the tent with blood dripping from his sword.

Three more times the terrifying request was made, with three more brave and willing volunteers offering their lives to God. The crowd became more and more horrified wondering where it was going to end, many ran off in terror.

The Guru called after them to stay saying he wished to show them something. As the crowd settled nervously to watch what would happen next, Gobind Singh went into the tent alone. When he reappeared he had with him the five volunteers all unharmed. He then presented each one with a Kirpan, a Kara, and Kaccha, and commanded that the five should not cut their hair – Kesh. He then gave each one a Kanga to keep their hair clean.

He announced that because of their bravery they would become a brotherhood known as the Khalsa, and from that time all in the brotherhood would be equal. To prove this all would have the same name: Singh for men, and women would have the name Kaur.

With all these special things, Guru Gobind Singh warned his followers, Sikhs would be easily noticed wherever they went, and so they must always be seen as brave and good.

As that day of Baisakhi drew to a close over two thousand people had joined the Khalsa and had dedicated their lives to God.

The donkey of Anandpur

The pots were stacked high and heavy on the tired old donkey's laden back. Working for the potter meant that Jumu spent every day from dawn to dusk struggling along with loads of clay or piles of pots. Sometimes the pain in his poor old back and tired wobbling legs was so bad he would bray in agony as he plodded on.

What made it even worse were the goads and giggles of the people prodding him at the road side, he hated that teasing. Couldn't they see his pain or hear his cries? Yet still Jumu patiently trudged on, it was important that he did a good job, the potter relied on his help.

It was really hot, getting on for midday when the hand gently reached down and patted his bowed head as he walked along. "Somebody cares!" thought the donkey, looking up to see Guru Gobind Singh passing through the city. Just for a moment the Guru stopped on his journey. The sad expression in the eyes of the donkey and the cruel jibes of the passers-by bothered him. He thought, "People seem to think it's alright to treat a donkey in that way, but they wouldn't dare tease and torment the animal like that if, say, it was a tiger." Then as he carried on his journey with that thought in his mind an idea came to him.

Later in the afternoon in the shade of the banyan tree Jumu was having his usual rest while the potter took a tea-break. Suddenly the tree began to rustle and two men crept around from behind it and fed Jumu a crisp apple. When the last juicy bit was swallowed they gently led him away very quietly so that no-one around noticed a thing.

The rescuers led Jumu along the quietest streets and alleys until he again came face to face with the Guru. Again his nose was gently patted, he felt he could trust this man. Why then was this old tiger skin being placed over Jumu's bent back, and stranger still, why was he being led back towards the city? Then, why oh why was he being set free in the middle of all these people? The same people who goad and tease him. This Guru had confused him.

Worse was to come. People began to scream and charge around in panic. Market stalls were tipped over and the fruit and vegetables rolled everywhere. As the stall holders ran off Jumu heard them scream, "Let's get out of here quickly, it's a tiger!" And soon, he had the market place all to himself.

The confusion vanished and all that Jumu could think about was the delicious feast surrounding him. So much to choose from, he could pick all his favourite vegetables.

His stomach full, the loyal Jumu thought about the potter and how he should be back at work. He made his way back to the banyan tree where he had been left, ready to be loaded with his next pile of pots. What a shock he got as he trotted up to the potter only to see him turn and run away screaming in terror at the sight of Jumu.

His head full of confusion, the forest seemed the only place for Jumu now, so he headed for the trees. Just as he reached the edge of the city a sudden beating of loud hunting drums terrified him. He ran as fast as he could towards the forest turning his head around just long enough to glimpse the hunting party chasing closely behind him. "I don't believe it," Jumu thought. "The Guru I thought was my friend is leading my enemies. How could he?" Jumu was shocked, bewildered and soon began to bray in fear. The hunting party stopped in their tracks at that hee-haw cry.

"That's no tiger", cried one of the hunters. "Just look what has happened to his stripes." The amazed hunters watched the tiger chasing round and round the nearby tree. Smiles spread across their

Follow-up activities

Arrange a visit to a Gurdwara. Prepare the children by discussion of basic Sikh beliefs.

Invite a Sikh into school to demonstrate to the children how to tie a turban. Discuss the skills involved. Let the children have a try.

Make a frieze of the Golden Temple using gold foil and other collage materials.

Work through a topic on hair. Is your hairstyle important to you? Why? Look at different hairstyles, collect pictures of fashionable styles. Can you find any hairstyles which are particularly linked with beliefs? Many people who are not Sikhs grow their hair very long, discuss the skills involved in plaiting and braiding hair. These skills are greatly valued in some communities. Ask parents to demonstrate.

Find out more about the Bangra dances of India and look at Indian musical instruments.

Discuss the problems that Sikhs have met in this country, for example joining the police force. How could the problems be resolved? The wearing of crash helmets became compulsory when riding a motorcycle. Why did this create a problem? How could this be resolved? Can you find other areas which would prove difficult to a Sikh? What other form of religious dress or customs would prove a source of difficulty in some jobs or in some school activities?

faces as the tiger skin hooked on to a branch to reveal poor frightened Jumu the potter's donkey. When he heard the roars of laughter coming from the hunting party Jumu realized that he was no longer in danger from them and began to feel much calmer.

The Guru stepped forward and reached out his hand to Jumu who was still puzzled about why his friend should be there. Then when that gentle hand was rubbing his nose

softly again Jumu felt he was right to trust this man and stood quietly, contented to listen whilst the Guru spoke to the crowd which had gathered.

Guru Gobind Singh told his followers to always remember the donkey. "Jumu still acted like a donkey even though to you he looked like a tiger. So you must remember that when you wear our Khalsa uniform you must be sure to act like a Sikh, it is not enough just to look like one."

Bibliography

Buddhism

The Buddhist World, Anne Bancroft, Macdonald, 1984.
Festivals of the Buddha, The Living Festivals Series, Anne Bancroft, RMEP, 1983.
Prince Siddhartha, Jonathan Landaw & Janet Brooke, Wisdom Books, 1984.
Our Culture – Buddhist, Jenny Wood, Franklin Watts, 1988.
A Life of Buddha for Children, Christina Albes, The Buddhist Publishing Society, 1974.
Life of Buddha-Buddhism for Primary, Ven Pemaloka, Singapore Buddhist Mission, 1983.
The Life of Buddha, John Snelling, Wayland, 1987.
The Story of Buddha, Jonathan Landaw, Helmkunt Press.

Hinduism

I am a Hindu, Aggrwal & Fairclough, Franklin Watts, 1986.
Hinduism, Dictionaries of World Religions, Patricia Bahree, Batsford Educational, 1984.
The Five Sons of King Pandu – The Story of the Mahabharata, retold by Elizabeth Seeger, Dent, 1970.
Hindus and Hinduism, Beliefs and Believers, Partha and Swasti Mitter, Wayland, 1982.
Hinduism, I.G. Edmonds, Franklin Watts, 1979.
The Living Festivals Series – Holi, Janis Hannaford, RMEP, 1983.
The Living Festivals Series – Divali, Howard March, RMEP, 1983.
Wedding Day, Joan Solomon, Hamish Hamilton, 1985.
The Hindu World, Patricia Bahree, Macdonald, 1984.
Stories from the Hindu World, Jamila Gavin, Macdonald, 1986.
City Links – Hindu Stories (5), June Jones, Blackie, 1987.
Sweet-tooth Sunil, Joan Solomon, Hamish Hamilton, 1985.

Christianity

The Christian World, Alan Brown, Macdonald, 1984.
The Christmas Book, Susan Baker, Macdonald, 1980.
The Easter Book, Jenny Vaughan, Macdonald, 1980.
Children's Prayers from around the World, Lion Books, 1981.
The Living Festivals Series – Christmas, Antony Ewens, RMEP, 1982.
The Living Festivals Series – Easter, Noma Fairbairn & Jack Priestly, RMEP, 1982.
The Living Festivals Series – Hallowe'en, All Souls & All Saints, Antony Ewens, RMEP, 1982.
The Living Festivals Series – Holy Week, Noma Fairbairn and Jack Priestly, RMEP, 1982.
The Living Festivals Series – Shrove Tuesday and Ash Wednesday, Margaret Davidson, RMEP, 1982.
Learning about the Church, Felicity Henderson, Lion Books, 1984.
Here are the people, Peter Watkins and Erica Hughes, Franklin Watts, 1984.
Colin's Baptism, Olivia Bennett, Hamish Hamilton, 1986.
Mother Teresa, Charlotte Gray, Exley, 1988.
The Christian Church, Christopher Wright, Batsford, 1982.
Christians and Christianity, Beliefs and Believers, Leonard F. Hobley, Wayland, 1979.
Easter Book, Mary Batchelor, Lion Books, 1987.
How our Bible came to us, Meryl Doney, Lion Books, 1985.

Islam

The Muslim World, Richard Tames, Macdonald, 1982.
Stories from the Muslim World, Huda Khattab, Macdonald, 1987.
City Links – Muslim Stories, June Jones, Blackie, 1986.
Shabnam's day out, Joan Solomon, Hamish Hamilton, 1980.
Gifts and Almonds, Joan Solomon, Hamish Hamilton, 1980.
A Muslim Family in Britain, Steve Harrison and David Shepherd, Pergamon Press, 1980.
Islamic Worship, Founders of Faith, R. Bruce, Holt, Rinehart & Winston, 1985.
Muhammad, Founders of Faith, R. Bruce, Holt Rinehart & Winston, 1984.
The Story of Islam, Antony Kamm, Cambridge, 1976.
Living in Makkah, City Life, Shadiya Suich, Macdonald, 1987.
Today's World – Islam, Christopher Barlow,

Batsford, 1982.
The Living Festivals – Ramadan & Id-ul-fitr, Janis Hannaford, RMEP, 1983.
The Life of Muhammad, Religious Stories, Maryam Davis, Wayland, 1987.
Muslim Festivals, Festivals, M.M. Ahsan, Wayland, 1985.
Picture reference book of the world of Islam, Hodder & Stoughton, 1976.

Judaism

The Jewish World, Douglas Charing, Macdonald, 1983.
Stories from the Jewish World, Sybil Sheridan, Macdonald, 1987.
Sam's Passover, Lynne Hannigan, A. & C. Black, 1985.
Jewish Worship, World Religions, J. Rose, Holt, Rinehart & Winston, 1985.
Dictionary of World Religions – Judaism, Angela Wood, Batsford, 1984.
I am a Jew, Clive Lawton & Chris Fairclough, Franklin Watts, 1986.
Being a Jew, Looking into World Religions, Angela Wood, Batsford, 1987.
Judaism, Religions of the World, Myer Domnitz, Wayland, 1986.
The Living Festivals Series – Passover, Lynne Schofield, RMEP, 1982.
The Living Festivals Series – Chanukah, Lynne Schofield, RMEP, 1982.
Israel – The land and its people, Countries, Danah Zohar, Macdonald, 1977.
Passport to Israel, Clive A. Lawton, Franklin Watts, 1987.
The Ancient Jews – How they lived in Canaan, Linda Matchan, Canongate, 1980.

Sikhism

Understanding your Sikh Neighbour, by Piara Singh Sambhi, Lutterworth Educational,

Thinking about Sikhism, W. Owen Cole, Lutterworth, 1980.
Sikh Festivals, Dr Sukhbir Singh Kapoor, Wayland, 1985.
Guru Nanak and the Sikh Gurus, Ranjit Arora, Wayland, 1987.
Sikhs and Sikhism, Beliefs and Believers, Sukhbir S. Kapoor, Wayland, 1982.
The Living Festival Series – Guru Nanak's Birthday, Margaret Davidson, RMEP, 1982.
A Sikh Family in Britain, W. Owen Cole, Pergamon, 1973.
Our Sikh Friends, Anne Farncombe, National Christian Education Council, 1978.
The Sikh World, D. Singh and A. Smith, Macdonald, 1985.
Stories from the Sikh World, Rani and Juanu Singh, Macdonald, 1987.
Bobbi's New Year, Joan Solomon, Hamish Hamilton, 1980.

General Interest

Religious Topics Series, Jon Mayled, Wayland, 1986.
Holy Books
Religious Symbols
Feasting and Fasting
The History of Religions
Religious Services
Religious Beliefs
Religious Food
Family Life
Religious Teachers and Prophets
Initiation Rites
Religious Festivals
Festivals in World Religions, Alan Brown, Longman, 1986.
Beginnings – Creation Myths of the World, Penelope Farmer, Chatto and Windus, 1978.

In the Beginning – creation myths from around the World, Helen Cherry and Kenneth McLeish, Longman, 1984.
Religions, Topics, Jenny Vaughan, Wayland, 1986.
Religions, My First Library, Robert Fisher, Macdonald, 1987.
Religions – a book of beliefs, Myrtle Langley, Lion Books, 1981.
Cults and New Faiths, John Butterworth, Lion Books, 1981.
The New Religious World, Anne Bancroft, Macdonald, 1985.
Faiths and Festivals, Martin Palmer, Ward Lock, 1984.
Worlds of Difference, Martin Palmer and Ester Bisset, Blackie, 1985.
Festivals and Celebrations, Rowland Purton, Basil Blackwell, 1987.
World Religions: A handbook for teachers, edited by W. Owen Cole, The Commission For Racial Equality, 1977.
World Studies 8–13 – A Teachers' Handbook, Simon Fisher and David Hicks, Oliver and Boyd, 1986.
Let's Celebrate!, Caroline Parry, Kids Can Press, 1987.
Exploring Religion Series, Olivia Bennett, Bell & Hyman, 1985.
People
Buildings
Worship
Writings
Festivals
Signs and Symbols

Indices

Festivals and Celebrations

People

Projects and illustrations

Page numbers in **bold** denote illustration.

Religious Names and Terms

Songs, prayers and poems

Stories and features

Acknowledgements

The publishers have made every effort to trace the ownership of all copyrighted material and to secure permission from holders of such material. They regret any inadvertent error and will be pleased to make the necessary corrections in future printings.

Thanks are due to the following for their kind permission in allowing us to reprint material.

Samantha Paranahews for *Hoping for a Better Life* (p. 8).

Unwin Hyman for *Rainy Nights* by Irene Thompson (p.45) and *Snowdrops* by Mary Vivian (p. 9) both from Book of 1000 poems.

Mary Anne Hoberman for *Hello* (p.13).

Shel Silverstein and Random House for *No Difference* (p. 14) from Where the Sidewalk Ends and *This Bridge* (p. 82) from A Light in the Attic.

John Meeks and Colin Radcliffe for *Pete the Lonely Mongrel Dog* (p. 18) from The Jolly Herring published by A & C Black.

The Salvation Army for *Days* by John Gowans (p. 20) © Salvationist Publishing and Supplies Ltd.

David Grimshaw for *Super-walk '88* (p. 22).

Rowland Purton and Basil Blackwell for *Prayers from Dear God* (pp. 23, 37, 77).

The Blackie Publishing Group for *The Old Brown Horse* by W. K. Holmes (p. 30) from In Poem Town Book III.

Sandra Kerr for *Try Again* (p. 35). Words and music by Sandra Kerr.

Bantam Books for *The Old Woman* by Joyce Johnson (p. 40).

Brian Patten for *Billy Dreamer's Fantastic Friends* (p. 42) and *The Bossy Young Tree* (p. 93) from Gargling with Jelly published by Puffin.

Ralph McTell for *I live in the city* (p. 44).

Marjorie Kinnan Rawlings for the extract from *The Yearling* (p. 62) published by Piccolo.

John Pedley for the extract adapted from Stories of Great Lives: Test Match published by Blandford (p. 68).

Grenville Kleiser for the prayer on page 75 from Short Prayers for the Long Day published by Collins.

Oxfam for the map and statistics on page 79.

Richard McKenzie and Chris Barrett for *There is no more* (p. 80), Planet Earth Poetry competition 1988 organized by Puffin.

Carolyn Askar for *The Rainbow People* (p. 80) and reproduced with permission.

Christian Aid Publications for the adaptation of *The Banana Game by Steve Pratchett* (p. 81).

Michael Hollins and Eta Gullick for *The prayer of and African Christian* (p. 81) from The One Who Listens published by Mayhew McCrimmon.

Hodder and Stoughton for *Travellers* by Arthur St. John Adcock (p. 82).

Timothy Dudley-Smith for the extract from *Praise the Lord for Times and Seasons* (p. 84) from Come and Praise published by BBC Books.

Kids Can Press for *The Iroquois Green Corn Festival* (p. 85) from Let's Celebrate text © 1987 Caroline Parry. Reprinted by permission of Kids Can Press Ltd, Toronto, Canada.

Hazel Charlton for *I listen and I listen* (p. 88) from Come and Praise published by BBC Books.

Kit Wright for *The Song of the Whale* (p. 90) from Hot Dog published by Puffin.

Wally Whyton for *Leave them a Flower* (p. 92) from The Jolly Herring published by A & C Black.

The Independent for the extract from the article about Greenpeace (p. 95).

Maxine Kumin for *The Microscope* (p. 96) from Presenting Poetry 1 published by Oliver & Boyd.

Stanier and Bell for *World Harvest* by Richard Graves and Cecily Taylor (p. 114) and *Child for the World* by David Medd (p. 115). Reproduced by permission of Stanier & Bell Ltd.

S. S. Grossman and S. E. Goldfarb for *My Dreidel* (p. 145) and Lois Birkenshaw for *Eat Good Food* (p. 61) both from Music for Fun Music for Learning published by Holt, Reinhart Winston of Canada.

Photographs

Barnaby's Picture Library: 53, 75, 79, 115, 121, 129, 141, 143

John Campbell/Macdonald Children's Books: Cover

Daily Mirror/A. Sidey: 95

Susan and Richard Greenhill: 127, 131, 133

Geoff Howard: 106, 117

Alan Hutchinson Library: 109

Kallaway: 51

Frank Lane: 91

Macdonald/Aldus Archive: 104

Bury Peerless: 123, 149

E H Rao/NHPA: 73

Reflex/P Cavendish: 105

Swedish Tourist Office: 119

Doreen Vause/Liz Beaumont: 15, 19, 23, 43, 83, 87

Whitbread: 65

The publisher would also like to thank Ann Wilkins, head teacher, the staff, and the children of Furzedown School in London for their enthusiastic participation in the shooting of the cover photographs.